AUDIT COMMITTEE ESSENTIALS

CURTIS C. VERSCHOOR

WILEY

John Wiley & Sons, Inc.

This book is printed on acid-free paper. ♾

Published by John Wiley & Sons, Inc., Hoboken, New Jersey.
Published simultaneously in Canada.

Library of Congress Cataloging-in-Publication Data:

Verschoor, Curtis C.
Audit committee essentials / Curtis C. Verschoor.
p. cm.
Includes index.
ISBN 978-0-471-69959-0 (cloth)
1. Audit committees–United States. 2. Auditing, Internal–United States.
3. Boards of directors–United States. I. Title.
HF5667.15.V4714 2008
657'.458–dc22 2007049363

Printed in the United States of America
10 9 8 7 6 5 4 3 2 1

To my ever-supportive wife
Marie K. Verschoor

Acknowledgements

Every successful project is a result of the influences and hard work of many people.

I am grateful for the continuing support of the School of Accountancy and MIS of DePaul University and Ledger & Quill. Also, an ambitious work like *Audit Committee Essentials* would not have been possible without the excellent library support of the dedicated professionals at DePaul. Brian DeHart was able to find needed materials online faster than I ever could have hoped.

Alex Lajoux, the Chief Knowledge Officer of the National Association of Corporate Directors was the person who encouraged me to write my first work on audit committees: *Audit Committee Guidance for the 1990s.* Later, Bonnie Ulmer and the folks at the Institute of Internal Auditors Research Foundation were kind enough to publish *Audit Committee Briefing*, and also *Governance Update 2003: Impact of New Initiatives on Audit Committees and Internal Auditors.* I especially appreciate the helpful comments on this manuscript from the Research Foundation's reviewers.

Judy Howarth at Wiley and her editorial group were extremely helpful in pointing out questions and comments and John DeRemigis at Wiley just would not take "No" for an answer, so can take credit for actually making the book happen. Of course, I am fully responsible for any errors or omissions that may have crept through the rigorous publishing process.

Contents

About the Author

Dr. Curtis C. Verschoor, CIA, CPA, CFE, CMA, is the Ledger & Quill Research Professor in the School of Accountancy and Management Information Systems and Wicklander Research Fellow in the Institute for Business and Professional Ethics, both at DePaul University, Chicago. He is also a Research Scholar in the Center for Business Ethics at Bentley College in Waltham, Massachusetts, a Fellow of the Corporate Governance Center at Kennesaw State University, Kennesaw, Georgia, and an Honorary Visiting Professor in the Centre for Research in Corporate Governance at the Sir John Cass Business School, City University of London. He is a private investor as well as a consultant, author, speaker, and expert witness on subjects including governance, ethics, audit committees, internal controls, and auditing management.

Currently Dr. Verschoor serves on the board of directors of nonprofit organizations and chairs the audit committee of one. He is a contributing editor for several academic and practitioner journals. He received undergraduate and MBA degrees from the University of Michigan at Ann Arbor and a doctorate in business from Northern Illinois University.

Prior to his career in academia, his financial career in industry included service as the corporate controller of both the Colgate-Palmolive Company and Baxter International, the CFO of a small diversified public corporation, and the chief internal audit executive of The Singer Company. Previously, he was the national director of education of Touche Ross & Co., a predecessor of Deloitte, LLP.

Dr. Verschoor has been widely quoted in various media including the *New York Times, Wall Street Lawyer, Houston Chronicle, Chicago Tribune*, and *Dallas Morning News*. He has also written books, monographs, columns, and articles in prominent journals, including the *Journal of Accountancy, Strategic Finance, Directors' Monthly, Internal Auditor, Management Accounting, Internal Auditing, Accounting Today, Bank Management,* and *CPA Journal.*

His most recent book is *Ethics and Compliance: Challenges for Internal Auditing.* Previous books include *Audit Committee Briefing: Understanding the 21st Century Audit Committee and Its Governance Roles*, *Governance Update 2003: Impact of New Initiatives on Audit Committees*, and Institute of Internal Auditors, *Audit Committee Briefing—2001: Facilitating New Audit Committee Responsibilities.*

He is an active volunteer in several professional organizations, presently serving on the Professional Conferences Committee of the Institute of Internal Auditors and the Ethics Committee of the Institute of Management Accountants. His biography is contained in the current *Who's Who in America*, *Who's Who in the Midwest*, *Who's Who in Education*, and *Who's Who in Finance*.

Dr. Verschoor can be reached at curtisverschoor@sbcglobal.net.

About The Institute of Internal Auditors

The Institute of Internal Auditors (IIA) is internationally recognized as a trustworthy guidance-setting body. Serving members in 165 countries, The IIA is the internal audit profession's global voice, chief advocate, recognized authority, acknowledged leader, and principal educator on governance, risk, and internal control.

The IIA sets, stewards and promulgates the *International Standards for the Professional Practice of Internal Auditing (Standards)*. The Institute also provides various levels of accompanying guidance; offers leading-edge conferences, seminars and Web-based training; produces forward-thinking educational products; offers quality assurance reviews, benchmarking, and consulting services; and creates growth and networking opportunities for internal auditors throughout the world. The IIA also certifies professionals through the globally recognized Certified Internal Auditor® (CIA®), and provides specialty certifications in government, control self-assessment, and financial services.

The IIA's Web site, *www.theiia.org*, is rich with professional guidance and information on IIA programs, products, and services, as well as resources for IT audit professionals. The Institute publishes Internal Auditor, an award-winning, internationally distributed trade magazine and The IIA's other outstanding periodicals address the profession's most pressing issues and present viable solutions and exemplary practices.

The IIA Research Foundation (IIARF) works in partnership with experts from around the globe to sponsor and conduct research on the top issues affecting internal auditors and the business world today. Its projects advance the internal audit profession globally by enhancing the professionalism of internal audit practitioners. It also provides leading-edge educational products through the IIARF Bookstore.

Preface

This book is intended to provide guidance on the subject of governance of corporations and similar organizations that is authoritative yet concise and easy to understand. It is primarily oriented toward the needs of those who have no legal training but who need to keep abreast of the rapidly changing governance requirements and responsibilities of audit committees. Its writing style especially avoids use of legalese. The volume contains not only authoritative information about legally mandated matters affecting audit committees but also the many best practices that are being advanced by thought leaders in the field of governance. Requirements and responsibilities are set forth within the context of the United States of America unless specifically mentioned otherwise.

The volume is intended to cover audit committees in both for-profit and not-for-profit corporations, although most of the specific legal requirements for audit committees involve public companies and are based on U.S. statutes. In some state jurisdictions, however, not-for-profit entities are being required and in other states encouraged to adopt the practices of public companies as best practices of governance.

The work should be especially valuable to audit committee members and chairpersons, consultants to audit committees, professional accountants, and auditors. It is also designed to provide the necessary indoctrination to board members or trustees who are newly assigned to service on the audit committee. Because audit committee members are also members of the board of directors of their organization, there is considerable coverage of matters of interest to all board members.

Readers should take the contents of this volume as an educational resource that may not be applicable to every entity or to every situation. The book is not intended to be a substitute for professional advice that considers the context of and is tailored to a specific environment, facts, and circumstances. Application of its contents to specific corporate circumstances should be done only with the assistance of a professional advisor who can take into account the facts and context of a particular situation. Each chapter concludes with a listing of the key points it contains.

Chapter 1, "Evolution of Audit Committees," describes the historical development of audit committees from their origins in the early 1940s to the present. It outlines the various U.S. legislative and private sector initiatives arising from earlier scandals that have resulted in the lengthy and growing menu of responsibilities audit committees have today. In many cases, the full board has been designated specific responsibilities and has decided to delegate to a committee some that require particular expertise and experience. While retaining ultimate responsibility, the board is implementing some of its duties by placing considerable reliance on the work of the audit and other standing committees. The responsibilities assigned to the audit committee have increased in recent years and are expected to continue to do so in the future.

The contents of Chapter 2, "Full Board Responsibilities and Effective Board Processes," acknowledge the fact that audit committee members must perform all of the required functions of a director or trustee of an organization as well as those of a member of a board standing committee. Board members have both general and specific responsibilities. The general responsibilities include the duties of care and loyalty. Additional general duties of disclosure and of good faith have resulted from court decisions. More specific duties have evolved over time, usually as a result of legislation. These duties usually also include best practices that boards of directors should embrace as well as the requirement that boards should regularly assess their effectiveness as a whole and strive for continuous improvement. Chapter 2 captures information from authoritative legal sources for coverage of required board-level responsibilities and discussion of most effective processes at the full board level. These sources include the Model Business Corporation Act, the *Principles of Corporate Governance*, and the 2007 edition of the *Corporate Director's Guidebook*. The chapter also includes recommendations from audit committee thought leaders including those at PricewaterhouseCoopers, the Conference Board, and the KPMG Audit Committee Institute.

Chapter 3, "Personal Characteristics of Effective Boards and Members," describes the personal qualities of directors that will enable them to be most effective. The source of these concepts is same legal and thought-leading authorities. Characteristics of an effective board member include a willingness to invest the time and effort involved to become familiar with the industries in which the corporation operates, plus the expenditure of sufficient time and possession of the necessary subject matter interest to be an active participant in all deliberations. Above all, directors need independence yet tact, to avoid overrelying on everything management presents to the board without sufficiently considering its aspects in enough detail. An effective board member must maintain good faith, provide general oversight on behalf of shareowners, exercise informed judgment, and demonstrate dedication to the corporation's best interests. Board members should also regularly assess their effectiveness and strive for continuous improvement.

Chapter 4, "Duties of Audit Committees Prescribed by Law, Regulation, or Rule," provides an outline discussion of specific duties of audit committees that are prescribed by law, regulation, or rule. These duties are set forth in authoritative sources and are largely the result of Securities and Exchange Commission (SEC) regulations implementing specific statutes as well as the rules of the principal stock exchanges that have been approved by the SEC. The stock exchange rules flesh out and put into place the audit committee requirements of Sarbanes-Oxley and those contained in earlier legislation as well as earlier private sector recommendations, such as those resulting from the 1999 Blue Ribbon Committee on Improving the Effectiveness of Audit Committees. Major legally required responsibilities of audit committees include oversight of the external audit firm and its work, receipt of confidential information from employees and others, oversight of processes related to financial and other disclosures as well as internal control and management of business risks. Later chapters discuss the more important of these duties.

Chapter 5, "Overview of Additional Duties of Audit Committees Considered to Be Best Practices," presents an overview of the audit committee duties that have emerged as best practices by means of the reviews and analyses of corporate governance leaders and subject matter experts. These include oversight of internal auditing activities and of ethics and compliance programs. Sarbanes-Oxley requires public companies to have an ethics code, and the stock exchanges, most especially the New York Stock Exchange, have fleshed out this requirement to include directors, officers, and employees. As examples of an actual code of conduct, the Google, Inc. and United Parcel Service codes of conduct are attached as exhibits to this chapter. The Google code demonstrates how one company describes the ethical climate that it considers crucial to its success and is widely recognized as important in today's business environment. An example of a more legalistic code of conduct is that of United Parcel Service. The majority of both the legally required duties discussed in Chapter 4 and those of best practice in Chapter 5 apply equally to private and not-for-profit organizations as well as publicly held companies. A number of these duties involve internal auditing, a subject that is covered further in Chapter 9.

Chapter 6, "Necessary Characteristics of Audit Committees and Members," describes both legally required and best practice guidelines of the educational and experience aspects and other personal characteristics that audit committees and their members should possess. This chapter continues to use the same authoritative legal and other sources noted earlier to outline the background required or best suited for membership on an audit committee. Additional private sector sources are introduced to provide context and further explanation.

The importance and content of an appropriate charter or mission statement for the audit committee is the subject of Chapter 7, "The Audit Committee and Its Charter." Public companies are required to publish their audit committee charter every three years, or more often if revised. Audit committees are usually tasked to review the contents of their charter on an annual basis. A sample audit committee charter from a legal and regulatory perspective is attached as an exhibit to this chapter, indicating the statutory or regulatory requirement from which responsibilities and duties arise. Excerpts from the audit committee charters of additional companies are also attached to indicate how some company audit committees are describing required duties in a manner that can be considered to be best practices.

The goal of Chapter 8, "Audit Committee Oversight of Financial Statements and Financial Disclosures," is to provide further guidance concerning some of the most important audit committee responsibilities, those that deal with financial statement preparation and financial and other disclosures to the public. Based on legislative requirements and those of the Blue Ribbon Committee mentioned earlier, professional external auditing standards require that the external auditor communicate specific information to the audit committee, including the auditor's evaluation of the quality and not just the acceptability of the accounting principles that the organization has chosen to use in its financial statements. This information is intended to assist audit committees in their oversight responsibilities relating to financial statement preparation and financial and other public disclosures.

The relationships of the audit committee with the organization's internal auditing activity outlined in other chapters are further developed in Chapter 9, "The Audit Committee and Internal Auditing." The objectives of both internal auditing and the audit committee are complementary, and effective coordination produces symbiotic benefits for each and the organization as a whole. This chapter notes that best practices suggest that a direct functional reporting relationship exists between the chief audit executive and the audit committee. This relationship allows the audit committee's oversight of the development of the risk-based plan of audit engagements to assure that adequate resources are provided to internal auditing and that they are directed to the appropriate areas of the organization.

Chapter 10, "The Audit Committee and Risk Management," discusses in greater detail the recommendations for audit committees to oversee an organization's risk management efforts. "The Audit Committee and Risk Management" covers authoritative guidance published in 2004 by the Committee of Sponsoring Organizations of the Treadway Commission (COSO). The chapter also describes the context of risk management for audit committees.

This chapter outlines the principal content of risk management processes and explains that the audit committee needs to determine that obstacles do not hinder achievement of the organization's goals. The audit committee also needs to be assured that processes are in place to consider transferring or mitigating all business risks that have more than a low likelihood and low expected impact. The chapter outlines terminology used in the risk context, what constitutes enterprise risk management, and the benefits its use should bring to organizations.

Additional guidance concerning audit committee responsibilities for internal control is presented in Chapter 11, "The Audit Committee and Internal Control." The chapter discusses control concepts set forth in 1993 by COSO and the management assessment and reporting on internal control over financial reporting and related external auditor opinion that is legally required for public corporations under Sarbanes-Oxley. The chapter discusses both the SEC interpretive guidance to management on its internal control assessment as well as Audit Standard No. 5 issued by the Public Company Accounting Oversight Board (PCAOB) that guides the external auditor's examination. It concludes with an internal control evaluation tool developed by the American Institute of Certified Public Accountants (AICPA) for use by audit committees.

Chapter 12, "The Audit Committee and Ethics-Related Initiatives," discusses the critical importance that an ethical culture has to strong corporate governance. It also covers the responsibilities that audit committees have for overseeing the ethics-related programs of the organization, including the system for receiving information reported confidentially concerning matters of accounting, auditing, and internal control.

The subject matter of Chapter 13, "The Audit Committee and Information Technology," involves some of the more important risks that audit committees are being asked to monitor. These responsibilities include oversight of the security and functioning of information processing systems as well as information technology (IT) and Internet-based applications that may be used in manufacturing and marketing the firm's products or providing the firm's services. Although audit committee members are not expected to be IT experts, they should be aware of the basic fundamentals of IT security, the necessary general controls over IT systems, and how to assure themselves that IT risks are being appropriately mitigated and the opportunities for use of IT are being effectively exploited.

Chapter 14, "Audit Committee Issues in Not-for-Profit Entities," covers aspects of not-for-profit organizations and specialized issues affecting audit committees of these entities. One such issue is the protections that state legislation and the federal Volunteer Protection Act of 1997 provide for board and audit committee members from being held financially liable for their acts of ordinary negligence under certain conditions. The chapter also outlines the Internal Revenue Service tax forms that must be filed by tax-exempt organizations and briefly introduces the specialized requirements and auditing standards that are involved with organizations receiving funding from the federal government.

Chapter 15, "Audit Committee Resources," consists of an annotated listing of information sources that readers can use to gain additional and more in-depth insight on particular issues affecting audit committees. These sources include Web sites of organizations having a wealth of information about topics of interest and importance to audit committees.

The volume concludes with a glossary of terms and a detailed index.

Chapter 1

Evolution of Audit Committees

Audit committees have had an important role in the governance of corporations since their inception in the early 1940s, and their visibility and contributions have greatly increased in the past few years. Audit committees have been described as organizations' guardians of financial integrity. From a regulatory perspective, the governmental agency empowered to regulate the issuance and trading of securities of public corporations, the Securities and Exchange Commission (SEC), has been involved with the establishment and oversight of audit committees in public companies since their beginning years.

Interestingly, however, the stock exchanges, as self-regulatory agencies, have been directly involved in putting into place many of the detailed requirements that the SEC mandated that audit committees of public companies follow. A body of best practices beyond legal and regulatory requirements has also grown up as a result of the work of thought leaders from the legal, investment, and auditing professions.

The public accounting profession through the American Institute of Certified Public Accountants (AICPA) has also long actively supported the need for an important role for audit committees. Because of the increased emphasis placed on the governance of corporations in the postmillennium years, particularly those that are publicly held, audit committees in many not-for-profit organizations have become more prevalent and have received greater attention and visibility. Their influence in organizations has matched this trend.

EARLY EVENTS

The New York Stock Exchange (NYSE) suggested, and the SEC endorsed, the concept of audit committees composed of nonexecutive directors as early as 1940. At that time, the responsibilities envisioned for audit committees were quite narrow, basically being limited to the nomination of the external auditor and arranging some of the parameters of its engagement. The AICPA was also active in the discussion of the need for audit committees and in 1967 issued a policy statement recommending that public corporations establish audit committees composed of outside directors.

In 1974, the SEC required proxy statement disclosure of the existence and composition of audit committees in all public corporations where they were in place.

The NYSE issued a white paper at approximately the same time that strongly recommended the formation of an audit committee by each company listed on that exchange.

Several important developments took place in the late 1970s. The AICPA Special Committee on Audit Committees renewed its earlier support for establishment of an audit committee composed entirely of independent directors. In early 1977, the NYSE enacted a listing requirement that all companies listed on that exchange appoint an audit committee of nonemployee or independent directors as a condition of continued listing on the exchange. The SEC was instrumental in bringing this initiative to fruition.

The NYSE clarified in 1978 its independence requirements for audit committee members. Audit committees had to consist solely of directors "independent of management and free from any relationship that would interfere with the exercise of independent judgment as a committee member."[1] At about the same time, the American Stock Exchange (ASE) also made a nonbinding recommendation that all of its listed companies should form independent audit committees. As noted later in this chapter, the National Association of Securities Dealers Automated Quotation System (Nasdaq) stock market established an audit committee requirement in 1989.

It should be borne in mind that in the 1970s, the influence of nonexecutive directors was substantially less than it has become in recent years. The idea that the major function of a board of directors is to represent the interests of shareowners was not prevalent. Thus, audit committee members were likely to be the only independent members of the board. In many cases, even total independence of the audit committee from management was more of a goal than an actuality.

An early endorsement by the legal profession of the concept of audit committees in public corporations appeared in the 1978 edition of the *Corporate Director's Guidebook* published by the American Bar Association (ABA). Two years later, the ABA Committee on Corporate Laws published specific recommendations for the membership, responsibilities, and potential liabilities of audit committees and their director-members. Later chapters discuss the contents of subsequent versions of the *Corporate Director's Guidebook* published by the ABA.

SEC REGULATORY, LEGAL, AND PRIVATE SECTOR INITIATIVES

The SEC continued its support for independent audit committees throughout the 1970s and sponsored public hearings related to corporate accountability and the adequacy of internal controls in U.S. corporations. The SEC stressed the "vital importance of an independent audit committee to the proper functioning of the corporation."

[1] NYSE Listed Company Manual §303.00. See www.nyse.com.

According to the securities laws, the current definition of an audit committee is:

a) A committee (or equivalent body) established by and amongst the board of directors of an issuer for the purpose of overseeing the accounting and financial reporting processes of the issuer and audits of the financial statements of the issuer: and
b) If no such committee exists with respect to an issuer, the entire board of directors of the issuer.[2]

Several attempts in the late 1970s to require greater disclosure of internal control adequacy and audit committee performance failed to receive support from the business community and were withdrawn. The last and most sweeping attempt would have required management to assess and report publicly on the effectiveness of internal control systems and also management's responses to internal control recommendations made by either internal or external auditors.

The formation in 1985 of the National Commission on Fraudulent Financial Reporting, also known as the Treadway Commission, after its chairman, resulted in renewed interest in audit committees on the part of financial statement users, preparers, auditors, legislators, regulators, and the general public. The Treadway report showed how audit committees could prevent or detect fraudulent financial reporting and contained 11 specific recommendations as to how this could be accomplished, including the recommendation concerning a management assessment of internal controls.

Appendix I to the Treadway report sets forth good practice guidelines for audit committees. These recommendations include the issues that audit committees should (1) be informed and vigilant, (2) have their duties and responsibilities set forth in a written charter, and (3) be given the resources and authority adequate to discharge their responsibilities. Additional guidance elsewhere in the Treadway report involves these recommendations that the audit committee should:

- Not consist of fewer than three members
- Include private meetings with the internal auditor and the external auditor
- Report to full board
- Require expanded knowledge of company operations
- Include corporate and/or outside counsel in meetings
- Possess knowledge of audit plans—of both external and internal auditor
- Require knowledge of electronic data processing and review of security practices
- Approve controls for use of other auditors in addition to principal auditor

[2] Securities Exchange Act of 1934, §3(a)(58).

- Provide oversight of sensitive areas such as officers' expenses and perquisites
- Oversee any areas requiring special attention[3]

Pursuant to Treadway recommendations, in 1989, the Nasdaq stock market required its listed companies to establish and maintain an audit committee of which the majority of members are independent directors.

After several years of deliberations, the American Law Institute, an organization consisting of judges, attorneys, and legal academics, adopted in 1992 but published in 1994 its *Principles of Corporate Governance: Analysis and Recommendations*.[4] This two-volume work includes recommendations of the appropriate duties that should be undertaken by boards of directors and audit committees. The recommendations for duties of the board of directors as a whole are contained in Chapter 2 and those for audit committees are discussed in Chapter 4. Some of these recommendations became the basis of changes put into practice in later pronouncements of other statutes or recommended by other groups.

A Delaware Chancery Court decision, the *in re Caremark International* case in 1996, established the principle that

> a director's obligation includes a duty to attempt in good faith to assure that a corporate information and reporting system, which the board concludes is adequate, exists, and that failure to do so under some circumstances may, in theory at least, render a director liable for losses caused by non-compliance with applicable legal standards.[5]

This decision is most important to audit committees as usually they oversee the organization's information-gathering and dissemination functions, including relationships with internal and external auditors.

In 2003, the Delaware Supreme Court upheld the lower court's articulation of a new duty of corporate directors in the *in re The Walt Disney Company* case.[6] In this case, which involved whether the directors adequately considered the amount of compensation awarded to Michael Ovitz upon his discharge, was called the duty of good faith. The court held that directors who take an "ostrich-like approach" to corporate governance and "consciously and intentionally disregard their responsibilities, adopting a 'we don't care about the risks' attitude" may be held liable for breaching their duty to act in good faith. The court specifically noted the importance of the duty of good faith, in addition to the duties of due care and of loyalty, as primary guidelines for legally evaluating the conduct of directors.

---

[3] National Commission on Fraudulent Financial Reporting, Report of the National Commission on Fraudulent Financial Reporting (Treadway Report), October 1987, p. 179.

[4] American Law Institute, *Principles of Corporate Governance: Analysis and Recommendations* (St. Paul, MN: American Law Institute Publishers, 1994).

[5] *In re Caremark Int'l Inc.*, 698A.2nd 959 (Del. Ch. 1996).

[6] *In re Walt Disney Co. Derivative Litig.*, 907 A.2nd 693 (2005 Del. Ch.).

REGULATION ARISING FROM BANKING SCANDALS

A significant force in the development of audit committees resulted from the banking scandals of the late 1980s. A study of bank failures by the U.S. General Accounting Office (GAO) (now called the U.S. Government Accountability Office) showed that audit committees of even the largest banks were not sufficiently independent, lacked the expertise to accomplish their responsibilities, and did not receive assessments of key bank operations. The GAO recommended a strengthened role for audit committees in insured banks and savings institutions.

Many of the GAO's recommendations were enacted in December 1991 in the Federal Deposit Insurance Corporation Improvement Act (FDICIA). Under the act, the management of insured institutions are required to increase their activities that are designed to maintain effective internal controls over financial reporting, safeguarding assets, and compliance with relevant laws and regulations. Each year, the management of insured financial institutions must assess and issue a public report on the effectiveness of internal controls over financial reporting. The institution's external auditor must provide an attestation opinion on management's report. This requirement is the forerunner of a similar requirement contained in Sarbanes-Oxley. As a result of this increased emphasis, audit committees of insured institutions are also tasked to higher levels of oversight of the financial reporting, internal controls, and internal and external auditing of insured financial institutions.

STOCK EXCHANGE INITIATIVES

In late 1998, another landmark development affected audit committees. The SEC believed that the quality and related oversight of corporate financial reporting required a significant overall review and upgrade. Consequently, a Blue Ribbon Committee was formed by the New York Stock Exchange and the Nasdaq stock market. Using fast-track methods, the committee issued its report of 10 major recommendations in February 1999.[7]

The *Report and Recommendations of the Blue Ribbon Committee on Improving the Effectiveness of Corporate Audit Committees* (*Blue Ribbon Committee Report*) focused on the need for total independence and for financial literacy of all audit committee members and the benefits of a formal written charter for the audit committee. The report also included several best practices for audit committee relationships with the external audit firm and recommended specific interactions between the audit firm and the committee. The recommendations in the report were largely put into place as mandatory requirements by means of a series of SEC releases and

[7] Blue Ribbon Committee on Improving the Effectiveness of Corporate Audit Committees, *Blue Ribbon Committee Report*, New York Stock Exchange and the National Association of Securities Dealers, 1999.

stock exchange rules and through AICPA auditing standards that were issued later in 1999 and early 2000.

In the regulatory releases by the SEC and AICPA implementing the *Blue Ribbon Committee Report*, external auditors were directed to be primarily accountable to audit committees and provide them with information that would allow a candid discussion of the accounting judgments that were made by management and reflected in the financial statements. Also, management is required to provide more information to the audit committee regarding its evaluation of the company's risk and control structure, together with supporting information concerning the contents of periodic financial statements.

Additional initiatives from the report led to four more requirements for public companies:

1. Proxy statements must include an annual report of audit committee activities.
2. Proxy statements must include the audit committee's charter at least once every three years and more often if changes are made.
3. External auditors must be engaged to perform a formal current review of interim financial statements each quarter.
4. Proxy statements must include a breakdown of the total fees paid to external auditors for auditing, tax services, and other services.

The fee disclosure requirement exposed many examples (prior to 2002) where external auditors received fees for providing consulting services that some times approached or even exceeded what they received for auditing the corporation's financial statements. Since the firms were well aware that providing consulting services to clients was much more profitable than the "commodity" of auditing financial statements, the large fees for nonaudit services tended to threaten the independence or at least the appearance of independence of external audit firms. The SEC felt very strongly that large consulting fees impaired the independence of external auditors. Public hearings were held, but at the time, the external audit firms successfully resisted any regulatory limits on the amount of consulting that could be provided to their audit clients.

SARBANES-OXLEY ACT OF 2002

The early years of the twenty-first century saw a number of accounting and auditing-related scandals, including Waste Management, Enron, HealthSouth, and WorldCom. These led to the passage of the Sarbanes-Oxley Act of 2002, portions of which are discussed at greater length in subsequent chapters. This legislation has been called the most significant change in the governance of publicly held corporations since passage of the securities laws of the mid-1930s. The major thrust of the legislation was to establish the Public Company Accounting Oversight Board (PCAOB) to regulate and monitor the practice of public accounting as it relates to publicly held companies. A major function of the PCAOB is to inspect the auditing and quality control practices of firms that audit publicly held companies.

Sarbanes-Oxley also took away from the AICPA, the trade or membership association of certified public accountants, the self-governance functions of public accountants, such as setting ethical, quality, and auditing standards and inspecting firms' performance to assure their proper use. These functions are now provided by the PCAOB, an independent government agency under the oversight of the SEC. Sarbanes-Oxley Section 201(g) prohibits external auditors from performing certain services for their audit clients, including all internal auditing and almost all consulting. Sarbanes-Oxley Section 201(h) requires audit committee to approve in advance any taxation and other nonauditing services that external auditors provide to their audit clients.

Sarbanes-Oxley also contains provisions requiring public corporations to improve their governance practices. The stock exchanges have set forth rules detailing many of the specific actions legislated by this statute. These rules mandate independence and financial competency requirements for audit committees, including financial literacy for all members and financial expertise for one or more members. The act also clarifies the role of all independent directors. Sarbanes-Oxley Sections 302 and 404 require management to certify the completeness and accuracy of periodic financial statements and assess the effectiveness of the corporation's disclosure and internal controls.

Other provisions of Sarbanes-Oxley require companies to establish confidential mechanisms to allow employees to communicate suspected wrongdoing to audit committees (whistleblowing) and to develop and implement a code of ethics for senior financial officers. (The stock exchanges have extended this rule to directors and all employees.) Sarbanes-Oxley also establishes greater criminal penalties for securities fraud, requires attorneys to inform authorities when unlawful conduct takes place, and provides employment protection for employee whistleblowers. More detailed coverage of the provisions contained in Sarbanes-Oxley that affect audit committees is contained in later chapters of this volume.

One important indication of the effect of Sarbanes-Oxley on the work of audit committees is the significant increase in the annual average number of audit committee meetings that take place. Survey research by executive search consulting firm Korn/Ferry shows that the annual average number of audit committee meetings for Fortune 1000 corporations has more than doubled since 2000, before the enactment of Sarbanes-Oxley. In 2000, the average number of meetings held was 4 per year; by 2006, that number had increased to 9 per year.[8] A later survey by consulting firm Huron Consulting Group notes that from 2002 to 2006, the average annual number of audit committee meetings doubled from about 5 to 10 meetings. In 2006, 60% of public companies held 9 or more meetings of their audit committee, up from 7% in 2002. The number of audit committees in public companies

---

[8] Korn/Ferry International, 33rd Annual Board of Directors Study, 2007, p. 16, and 2001, p. 13.

holding 4 or fewer meetings in 2006 dropped to only 3%, down from 44% in 2002.[9]

The substantial cost of implementing some Sarbanes-Oxley requirements has also drawn widespread criticism, particularly Section 404 of the act. This provision requires an annual assessment by management of internal controls over financial reporting and an attestation opinion by the external audit firm. The earlier calls for repeal of portions of Sarbanes-Oxley, particularly Section 404, have subsided. SEC and PCAOB efforts to reduce costs of compliance resulted in two postponements of the effective date for smaller companies to comply with this section. The latest postponement occurred in December 2006, when the deadline for smaller companies to file a management assertion concerning internal control over financial reporting was delayed until fiscal years ending after December 31, 2007. The requirement for an external auditor opinion for such companies was delayed until fiscal years ending after December 31, 2008.

In 2007, the subject of the cost of compliance with Sarbanes-Oxley Section 404 has received attention at both the SEC and the PCAOB. The SEC has published interpretive guidance for management to use in its assessment of internal control over financial reporting. Concurrently, the PCAOB has developed and issued guidance to external auditors in the form of Audit Standard No. 5, which replaces Audit Standard No. 2. Each of these pronouncements describes the need for both management and external auditors to take a top-down and risk-based approach to their tasks and avoid unnecessary work. If entity-wide internal controls are adequate to address a particular risk, no further testing need be done. Chapter 11 presents additional discussion of audit committee involvement with compliance with the provisions of Sarbanes-Oxley Section 404.

DIRECTORS' LIABILITY

Directors may incur personal liability for failure to follow their duties of due care or loyalty or for failure to satisfy regulatory legal requirements, such as those set forth in securities laws. These requirements are discussed in later chapters. Most corporations provide indemnification rights to directors and officers for acts performed in the course of their responsibilities. Directors' and officers' insurance is also commonly provided, although some areas of activity often are excluded under a typical policy.

Most litigation against directors has been brought alleging a breach of loyalty rather than a duty of care. Diligent pursuit of the guidance set forth in this volume is likely to be sufficient to avoid liability. As noted elsewhere, if directors avoid conflicts of interest and act in good faith, discharge their responsibilities with informed judgment, with the measure of care that a person in a similar position

[9] Huron Consulting Group, *2007 Audit Committee Research Report*, Huron Consulting Group, 2007, p. 4. At www.huronconsulting.com/library/ accessed January 2008.

would use, and in a manner they believe to be in the best interests of the corporation, they should avoid personal liability.

Federal law provides some protection against liability for unpaid directors of not-for-profit organizations. The Volunteer Protection Act of 1997 shields volunteer directors from liability that could otherwise arise from a simple act of negligence. In some states, state laws also prohibit unpaid directors that serve a not-for-profit charitable organization from being sued for malpractice. This subject is further discussed in Chapter 14.

PRIVATE COMPANY AND NOT-FOR-PROFIT GOVERNANCE INITIATIVES

Although the headlines detailing governance scandals have involved events at large publicly held corporations, the pressure for improved disclosure and greater transparency has been felt by not-for-profit organizations as well. Charitable organizations realize that their continued existence and ability to attract donations depends on the trust that givers have that their funds will be utilized in an appropriate manner for the purpose for which they were contributed. The fact that many such organizations consist of locally managed chapters having limited interface with a national headquarters makes good governance an especially high priority.

Although Sarbanes-Oxley applies directly only to publicly held for-profit corporations, because of the reasons just set forth, many private and not-for-profit corporations have chosen to adopt some or all of its provisions as best business practices. Adopters include some large health care providers and some large 501(c)3 organizations. More than three-quarters (78%) of private company respondents to a 2005 survey by attorneys Foley & Lardner have instituted governance reforms, compared with 60% in a similar 2004 survey.[10]

In the main, the Sarbanes-Oxley provisions that have been adopted by a number of private and nonprofit corporations are those that are relatively inexpensive to put into place. For example, a number of nonprofit organizations have instituted one or more of these policies:

- The chief financial/chief executive officer makes certifications concerning financial statements and internal and disclosure controls.
- All members of audit committees are independent directors and manage all relationships with the external auditor.
- A financial expert is designated on the audit committee.
- A code of ethics is implemented for the organization or at least for the senior management and finance officers.

[10] Foley & Lardner LLP presentation attended in person by the author, "The Impact of Sarbanes-Oxley on Private and Non-Profit Companies," 2005 National Directors Institute, March 10, 2005, Chicago.

- Mechanisms are established for confidential employee whistleblowing.
- Audit committee approval is required for nonaudit services provided by the external auditors.

California has enacted a Nonprofit Integrity Act of 2004, which raises compliance issues for charities that are required to register with the California Attorney General. Even out-of-state charities that solicit donations, conduct charitable activities, have employees, maintain an office, hold funds or other property, or hold board meetings in California are likely to be subject to this act. This legislation requires charities with revenue of at least $2 million to have an audit committee that makes recommendations regarding the retention or termination of the external auditor. A provision also requires review of the external audit and conferring with the external auditor to ensure that the organization's financial affairs are in order.

Some observers have called this phenomenon the adoption of Sarbanes-Oxley—Lite. Additionally, several state legislatures including New York have considered bills that would make some Sarbanes-Oxley provisions mandatory for nonprofit organizations headquartered in their state. The U.S. Senate has also held hearings on the subject of improving the governance of not-for-profit organizations. Chapter 14 further discusses issues for audit committees of not-for-profit entities.

FUTURE OUTLOOK

In view of the many calls by investors and the general public for better governance on the part of publicly held corporations, increased oversight burdens have been placed on their boards of directors. Although not legally required to, the boards of directors or trustees of many privately held and not-for-profit corporations have also adopted a number of these practices as a measure of best corporate practice.

As a consequence, audit committees must assume primary responsibility for some of the most important duties of the boards of directors and report regularly to the full board. Additionally, legislative and regulatory initiatives have assigned audit committees specific responsibilities to oversee many of the most critical of the newly recommended or required responsibilities on behalf of the full board.

Another factor motivating improved governance is that corporations perceived to have inadequate corporate governance are being penalized in the marketplace. In fact, several financial service organizations now evaluate and publish the quality of the governance structure of public corporations to guide investors and creditors. The financial rating agencies also utilize governance as one of the measures of financial quality and strength. Thus, corporations with inadequate governance are likely to bear the burden of a higher cost of capital.[11] For example, Moody's framework for U.S. and Canadian corporate governance assessment states that:

[11] For example, see Moody's series of Special Comments on issues of corporate governance on www.moody's.com accessed January 2008.

> Corporate governance can be seen as an important analytic element of management quality. To the extent that shareholders as well as creditors and others have confidence that proper systems of management accountability and incentives are in place, they can have greater confidence in the present management of the company. In theory, they also can be more confident that, should management fail to meet emerging challenges, managers will be held accountable, either through early action by the board of directors, or through pressures, up to and including hostile takeover, in the marketplace for corporate control.[12]

Audit committees are also becoming more involved with processes involving the management of risks the organization chooses to accept. Oversight of risk management—for example, the avoidance of the chance of costly litigation to defend against accusations of bias based on gender, age, and other categories of employees—is gaining importance for audit committees.

In view of the continuing existence of negative public attitudes toward business in general and toward the top levels of management of corporations in particular, the actions of audit committees and boards of directors concerning the governance of their organizations are likely to remain in the public spotlight for years to come. The audit committee should schedule meetings that are free from unreasonable time constraints. The days of board standing committee meetings occurring just "a few hours before the regular board meeting" are long gone. With the prominence audit committees have gained comes a responsibility for members to be sure that they maintain their knowledge of important topics and current developments through continuing education and development. Audit committees should also avail themselves of consulting advice and legal counsel when appropriate.

KEY POINTS IN CHAPTER 1

1. The audit committee is one of the key standing committees of the full board of directors. A primary responsibility is the oversight of a company's financial integrity.
2. The subject of organizational governance has vastly increased in importance since the business scandals of the early 2000s.
3. Audit committees have been in existence only since the early 1940s.
4. Together with responsibilities of boards of directors as a whole, audit committee responsibilities have increased substantially, particularly in recent years. Board member responsibilities are discussed more fully in Chapter 2; audit committee member responsibilities, in Chapter 4.
5. Although the concept of independence from management is important for all members of boards of directors, it is critically important for audit committee members.

---

[12] Moody's, Rating Methodology, *U.S. and Canadian Corporate Governance Assessment*, August 2003. On www.moody's.com accessed January 2008.

6. Rules and regulations implementing the recommendations of the Blue Ribbon Committee on Improving the Effectiveness of Corporate Audit Committees has increased the transparency of the activities of public company audit committees and set forth new responsibilities. New auditing standards recommended by the committee require external auditors to present information about the use of accounting that may be new and not well covered by existing accounting rules, use of accounting estimates that may not be well supported, and use of accounting principles that may not the most desirable in the circumstances.
7. The Sarbanes-Oxley Act of 2002 has dramatically changed the landscape of the corporate governance of publicly held corporations. Management responsibilities have been expanded, and the resulting SEC and stock exchange listing standards have greatly increased the responsibilities of audit committees.
8. The breadth of audit committee responsibilities in many companies has expanded from oversight of financial statement preparation to include monitoring of processes relating to governance, risk management, ethics and compliance, internal controls, financial disclosures, and information technology.
9. The governance of not-for-profit organizations has also come under greater public scrutiny. Many have appointed audit committees and adopted some of the Sarbanes-Oxley and similar requirements applicable to public corporations. This trend is particularly true in industries that deal with the federal government, such as those providing health care services.
10. Future demands on audit committees are likely to increase as revelations of new accounting-related scandals emerge, such as the backdating of stock option grants.
11. The trend toward increased breadth in the responsibilities of audit committees beyond merely accounting, auditing, and financial reporting is likely to continue and include areas of compliance, ethics, risk management, and information technology.

Chapter 2

Full Board Responsibilities and Effective Board Processes

In addition to their duties as committee members, directors selected for service on board standing committees have the same responsibilities as do all members of the board. This chapter outlines the principal legally required and recommended best practice duties of the full board as well as individual board members. Information in this chapter pertains to for-profit corporations of all sizes, whether they are public or private. It is also relevant to not-for-profit entities.

INTRODUCTION

Members of an audit committee are regular board members who have also been chosen to serve as a member of a standing committee of the board. Standing committees, such as the audit committee, are created to meet separately from the full board and achieve specific objectives and perform specialized tasks in accordance with provisions of the bylaws of the corporation. For example, board committees may accomplish some duties more effectively than the full board where specialized knowledge or experience is required.

Also, board committees may be assigned to perform details of various specific oversight functions on behalf of the full board and periodically report back to the full board the results of their activities. This relieves the full board from delving fully into details of each and every matter affecting the corporation. In setting forth various duties, the articles of incorporation and bylaws must conform to the corporation law in the state in which the corporation is organized. State laws governing not-for-profit corporations differ from those for regular corporations, but the requirements of director characteristics and responsibilities as well as effective board processes are similar.

RESPONSIBILITIES OF THE BOARD OF DIRECTORS

A corporation is an entity created under the laws of a particular state under which the corporation was organized. All corporate powers are exercised by or under the authority of the board of directors of the corporation. In other words, the board is the repository of all of the powers, rights, and responsibilities that a corporation has set forth in its articles of incorporation. The business of the corporation is to be managed by or under the direction and subject to the oversight of its board of directors as described in the corporation's bylaws.

GENERAL RESPONSIBILITIES OF DIRECTORS

The primary responsibility of a board of directors is to "direct" corporate operations by providing general direction to management rather than to perform the functions of management by themselves. The increasing importance of the full board in determining the affairs of a corporation relative to senior management is highlighted by the fact that companies listed on the New York Stock Exchange are required by rule to have a majority of independent directors. The commentary to this rule notes that "[e]ffective boards of directors exercise independent judgment in carrying out their responsibilities. Requiring a majority of independent directors will increase the quality of board oversight and lessen the possibility of damaging conflicts of interest."[1]

Since audit committee members are members of the board as a whole, duties of all board members in general also apply to those directors who serve as chair or member of the audit committee. The fifth edition of the *Corporate Director's Guidebook* is a publication of the American Bar Association (ABA) Committee on Corporate Laws, ABA Section of Business Laws.[2] The committee is composed of practicing lawyers, law professors, law school deans, and judges, all having significant expertise in corporation law, from throughout the United States. The *Guidebook* is believed to represent the best expression by the legal profession of legally required and best practices on the subject of corporate governance in general and audit committees in particular.

The 2007 edition of the *Corporate Director's Guidebook* sets forth the responsibilities of the board as a whole as well as directors individually. It notes that the board's principal responsibilities are to promote the best interests of the corporation. This is accomplished by providing general direction for the management of the corporation's business and affairs.

The *Guidebook* sets forth the basic premise that the major functions of a board of directors can be split into two categories: making decisions and providing oversight. The second of these functions means giving advice concerning and monitoring the progress of management's actions, but not being directly involved with determination of tactics and execution of strategies. The distinction between the responsibilities of a board versus those of management is clear. Boards of directors have been invited to have their "nose in but their fingers out." This phrase refers to

---

[1] NYSE, Inc., Listed Company Manual § 303A¶ 1. See www.nyse.com

[2] Excerpted from *Corporate Director's Guidebook, Fifth Edition*, 2007, published by the American Bar Association Section of Business Law. Copyright © 2007 by the American Bar Association. Reprinted with permission.

the fact that as part-timers, directors cannot micromanage the corporation's affairs and should not interfere with the management functions of the officers they have selected as they execute board-approved strategies. The contribution of the board of directors to corporate governance should be limited to oversight together with making the decisions reserved to it by the bylaws.

The Conference Board, a business membership and research organization, published in 2007 a revision to its guidance on the subject of governance.[3] This research report notes that

> the board should have a set of written guidelines in place to articulate corporate governance principles and the roles and responsibilities of the board and management. These guidelines should be reviewed at least annually. By elaborating on directors' basic duties, the guidelines help the board and its individual members understand their obligations as well as the general boundaries within which they should operate.[4]

In addition, the difference between director oversight and management responsibility should be clear (e.g., significant expenditures require board review or approval), but boards should not micromanage or second-guess operational decisions made by management.

Boards need to participate in significant determinations, ask questions, become well informed about the corporation as well as about specific issues, and apply good business judgment in making determinations. As noted, the general duties of a director involve both providing general oversight of the conduct of the corporation's affairs and making important high-level decisions that affect the operation of its business. These two areas of duties might in some cases be mutually exclusive. Director decision making generally involves considering and, if warranted, approving corporate policy and strategic goals and taking specific actions, such as evaluating and selecting top management, approving major expenditures, and acquiring and disposing of material assets.

The contents of this volume are concerned primarily with oversight functions. Oversight functions involve monitoring the corporation's business and affairs, including, for example, financial performance, management performance, and compliance with legal obligations and corporate policies. These duties include the directors' evaluation of the performance of senior management and determination of their compensation, the review of financial and other periodic reports to shareholders and others, and a general overall monitoring of management's performance in handling the affairs of the corporation.

Aspects of the other main function of the board of directors, decision making, involve matters of the corporation as a whole: declaring dividends, helping management to set the organization's overall strategy and objectives, considering and

[3] Conference Board, *Corporate Governance Handbook 2007: Legal Standards and Board Practices*, Research Report R-1045-07-RR. (New York: Conference Board, 2007)

[4] Id., p. 17.

approving major mergers and acquisitions or divestments, electing officers, and assuring management succession. As already noted, the board's oversight functions mainly concern monitoring of the corporation's affairs. The oversight processes should emphasize issues of assuring complete financial and other reports to the shareowners and the public, total compliance with applicable laws and regulations, attention to the management of business risks, and the quality of performance resulting from the execution of strategic plans.

Board of director oversight also includes assuring there is proper periodic reporting of operating results to the shareowners. In performing these responsibilities, directors must protect the interests of the corporation by adhering to high standards of ethical conduct. They also should continue to be aware of new developments in the field of corporate governance.

The 2007 *Corporate Director's Guidebook* gives special emphasis to the subject of ethics, noting:

> The board is the guardian of the corporation's integrity. The board encourages senior management to establish the proper "tone at the top" by setting clear expectations for the corporation's ethical behavior and conduct of its business in compliance with law.[5]

IMPORTANCE OF BEING FULLY INFORMED

It is clear that management has to be totally in charge of running the business on a day-to-day basis. It is also well established, however, that a director's fiduciary responsibilities to actively participate in processes of review and evaluation of management's performance must be based on current and complete knowledge. This knowledge should be gathered by active inquiry and discussion, not passive acceptance of information contained in formal management presentations. The need for directors to be fully informed for both decision making and providing oversight is expressed in the Conference Board's *Corporate Governance Handbook* in this way:

> The effectiveness of the board ultimately depends on the quality and timeliness of information received by directors. The board and management should agree on the type of information the board needs to make informed decisions and perform its oversight function. This should include material on business and financial performance, strategic issues, and information about material risks and other significant matters facing the company. Information for board meetings should be distributed enough in advance of the meetings to permit directors to read, absorb, and consider it. Besides formal processes, boards and management should develop informal communication and reporting channels.[6]

[5] Id., p. 12.
[6] Conference Board, *Corporate Governance Handbook*, 2007, p. 19.

In addition to having current and complete information concerning the corporation's operations, directors must also have a full understanding of the competitive environment in which the company is operating as well as its strategies in dealing with it. The *Corporate Director's Guidebook* notes that a director's understanding and knowledge of the corporation and its industry should include:

- The corporation's business activities;
- The key drivers underlying the corporation's profitability and cash flow—how the corporation makes money—as a whole and also in its significant business segments;
- The corporation's operational and financial plans, strategies, and objectives and how they further the goal of enhancing shareholder value;
- The corporation's economic, financial, regulatory, and competitive risks, as well as risks to the corporation's physical assets, intellectual property, and personnel;
- The corporation's financial condition and the results of its operations and of its significant business segments for recent periods; and
- The corporation's performance compared with that of its competitors.[7]

SPECIFIC RESPONSIBILITIES OF DIRECTORS

Another authoritative governance reference, the *Principles of Corporate Governance*, published in 1994 by the American Law Institute (ALI), a group of prominent judges, law school deans, and practicing attorneys, sets forth the principal functions that a board of directors should perform.[8] They are:

1. Select, regularly evaluate, fix the compensation of, and, where appropriate, replace the principal senior executives;
2. Oversee the conduct of the corporation's business to evaluate whether the business is being properly managed;
3. Review and where appropriate, approve the corporation's financial objectives and major corporate plans and actions;
4. Review and, where appropriate, approve major changes in, and determinations of other major questions of choice respecting, the appropriate auditing and accounting principles and practices to be used in the preparation of the corporation's financial statements;
5. Perform such other functions as are prescribed by law, or assigned to the board under a standard of the corporation.[9]

[7] Excerpted from *Corporate Director's Guidebook, Fifth Edition*, 2007, published by the American Bar Association Section of Business Law. Copyright © 2007 by the American Bar Association. Reprinted with permission., p. 14.

[8] ALI, *Principles of Corporate Governance: Analysis and Recommendations* (St. Paul, MN: American Law Institute Publishers, 1994).

[9] Id., § 3.02, p. 86.

Written well before the scandals of the early 2000s, the work of these authoritative legal scholars under the auspices of the ALI prescribed significant responsibilities for boards of directors of large public companies. The ALI principles and suggested requirements are equally applicable to not-for-profit entities whose actions must pass muster in the court of public opinion as well sometimes in a court of law. The recommendations contained in the *Principles* have been largely incorporated in provisions of the Model Act for Corporations that has been adopted in the corporation statutes of a wide majority of states.

It is interesting to note that the ALI deemed function number 4, dealing with accounting principles and practices, so important that it placed it within the purview of the full board, not just the audit committee. The content of the ALI recommendations regarding functions of the audit committee is discussed later in this volume.

BEST PRACTICES BOARDS SHOULD EMBRACE

The National Association of Corporate Directors (NACD),[10] a membership organization of directors that is devoted to improving corporate governance, publishes Blue Ribbon Commission reports on various governance topics, including director professionalism. The latest edition of the NACD's report on director professionalism was released in 2005.[11] According to the NACD, specific tasks boards should undertake include:

- Approve a corporate philosophy and mission.
- Select, monitor, evaluate, compensate, and—if necessary, replace the CEO and other senior executives. Ensure management succession.
- Review and approve management's strategic plans, including developing a depth of knowledge of the business being served, understanding and questioning the assumptions upon which such plans are based, and reaching an independent judgment that the plans can be realized.
- Review and approve the corporation's financial objectives, plans, and actions, including significant capital allocations and expenditures.
- Review and approve material transactions not in the ordinary course of business.
- Monitor corporate performance against the strategic and business plans, including overseeing the operating results on a regular basis to evaluate whether the business is being properly managed.
- Ensure ethical behavior and compliance with laws and regulations, auditing and accounting principles, and the corporation's own governing documents.

[10] See www.nacdonline.org.

[11] National Association of Corporate Directors, *Report of the NACD Blue Ribbon Commission on Director Professionalism*, 2005 ed. (Washington, DC: NACD, 2005).

- Assess the board's own effectiveness in fulfilling these and other board responsibilities.
- Perform such other functions as a prescribed by law, or assigned to the board in the corporation's governing documents.[12]

This listing of recommended tasks provides insights from the perspective of an organization that wishes to set best practice standards for director behavior. Thus, the list includes topics that are not included in strictly legal requirements, such as an expressed need for a depth of knowledge about the organization's strategic plan, approval of a corporate philosophy and mission, desirability of board self-evaluation, and an emphasis on ethical behavior and compliance with laws and regulations. The NACD believes these best practice recommendations are equally applicable to not-for-profit and privately held organizations.

OVERVIEW OF CURRENT LEGALLY REQUIRED BOARD MEMBER DUTIES

The Model Business Corporation Act for regular for-profit corporations has been adopted by more than 30 states. The Model act provides the baseline standard that every director must follow to discharge his or her fiduciary duties as a director, including duties as a member of a committee. Although the state corporation statutes do not specifically define the board's responsibilities for overseeing the management of the corporation, the 2007 *Corporate Directors' Guidebook* outlines these tasks:

- Monitoring the corporation's performance in light of its operating, financial, and other significant corporate plans, strategies, and objectives, and approving major changes in plans and strategies;
- Selecting the CEO, setting the goals for the CEO and other senior executives, evaluating and establishing their compensation, and making changes when appropriate;
- Developing, approving, and implementing succession plans for the CEO and top senior executives;
- Understanding the corporation's risk profile and reviewing and overseeing risk management programs;
- Understanding the corporation's financial statements and monitoring the adequacy of its financial and other internal controls as well as its disclosure controls and procedures; and
- Establishing and monitoring effective compliance systems and policies for ethical conduct.[13]

---

[12] Id., pp. 3–4.

[13] ABA, *Corporate Director's Guidebook* (2007), p. 12.

Directors' specific attention to matters of business risk and compliance are relatively recent additions to the portfolio of director concerns. These areas are usually one of the primary concerns of the audit committee and are discussed at greater length concerning risk management in Chapter 10 and compliance in Chapter 12.

DUTIES OF CARE AND LOYALTY

A primary consideration of every board of directors is that all directors must always act in good faith and in the best interests of the corporation. This duty is characterized as the duty of loyalty, where directors must avoid both personal and financial conflicts of interest with the corporation. Directors are also expected to discharge their duties in a prudent manner with the care that a person in a like position would reasonably believe appropriate under similar circumstances. This mandate is often referred to as the duty of care. This precept provides that directors must discharge their duties "with the care that a person in a like position would reasonably believe appropriate under similar circumstances."[14] In other words, a director must act in a prudent manner for the benefit of the corporation, viewed in light of the director's knowledge and experience and the situation at hand.

The duty of care requires directors to regularly attend all meetings of the full board and any committees to which he or she is assigned and to be well informed about the business of the corporation. Similar provisions relating to the duty of loyalty and the duty of care apply to not-for-profit corporations and are contained in the not-for-profit corporation statutes of the various states of incorporation.

A qualification of the duty of care is the Business Judgment Rule, which flows from case law. This doctrine protects directors from personal liability relating to decisions made by directors so long as the director was disinterested in the matter, became fully informed on the subject, and acted in good faith and the honest belief that the action taken was in the best interests of the corporation.[15] In other words, the Business Judgment Rule protects directors from lawsuits that would use hindsight to speculate on the validity of a particular decision made by a board in a particular circumstance. Determination of any liability resulting from actions of directors in not-for-profit organizations depends on the provisions of the laws of the state of incorporation.

Aspects of the duty of care set forth in the 2007 *Corporate Director's Guidebook* include these matters:

- *Time commitment and regular attendance.* Personal attendance and full participation are required, not delegation through a proxy. For public companies, if a director's attendance at full board and committee meetings falls below 75%, that fact must be noted in the proxy statement at which directors stand for election.

[14] Id., p. 17.
[15] Id., p. 26.

- *Need to be informed and prepared.* Directors should not hesitate to request additional information and not be content to just listen to management presentations. The 1996 *Caremark International* decision established the principle that "a director's obligation includes a duty to attempt in good faith to assure that a corporate information and reporting system, which the board concludes is adequate, exists, and that failure to do so under some circumstances may, in theory at least, render a director liable for losses caused by non-compliance with applicable legal standards."[16] It can be assumed that members of the audit committee have an even more stringent obligation than do board members to be sure that adequate information systems exist that provide timely, reliable, and relevant information for decision making.
- *Right to rely on others.* Directors may rely on the work of other board committees, professional advisors, and others whom the director believes to be reliable and competent in the subject presented. These persons include management, legal counsel, and independent auditors, so long as the director has no knowledge that would make the reliance unwarranted. Again, directors should question professional advisors to make sure they fully understand the full context of information with which they are presented.
- *Inquiry.* When information indicates that potential problems or issues may exist, directors should pursue the matter and make inquiries and follow up until they are reasonably satisfied that management is dealing with the issue appropriately. Even when there are no red flags, directors should satisfy themselves that there are programs designed to identify and manage business risks and compliance with corporate policies, laws, and regulations.
- *Disclosure among directors.* When decisions are made and for effective oversight, a candid discussion among directors and with management is essential. Each director should disclose information known to be material to the decision-making or oversight responsibilities of the board or its committees.[17]

The duty of loyalty has a number of specific applications that are set forth in the 2007 *Corporate Director's Guidebook*, including:

- *Acting in good faith.* The fundamental requirement of loyalty is that a director must believe in good faith that his or her actions are in the best interests of the corporation.
- *Conflicts of interest.* Directors should not participate in the discussion or voting on matters in which they may have a personal interest. The appearance of a conflict is as important as the actuality. Favoritism, nepotism, and the like have no place in the governance of either a public company or a charitable not-for-profit.

[16] *In re Caremark Int'l Inc.*, 698A.2nd 959 (Del. Ch. 1996).

[17] ABA, *Corporate Director's Guidebook* (2007), pp. 18–21.

- *Fairness to the corporation.* Disinterested directors should consider the fairness of a transaction that has conflict of interest or self-dealing elements.
- *Independent advice.* Independent advice may be helpful to determine the merits of a related party transaction.
- *Corporate opportunity.* Directors having access to a business opportunity related to the business of the corporation should typically make it available first to the corporation. Directors should not take personal advantage of their knowledge of a corporation's future plans.[18]

Most successful lawsuits against directors have been based on a breach of the duty of loyalty rather than a breach of the duty of care. This may be due to the relatively greater ease to demonstrate a conflict of interest than lack of attention or inquiry.

The earlier 2004 edition of the *Corporate Directors Guidebook* contained a helpful parsing of the language of the duties of directors as they relate to the duties of loyalty and of care in all corporations whether they are organized as for-profit or not-for-profit and if for-profit are then either publicly held or private corporations:

- *Acting in good faith*—acting honestly; dealing fairly; a lack of good faith will be evidenced by acting, or causing the corporation to act, for the director's personal benefit or acting with the intent to violate applicable law, or failing to act in the face of a known duty to act, in a manner that demonstrates an intentional disregard of, or extreme inattention to, the director's duties;
- *Reasonably believes*—although the director's personal belief is subjective, the qualification that it must be "reasonable"—that is, based upon a rational analysis of the situation understandable to others—makes the standard of conduct also objective, not just subjective;
- *Best interests of the corporation*—emphasizing the corporate director's obligation to the corporation and the requirement to avoid acting in a self-interested manner to the corporation's detriment;
- *Care*—expressing the need to pay attention, to ask questions and to act diligently in order to become and remain generally informed and, when appropriate, to bring relevant information to the attention of the other directors; in particular, these activities include reading materials and engaging in other preparation in advance of meetings, asking questions of management or advisors, requesting legal or other expert advice when desirable for a board decision until satisfied that all information significant to a decision is available to the board and has been considered, and when relevant, bringing the director's own knowledge and experience to bear;
- *Person in a like position*—avoids the implication of special qualifications and incorporating the basic attributes of common sense, practical wisdom and informed judgment generally associated with the position of corporate director; and

[18] Id., pp. 21–25.

- *Under similar circumstances*—recognizing that the nature and extent of the preparation for and deliberations leading up to decision-making and that the level of oversight will vary, depending upon the corporation's circumstances and the decision to be made.[19]

In 2004, changes were proposed to § 8.01 of the Model Act for Corporations by the same American Bar Association Committee that wrote the *Corporate Director's Guidebook*. These changes include revisions to the functions of a board of directors. In the case of public corporations, the board's oversight responsibilities are stated to include attention to:

- Business performance and plans
- Major risks to which the corporation is or may be exposed
- Performance and compensation of senior officers
- Policies and practices to foster the corporation's compliance with law and ethical conduct
- Preparation of the corporation's financial statements
- Effectiveness of the corporation's internal controls
- Arrangements for providing adequate and timely information to directors
- Composition of the board and its committees, taking into account the important role of independent directors[20]

This listing of clarifications in the full board's responsibilities responds to the governance failures of the early 2000s and recognizes the trend toward a broader and more principles-based statement of board responsibilities and duties. Analysis of the contents of the listing is also significant to audit committees in that many of the stated important new or augmented responsibilities involve areas for which they are likely to have primary responsibility and may be acting largely on behalf of the board as a whole. These areas include the topics of risk management, legal compliance, ethics, preparation and dissemination of financial information, internal control effectiveness, and disclosure of significant other information. Most of these topics will be discussed in greater detail in later chapters of this volume.

In a legal sense, as noted, directors are entitled to rely on information presented by management and others (absent any knowledge that would make that reliance unwarranted). This reliance includes information presented by professional advisors, such as attorneys and external auditors. However, because of the *Caremark* decision,[21] directors do need to be sure that a system is in place to provide them

[19] Excerpted from *Corporate Director's Guidebook*, Fourth Edition, 2004, published by the American Bar Association Section of Business Law. Copyright © 2004 by the American Bar Association. Reprinted with Permission.

[20] "Changes in the Model Business Corporation Act," *Business Lawyer* 59, no. 2 (February 2004). pp. 569–688.

[21] The 1996 *Caremark International* case in Delaware Chancery Court set forth new guidelines that require directors to inquire about unusual circumstances and be sure important matters come to their attention. Directors cannot just rely on management to keep them fully informed.

with necessary information to conclude that the information they are receiving regarding all important matters is relevant, reliable, timely, and complete. In this connection, directors also need to inquire about issues when alerted to circumstances suggesting that board attention is appropriate. Inattention to obvious red flags is an invitation to the plaintiffs' bar to file suit against directors for breach of one or more of their responsibilities.

ADDITIONAL DUTIES

Recent court decisions in some jurisdictions have described a new duty, the duty of disclosure, flowing from both the duties of care and loyalty. This concept requires directors to present shareholders with all material information known to them when requesting shareholders to vote approval of a proposal. It is significant to audit committee members because oversight of processes relating to public dissemination of information is usually delegated to the audit committee.

Another responsibility of corporate directors, known in court cases as the duty of good faith, was articulated in the 2003 Walt Disney case.[22] The Delaware Court of Chancery held that directors who take an "ostrich-like approach" to corporate governance and "consciously and intentionally disregard their responsibilities, adopting a 'we don't care about the risks' attitude," may be held liable for breaching their duty to act in good faith. The court specifically noted the importance of good faith, in addition to due care and loyalty, when considering director conduct.

Directors have a duty to keep confidential all information that the corporation has not made public. In addition to damaging the collegiality of the board and its bond of trust, unauthorized disclosure of information could subject the director so doing to personal liability or the corporation to litigation for violation of the securities laws.

Directors should also be aware of what some courts have called an emerging duty of candor that management (or other directors) owes to the board. Senior executives should keep directors apprised on a real-time basis of critical issues that affect the organization's strategic direction, are material to the board's oversight responsibilities, and are relevant to its decision making. Additionally, directors should probe management on issues they deem important in order to stay fully informed.

Further discussion of the legally required duties and responsibilities of the audit committee is contained in Chapter 4.

DIRECTORS' RIGHTS

To accomplish the proper oversight and decision-making functions that a director has, he or she is entitled to access to information and resources needed to do the job. The 2007 *Corporate Director's Guidebook* sets forth the most important rights:

[22] *In re Walt Disney Co. Derivative Litig.,* 907 A.2nd 693 (2005 Del. Ch.).

- Inspect books and records;
- Request additional information reasonably necessary to exercise informed oversight and make careful decisions;
- Inspect facilities as reasonably appropriate to gain an understanding of the operations of the business;
- Receive timely notice of all meetings in which a director is entitled to participate;
- Receive copies of key documents and of all board and committee meeting minutes; and
- Receive regular oral or written reports of the activities of all board committees.[23]

Sarbanes-Oxley also grants to the audit committee the authority to engage independent counsel and other advisors with the corporation required to pay the cost.

AREAS OF SPECIAL CONCERN FOR THE BOARD AS A WHOLE

The 2004 edition of the *Corporate Director's Guidebook* set forth six areas of special concern to the board as a whole, whether it serves a public corporation or a privately held or not-for-profit entity. These areas were quality of disclosure, compliance with law, approval of commitments and compliance with contractual obligations, effectiveness of internal and disclosure controls, identification of business risks and protection of assets, and counseling of directors. It is very interesting to note that the first five of these six responsibilities are likely to relate to a board member's reliance on the work of the audit committee. These concerns are believed to be still relevant and will be covered in greater detail in later chapters of this book.

In the 2007 edition of the *Guidebook*, the authors chose to emphasize most of these issues under the heading "Risk and Compliance Oversight." These issues are:

1. *Risk Management.* The board (or more likely the audit committee) should receive periodic reports concerning the corporation's identification, assessment, and decision processes for financial, industry, and other business risks.
2. *Compliance with Law.* Directors need to be sure that the corporation has adequate policies and procedures designed to provide assurance that there is compliance with corporate policies as well as all relevant laws and regulations. These policies include those pertaining to: codes of business conduct; environmental and health and safety; anti-discrimination and employment; anti-trust and competition; insider trading; anti-bribery; and securities laws. The board should consider

[23] ABA, *Corporate Director's Guidebook* (2007), pp. 14–15.

whether the ethics and compliance function has adequate funding to accomplish its mission. In addition, directors also have specific legal responsibilities for compliance with the U.S. Sentencing Guidelines and Sarbanes-Oxley requires audit committees to be responsible for a system to receive complaints about internal control and accounting matters from employees without fear of reprisal.

3. *Quality of Disclosure.* Directors need to understand that filings with the SEC and public relations releases accurately set forth significant information about the company and its business affairs. Each director of a public company signs the annual Form 10-K filed with the SEC.
4. *Employee Safety, Health and Environmental Protection, and Product Safety.* Although these issues may involve legal compliance, they also can result in significant risk and material costs when they occur. Board level attention to environmental and similar social issues sends the message that ethics and compliance is valued at the highest level of the organization.
5. *Political Activity.* If corporate officers and employees are active in seeking to shape governmental processes, their actions should be monitored by the board.
6. *Crisis Management.* There should be assurance to the board that plans exist for dealing with a natural disaster or significant adverse corporate development. Board-level participation in the development of such plans is advisable.[24]

The *Guidebook* places these special areas of concern in the discussion of a board's legal framework of responsibilities so as to emphasize the importance of the various oversight roles that the board performs. In the case of public companies these roles are performed on behalf of all shareholders, but in the case of not-for-profit organizations are on behalf of the general public.

RECOMMENDED ELEMENTS OF BOARD PRACTICES AND PROCESSES

The NACD *Report on Director Professionalism* outlines eight practices and processes that facilitate directors' ability to fulfill their role and discharge their responsibilities as directors and committee members. Some of these are mandated by New York Stock Exchange rules. The practices and processes recommended by NACD are:

1. Establishing a governance committee to ensure that boards can effectively discharge their governance responsibilities.
2. Creating independent leadership roles, such as a non-executive chair or lead director.
3. Influencing the agendas for both committee and full board meetings.

[24] Id., pp. 27–32.

4. Determining effective, independent selection and compensation methods to ensure board accountability to shareholders and reinforce perceptions of fairness and trust.
5. Requiring stock ownership.
6. Establishing an evaluation process, to include three levels, CEO, board, and individual director.
7. Holding executive sessions, without management presence.
8. Accessing independent advice when required.[25]

As an organization devoted to improving corporate governance, it is not surprising that the NACD's perspective on directors leans toward best practices, not just simple compliance with legal requirements. The recommended processes are directed toward enhancing the independence of the board from management, some of which are NYSE requirements. These include appointment of an independent lead director or non-executive chair, holding executive sessions without management presence, and utilization of independent consultants, rather than placing total reliance on information furnished by management and accepting management recommendations without adequate review and oversight.

The Conference Board Directors' Institute, an adjunct entity of the Conference Board, publisher of *Corporate Governance Handbook 2007*, notes favorable outcomes of regular board executive sessions without management presence:

- Promote open dialogue among the independent directors and free exchange of ideas, perspectives, and information;
- Have a feedback mechanism to the CEO for important issues that may surface (the lead or presiding director can take the lead in providing CEO feedback);
- Be scheduled at regular intervals (most commonly following each full board meeting, although some boards may also hold a short pre-meeting executive session) to eliminate any negative inferences from convening these sessions; and
- Should be supplemented by additional off-line informational channels (such as dinners before board meetings) to help build trust and relationships among the independent directors.[26]

The world's largest pharmaceutical company, Pfizer, Inc., believes its board exemplifies corporate governance best practices. In *Building Trust—Leading CEOs Speak Out: How They Create It, Strengthen It, and Sustain It*, Pfizer former chairman and CEO Hank McKinnell describes the importance of trust in his company's strategy of corporate governance:

> We believe in transparency and fairness for all investors. We've lived and thrived on the maxim that an independent, inquisitive, hardworking and highly intelligent board

[25] NACD, *Report on Director Professionalism*, 2005 ed., pp. 5–8

[26] Conference Board, *Corporate Governance Handbook* 2007, p. 21.

of directors is ultimately the best guarantor of that transparency and fairness. Over the long term, such a board makes managing a major company such as Pfizer easier. We insist on making it easy for our board to get the information they need and to ask the hard questions that challenge and sharpen management's thinking.[27]

The large international auditing firm PricewaterhouseCoopers (PwC) has issued a focus paper titled "Building Blocks of Effective Corporate Boards"[28] on www.globalbestpractices.com that outlines what the firm believes are the best practices that leading boards are employing. This guidance is issued in the context of the changes that have occurred as a fallout of the regulatory reforms resulting from corporate scandals. PwC believes that board members have heightened their level of oversight in response to the increased scrutiny being brought by shareowners and others. Additionally, the firm believes that a second phase of governance transformation has begun, in which directors are seeking ways to better balance their role as compliance watchdogs with their role of participating in strategic planning and serving as a sounding board for management.

The PwC paper outlines eight actions it considers to be building blocks of effectiveness:

1. *Create an open and engaging boardroom atmosphere.* Build boards whose members work well in teams, possess good listening and problem-solving skills, are independent-minded, and have the diverse experience to address relevant industry concerns and related business issues.
2. *Maximize the value of the board's time commitment by establishing clear roles and responsibilities within an appropriate structure.* Establish clear guidelines on appropriate issues for the board to tackle and ensure a clear definition of board roles.
3. *Determine the information the board needs, and ensure it is delivered on a timely basis.* Establish a system that provides the board with the targeted information it needs in a user-friendly format to understand and address critical issues.
4. *Dedicate time to strategic issues.* Determine strategic priorities and schedule time to address those priorities, ensuring time is dedicated to emerging issues and future plans.
5. *Create a transparent, explicit, and accountable executive pay management, and pass the commonsense test in the public eye.* Devise executive compensation plans that can adjust to changing market scenarios, support the performance objectives and operating philosophy established by the board and senior management, and pass the commonsense test in the public eye.

[27] John A. Koten, *Building Trust—Leading CEOs Speak Out: How They Create It, Strengthen It, and Sustain It* (New York: Arthur W. Page Society, 2004), p. 216.

[28] PricewaterhouseCoopers Global Best Practices, *Building Blocks of Effective Corporate Boards*, 2007. At PwC Web site http://cfodirect.pwc.com/CFODirectWeb/Controller.jpf?ContentCode=MSRA-76SLGR&ContentType=Content.

6. *Actively engage in the CEO succession process.* Discuss CEO succession periodically to ensure a firm plan is in place—and committed to—for a replacement leader in case of a crisis situation and establish CEO selection criteria for a successor under normal circumstances that provides opportunities for all directors to interact with leading candidates.
7. *Assess the strength of the company's management talent.* Ensure the company has a strong talent pool of people whose skills are relevant to face ongoing and coming challenges.
8. *Monitor the company's enterprise risk management system.* Tap the deep and diverse expertise of the board to assess management's risk and control profile.

The paper concludes:

> As boards evolve from the passive, management-friendly networks of yesteryear to today's more engaged overseers, they have filled board seats with directors who are independent based on new regulations and rules and who bring more diverse business backgrounds and levels of experience. Executive leaders truly committed to running organizations of high integrity understand that a proactive board-management relationship is vital to setting a tone at the top that fosters an ethical working culture.[29]

The KPMG Audit Committee Institute (ACI), an arm of the large international auditing firm KPMG, has issued a white paper titled "Five Guiding Principles for Audit Committees."[30] ACI believes that certain guiding principles underlie the effectiveness of every audit committee, even as there should be variation among entities. These principles can help ensure that practices are applied effectively—that is, by the right people with the right information, processes, and perspectives.

The first four principles have long been important to audit committee effectiveness. The last one is mandated by Sarbanes-Oxley and is vital to the independence, objectivity, and integrity of a corporation's financial reporting process:

1. *Recognize that one size does not fit all.* When delegating oversight responsibilities to the audit committee, recognize that the needs and dynamics of each company, board, and audit committee are unique.
2. *Have the "right" people on the committee.* The board must ensure that the committee comprises the "right" individuals to provide independent, objective, and effective oversight.
3. *Monitor and insist on the right "tone at the top."* The board and audit committee must continually assess whether—and insist that—the "tone at the top" sets an expectation of integrity and accuracy in financial reporting.

[29] Id., p. 18.

[30] KPMG International, "Five Guiding Principles for Audit Committees," 2006. At www.kpmg.com/aci/docs/practices/ACI_5%20Guiding%20Principles-WebFINAL.pdf.

4. *Ensure the oversight process facilitates the committee's understanding and monitoring of key roles, responsibilities, and risks within the financial reporting environment.*
5. *Articulate and exercise the committee's direct responsibility for the external auditor as required by Sarbanes-Oxley.*[31]

ASSESSING THE EFFECTIVENESS OF THE BOARD AS A WHOLE

In order to assure that the board as a whole is acting effectively, there must be a clear understanding of the board's mission. In other words, the board needs to articulate the areas it wishes to oversee and how it wishes to accomplish this objective. The bylaws of the corporation also set forth specific functions the board is required to perform as well as the functions for standing committees, such as the audit committee. These guidelines will assist in determining how well the board and the committees have discharged their responsibilities.

This being said, it is likely that the personal chemistry and style of the board chair (and also, if one has been appointed, a nonexecutive lead director) will be important factors in assuring board effectiveness. This leader must be skillful in drawing out the expertise of all members of the board in a collegial and open manner. The 2005 NACD report on director professionalism provides three areas where boards should concentrate efforts to assure their reasonable success. They are:

1. *Delineation of board and management powers.* Boards need to continually focus on the oversight of critical functions and avoid drifting into management's domain. Once board powers are clearly understood and articulated, the board should assess what it is doing and how well it is doing it.
2. *Effective interaction between directors.* Creative interplay of abilities and temperaments should make a well-functioning board greater than the sum of its parts. Boards should be sure to take advantage of technology to share information between meetings.
3. *Director education and development.* Continuous improvement should result from effective assessment of performance.[32]

According to the NACD report, judgments about the effectiveness of the board as a whole should use these assessment criteria. The evaluation process should be:

- Controlled by the independent directors themselves
- Aligned with established evaluation processes and goals

[31] Id., pp. 1–3.

[32] NACD, *Report on Director Professionalism*, 2005 ed. p. 19.

- Tailored to meet the needs of the individual company and board
- Designed to ensure candor, confidentiality, and trust
- Regularly reviewed and improved as necessary, and
- Disclosed (process only) to shareholders and the public.[33]

Chapter 3 discusses the effectiveness and desirable personal characteristics of board members to best achieve their goals.

LIABILITY AND INDEMNIFICATION

According to the 2007 edition of the *Director's Guidebook*, directors may incur personal liability for breaches of their duty of care or their duty of loyalty, or for failure to comply with other legal requirements, such as the federal securities laws. Most corporations have charter or bylaw provisions mandating indemnification of directors in most circumstances except when the individual is responsible for corporate misdeeds. Most corporations also purchase director's and officer's liability insurance to cover the cost of defending their interests. These protections for directors are usually in place in not-for-profit as well as publicly held and private corporations. Also, unpaid directors of not-for-profit organizations have some protection from liability resulting from state and federal statutes. This subject is discussed more fully in Chapter 14.

KEY POINTS IN CHAPTER 2

1. Members of a board of directors must be actively involved in representing the interests of the shareowners in determining but not managing the high-level affairs of the corporation. Directors should provide oversight and suggestions, guidelines and metrics, but should not determine day-to-day tactics useful in achieving the strategic plans and goals of the organization.
2. Boards must deal with two different tasks: making high-level decisions for the corporation, including approving the strategic direction of the corporation, declaring dividends, approving major acquisitions and divestitures, selecting the senior officers, and planning for their succession. Directors' second major task is to determine the compensation and oversee the performance of the officers they have put into place to carry out the approved strategy, and then faithfully report the results of implementing it to shareowners and the public.
3. In all of their actions, all members of the board of directors must consider two important legal duties: the duty of care and the duty of loyalty.

[33] Id., p. 22.

4. The work of independent nonexecutive members of the board is receiving greater attention that includes all members of the key oversight committees, such as the audit committee.
5. A lead director should be elected who will convene executive sessions of the board without management presence and foster a collegial and open atmosphere where all board members are comfortable in expressing their views.
6. Many of the issues of special concern for board members involve areas where the audit committee has primary responsibility. These include:
   - Quality of disclosure
   - Compliance with laws and regulations
   - Approval of commitments and compliance with contractual obligations
   - Effectiveness of internal and disclosure controls
   - Identification of business risks and protection of assets
7. The compensation of senior management as well as the CEO is emerging as a critically important issue for compensation committee analysis and full board deliberation.
8. CEO succession planning is a significant board responsibility. The board should be knowledgeable of the quality of the talent of individuals at the level of management that reports directly to the CEO.
9. Considering the recent increase in the duties of board members and their higher level of expected performance, directors must devote considerable time and effort in order to be fully effective.
10. The areas of required board oversight are broadening to include risk management, ethics and compliance, and internal controls as well as full financial and other disclosures to the public.
11. The board and its standing committees should be provided independent expert consulting advice and legal counsel whenever necessary.
12. Periodic self-evaluation of board and individual director performance is a growing phenomenon. The board and individual directors should continually strive to improve their performance.
13. The bylaws of most corporations provide for avoidance of liability in most circumstances and also provide director's and officer's insurance.

Chapter 3

Personal Characteristics of Effective Boards and Members

In order to accomplish most effectively the legally required and best practice duties of a well-run board of directors, various legal mandates, stock exchange rules, and best business practice recommendations have set forth a number of desirable characteristics of individual board members and boards as a whole. This chapter outlines those characteristics and further discusses some of the effectiveness considerations that were introduced in Chapter 2.

INTRODUCTION

The *Principles of Corporate Governance* reference volume mentioned in earlier chapters also describes the largely independent nature of the recommended composition of the board of directors of a large publicly held corporation. It states:

> The board . . . should have a majority of directors who are free of any significant relationship with the corporation's senior executives .[1]

This recommendation, which was controversial when first made in 1994, has since been enacted in the requirements for companies listed on the New York Stock Exchange (NYSE) and Nasdaq. The stewardship nature of the board's responsibilities is of long-standing duration.

Consequently, the "old-fashioned board" that was mainly comprised of friends and associates of the chief executive officer (CEO) is definitely out of fashion. It cannot be expected that such individuals could perform totally objective oversight of management actions, perhaps some of the most important functions of the board. Many of the governance difficulties that have occurred in the past can be directly traced to the fact that the board of directors merely perfunctorily considered issues and gave rubber-stamp approval of the actual past and proposed future actions of management and did not engage in adequate review, deliberation, and consideration.

---

[1] American Law Institute, *Principles of Corporate Governance: Analysis and Recommendations* (St. Paul, MN: American Law Institute Publishers, 1994), § 3A.01, p. 110.

Nowadays, boards of directors are responding to public and investor pressures for improved corporate governance. Directors must be engaged in objective oversight, become fully informed before making decisions. They must commit sufficient time and energy to fulfill their fiduciary responsibilities to shareowners and other stakeholders.

ROLE AND AUTHORITY OF INDEPENDENT DIRECTORS

In the post-Enron era, directors who are totally independent of management are playing a greater role in the governance of all public corporations. The NYSE has set forth listing rules dealing with independent directors, including a definition. It notes that "[l]isted companies must have a majority of independent directors."[2] Nasdaq Rule 4350(c)(1) states similarly that "[a] majority of the board of directors must be comprised of independent directors as defined."[3] The exchanges also require all members of the key standing committees—audit, nominating/governance, and compensation committees—to be totally composed of independent directors. The matter of audit committee member independence is discussed in Chapter 6.

Annual proxy statements of public companies must identify which directors are considered to be independent. Analysis of 2006 Fortune 1000 proxies by executive search consulting firm Korn/Ferry indicates that the average percentage of outside directors was 80%, the same as in 2005. Korn/Ferry reports that 2005 was the first decrease in this relationship which had previously not changed since 1990.[4]

To motivate open discussion among independent and other nonmanagement directors and "to empower [them] to serve as a more effective check on management," NYSE Rule 303A.03 provides that "the non-management directors of each listed company must meet at regularly scheduled executive sessions without management."[5] Korn/Ferry notes that 94% of American companies embrace this practice. This is an increase from 66% in 1996.[6]

In the words of the fourth edition of the *Corporate Director's Guidebook* that are still relevant, individual directors should "become informed, participate, ask questions, apply considered business judgment and, when necessary, bring a matter to the board's attention."[7] Thus, every director must become familiar with the corporation's operating activities, products and markets, understand its key profit

---

[2] NYSE, Inc., Listed Company Manual § 303A¶ 1. See www.nyse.com.

[3] Nasdaq Manual online at www.complinet.com/nasdaq/display/display.html?rbid=1705&element_id=26, accessed May 2007.

[4] Korn/Ferry International, *33rd Annual Board of Directors Study*, Los Angeles: KFI, 2007, p. 11, and 2006, p. 11.

[5] NYSE, Inc., Listed Company Manual § 303A¶ 3. See www.nyse.com.

[6] Korn/Ferry, 2007, p. 21

[7] Excerpted from *Corporate Director's Guidebook, Fourth Edition*, 2004, published by the American Bar Association Section of Business Law. Copyright © 2004 by the American Bar Association. Reprinted with Permission.

drivers, and the strategies the corporation uses to earn profits, which is the principal reason for its existence.

As what could be called "independent insiders," nonexecutive directors need to understand the business(es) in which the organization is engaged. Participation in decision making and oversight is important, but that participation must be informed and analytical. In addition to participating in setting strategic directions, a director should evaluate the performance of senior management and the corporation as a whole, so that executives can be appropriately rewarded. Providing for succession of management is also an important responsibility of the board. Thus, board members need to get to know the qualifications and experience of various members of senior management.

The issue of putting into practice the board's recognized predominance over senior management has been demonstrated by the controversy over whether the CEO should also serve as the chair of the board, as is typical in U.S. public corporations. The downside of having a separate person serve as board chair is the appearance of dilution of the CEO's authority. Also, employees may be confused as to exactly who is in charge. The obvious advantages of the separation involve enhancing the independence of the board and improving the quality of oversight.

A compromise solution is to appoint a lead director whose duties include independence-increasing activities, including presiding over executive sessions of the board without management presence, and leading periodic formal evaluations of the CEO's performance. The 2006 Korn/Ferry director survey of the Fortune 1000 corporations notes that 78% of these large corporations have an elected or appointed lead director. Ten years ago, Korn/Ferry reports that only 24% had selected a lead director from the ranks of nonexecutive directors.[8]

CHARACTERISTICS OF AN EFFECTIVE BOARD MEMBER

One of the most important functions of the board's nominating or corporate governance committee is to determine and recommend to the board for its consideration appropriate candidates to fill board and committee vacancies. Although not included in the 2007 *Corporate Director's Guidebook*, this description from the 2004 edition is still relevant:

> The principal attributes of an effective corporate director include strength of character, an inquiring and independent mind, practical wisdom and mature judgment. In addition to these personal qualities, the [nominating] committee may want to establish individual qualifications such as technical skills, career specialization or specific background experience.[9]

[8] Korn/Ferry International 2007, p. 24.

[9] Excerpted from *Corporate Director's Guidebook, Fourth Edition*, 2004, published by the American Bar Association Section of Business Law. Copyright © 2004 by the American Bar Association. Reprinted with Permission.

Candidates for potential membership on standing committees, such as the audit committee, may require specialized knowledge. The major characteristics desirable for audit committees and their members are further discussed in Chapter 6.

The 2005 National Association of Corporate Directors (NACD) report on director professionalism presents five elements as key determinants of whether an individual should be included on a board and whether the person's presence is a positive force for the benefit of the corporation.[10] They are:

1. *Personal characteristics*. These are mainly high ethical standards and integrity.
2. *Informed judgment*. This includes the ability to provide wise, thoughtful counsel on a broad range of issues.
3. *Financial literacy*. Although required only for audit committee membership, this characteristic is important for all board members, in view of the fact that all members of the board have a responsibility for financial reporting.
4. *Mature confidence*. The member should value board and team performance over individual performance, show respect for others, and be willing to listen.
5. *High performance standards*. The person should have a history of achievements that reflects high standards.[11]

Earlier, the ideal candidate for membership on a large public board of directors was likely to be the CEO of another large public corporation. This is changing, due to the fact that best governance practices limit the number of boards upon which an individual can serve as well as the practice by boards of other corporations to insist that their CEO pay full-time attention to the challenges of leading their corporation. The 2006 Korn/Ferry survey notes that a majority of corporations—60%—limit the number of outside boards on which the CEO may serve. In 1995, only 11% had such a restriction.[12]

In recent years, the practice of inviting women and minorities to serve as board members has rapidly increased. Diversity of outlook in a corporation's boardroom is considered essential to a corporation's diversity of appeal in a diverse marketplace. Korn/Ferry reports that 85% of corporations have one or more women on their board compared with 69% in 1995 and that 76% have one or more ethnic minority members compared with 47% in 1995.[13]

As a best practice, the board should regularly engage in a formal self-evaluation of its effectiveness. Mandatory rotation of directors to new committee assignments and also off the board through mandatory retirement facilitates fresh insights and avoids a long-term overfamiliarity with issues that leads to inadequate independent analysis. The Enron board was notable for the fact that its directors and chairs of standing committees had served for many, many years without rotation.

---

[10] National Association of Corporate Directors, *Report of the NACD Blue Ribbon Commission on Director Professionalism, 2005 ed.* (Washington, DC: NACD, 2005).

[11] Id., p. 21.

[12] Korn/Ferry 2007, p. 21, and 2001, p. 21.

[13] Korn/Ferry 2007, p. 11 and 2001, p. 12.

CORE COMPETENCIES OF AN EFFECTIVE BOARD

The 2005 NACD report sets forth core competencies that the board as a whole should possess. These recommendations apply to nonpublic as well as not-for-profit corporations. Each board member should have characteristics that contribute to the total effort in one or more areas. The recommended competencies are:

- *Accounting and finance.* Boards need to ensure that shareholder value is protected through adequate controls and enhanced using meaningful measures of performance. Recent legislation and regulation have increased the attention that boards have had to pay to proper controls and financial reporting.
- *Business judgment.* Boards need members skilled in making good business decisions. Boards should provide advice and counsel to the CEO, but at the end of the day, they must be sure that the shareowner's interests are protected.
- *Management.* Boards need members who stay current with management trends, best practices, and how to apply them. Evaluation of the performance of senior management is a critically important board function.
- *Crisis response.* Boards need to have the capability of providing leadership in cases of emergencies. Many cases of emergencies have involved senior management, so that the board must be able to step in promptly.
- *Industry knowledge.* Boards need knowledge about industry-specific issues in order to be fully informed.
- *International markets.* Corporations with global operations need boards with international knowledge.
- *Leadership.* Boards need members who can attract management having the ability to motivate high-performing talent. Providing for succession management as well as properly motivating incumbent management is an important board function.
- *Strategy/Vision.* Since a key role of the board is to approve and monitor strategy, boards need members having skills and capacity to encourage innovation, conceptualize key trends, evaluate strategic decisions, and continuously challenge the organization to sharpen its vision.[14]

These characteristics illustrate the breadth of knowledge that is required for effective board processes. No one person could fulfill all of these requirements, yet the board as a whole should be able to do so. Nevertheless, it would be a mistake to create a board that is so large as to be unwieldy and not allow full and informed participation by all members.

---

[14] NACD, *Report on Director Professionalism, 2005 ed.*, p. 10.

SUMMARY OF THE DIRECTOR'S ROLE

The 2007 *Corporate Director's Guidebook* concludes by noting that "the core values associated with the corporate director's role—good faith, general oversight, informed judgment, and dedication to the corporation's best interests—continue to be the touchstone for evaluating all directors' conduct."[15] The final portion of the *Guidebook* sets forth a summary containing a number of basic points:

- A director must exercise independent judgment for the overall benefit of the corporations.
- To meet the duty of care, a director must be diligent and invest significant amounts of time and energy in monitoring management's conduct of the business and compliance with the corporation's operating and administrative procedures and should be satisfied that the proper procedures are in place.
- A director should be comfortable that the board is appropriately informed and has had the time to deliberate carefully before making decisions, unless the circumstances warrant otherwise.
- A director is entitled to rely on performance by others of properly delegated functions and on reports, opinions, information, and statements of the corporation's officers, legal counsel, accountants, employees, and committees of the board on which the director does not serve, when under the circumstances it is reasonable to do so.
- The duty of loyalty requires that directors not use their corporate position for unauthorized personal benefit, gain, or other advantage at the expense of the corporation and that they not disregard their director duties.
- Conflicts of interest (including corporate opportunities and a director's transactions with the corporation) are not inherently improper. The manner in which an interested director and the board deal with a conflict situation determines the propriety of the transaction and the director's conduct.
- A periodic review of indemnification, expense advance and insurance protections for directors is advisable.
- This Guidebook should not be viewed as a substitute for legal consultation and advice.[16]

KEY POINTS IN CHAPTER 3

1. Members of a board of directors should have high standards; should be ethical and have integrity; be able to provide wise, thoughtful counsel; have general financial literacy; and have mature confidence that values team performance over personal performance.

[15] Excerpted from *Corporate Director's Guidebook, Fifth Edition*, 2007, published by the American Bar Association Section of Business Law. Copyright © 2007 by the American Bar Association. Reprinted with permission, p. 113.

[16] *Corporate Director's Guidebook*, 2007, pp. 113–114.

2. Directors need to always act in the best interests of the corporation and must have sufficient information in order that their decisions use good business judgment and are well supported by facts and analysis. Becoming fully informed is a key aspect of a director's duty of care.
3. If the CEO is also the chair of the board, the board should appoint or elect an independent director to serve as lead director and formally evaluate the CEO's performance and preside over executive sessions of the nonexecutive directors without management presence.
4. Directors can rely on the information provided by management and by professional advisors, such as attorneys and auditors, except when there is reason to believe this reliance is unwarranted. Directors must be sure that there exists an effective system for communicating all relevant information to them.
5. Directors need to be knowledgeable about the industries in which the corporation's businesses operate, including how they earn profits. Breadth of knowledge is important.
6. Directors must be committed to serving as the fiduciary representatives of shareowners and other stakeholders.
7. Independence of thought and action is a critically important characteristic of both board and audit committee members. Yet directors need to act in a manner that preserves a collegial atmosphere of openness within the boardroom.
8. The personal characteristics required for serving as an effective member of the audit committee are very similar to those required of an effective member of the board as a whole.
9. Effective board members should evaluate their own performance as well as that of the full board and continually strive for improvement.
10. Directors should maintain their competence and professionalism through continuing education and development.

Chapter 4

Duties of Audit Committees Prescribed by Law, Regulation, or Rule

INTRODUCTION

As noted in Chapter 1, an audit committee, as a standing committee of the corporation, has been a part of the governance structure of corporations for only a relatively brief portion of the time that corporations have been in existence. However, as also noted earlier, the number of duties, together with the scope and importance of the role of audit committees, has greatly escalated in recent years. This trend has largely resulted from the aftermath of the prominent business scandals in the early postmillennium years.

Consequently, the number of audit committee meetings since 2000 in the average public company in the Fortune 1000 has more than doubled, according to the annual survey performed by executive search consulting firm Korn/Ferry International.[1] The 2007 edition of the *Corporate Director's Guidebook* also highlights the importance of audit committees by stating:

> [T]he audit committee has become a critical component of the corporate governance structure of public companies because it has general oversight responsibility for the public company's financial reporting process and internal controls. It also has the exclusive responsibility for retaining and overseeing the performance of the external auditor.[2]

These comments largely apply to the audit committees of private and not-for-profit corporations as well.

[1] Korn/Ferry International, 32nd Annual Board of Directors Study, (Los Angeles: KFI, 2007), p. 14, and 2001, p. 13.

[2] American Bar Association, *Corporate Director's Guidebook, Fifth Edition* (Chicago: ABA Committee on Corporate Laws, 2007), p. 57.

Many of the prominent failures of corporate governance in public companies that have taken place in recent years have involved breakdowns in areas where audit committees have had primary responsibilities. The colossal frauds that took place at Sunbeam, Waste Management, Enron, and WorldCom involved weak internal controls and deficient financial reporting that their audit committees failed to prevent and their external audit firms failed to discover. At Adelphia and Tyco International, major problems involved inadequate controls over loans made and/or perks provided to senior executives. The list of accounting and auditing-related scandals seems never-ending, with later discoveries at Fannie Mae, HealthSouth, and AIG. More recently, the number of both large and small public companies that have been publicly cited for the practice of backdating of stock option grants is surprising large.

These recent developments have resulted in significant increases in the number and importance of responsibilities that are usually assigned by-law to audit committees. The breadth of responsibilities is particularly true in mid-size public companies that have not appointed board committees to specialize in the oversight of risk management, ethics and compliance, and similar matters.

Regulatory requirements of necessary qualifications for membership on audit committees have been expanded to include specific qualities of independence and competence. As a consequence of new audit committee responsibilities and better understanding of their importance, the number and length of audit committee meetings has increased much more than that experienced by other standing board committees. Thus, it is critical that audit committee members avoid serving on too many other board committees and on the boards or audit committees of too many other corporations. As will be discussed, a number of public corporations have begun to limit the number of outside boards and standing committees upon which their chief executive officer may serve.

As a standing committee of the board of directors, audit committees are designated specific responsibilities in the corporate by-laws to fulfill on behalf of the full board. Additionally, audit committees of public companies are required by Securities and Exchange Commission (SEC) regulation and stock exchange rules to develop and publish for investor and public use a charter and mission statement that clearly sets forth their position and specific duties. Public company audit committees are also required by SEC rule to report annually their accomplishments in the corporation's proxy statement. Because of the number and significance of these responsibilities, it is important that reports of committee activities and decisions regularly flow to the full board, so that all directors are kept informed and can participate in decision making where necessary.

Chapter 1 set forth a brief historical outline of legislative, regulatory, and other developments affecting the evolution of audit committees. This chapter presents an overview of audit committee responsibilities and also audit committee composition from a legal and regulatory perspective.

HISTORICAL DEVELOPMENT OF MANDATED AUDIT COMMITTEE DUTIES

In light of the history of audit committee development, it is not surprising that a majority of audit committee duties that are prescribed by statute, regulation, or rule tend to deal with financial affairs, primarily the preparation and auditing of financial statements. More specifically, these duties now include direct and exclusive responsibility for the selection, evaluation for retention, and oversight of the performance of the external auditor. They also include oversight of the corporation's financial reporting to the public, evaluation of internal control effectiveness and reporting thereon, and compliance with laws and regulations.

The American Law Institute's *Principles of Corporate Governance* volumes provide further authoritative direction from a historical perspective as to the place of audit committees in the governance structure of a public corporation. Volume One of this Treatise states:

> Every large publicly held corporation should have an audit committee to implement and support the oversight function of the Board by reviewing on a periodic basis the corporation's processes for producing financial data, its internal controls, and the independence of the corporation's external auditor.[3]

It lists eight specific functions and powers that audit committees should have:

1. Recommend the firm to be employed as the corporation's external auditor and review the proposed discharge of any such firm;
2. Review the external auditor's compensation, the proposed terms of its engagement, and its independence;
3. Review the appointment and replacement of the senior internal auditing executive, if any;
4. Serve as a channel of communication between the external auditor and the board and between the senior internal auditing executive, if any, and the board;
5. Review the results of each external audit of the corporation, the report of the audit, any related management letter, management's responses to recommendations made by the external auditor in connection with the audit, reports of the internal auditing department that are material to the corporation as a whole, and management's responses to those reports;
6. Review the corporation's annual financial statements, any certification, report, opinion, or review rendered by the external auditor in connection with those financial statements, and any significant disputes between management and the external auditor that arose in connection with the preparation of those financial statements;

[3] American Law Institute, *Principles of Corporate Governance: Analysis and Recommendations* (St. Paul, MN: American Law Institute Publishers, 1994), Part 3.05, p. 103.

7. Consider, in consultation with the external auditor and the senior internal auditing executive, if any, the adequacy of the corporation's internal controls;
8. Consider major changes and other major questions of choice respecting the appropriate auditing and accounting principles and practices to be used in the preparation of the corporation's financial statements, when presented by the external auditor, a principal senior executive, or otherwise.[4]

A very lengthy discussion and consultation process took place during the development of the *Principles*. Final approval of their premises and language took years to work out, and the concepts contained in the *Principles* were considered to be far-reaching when they were finally adopted in 1992, In spite of these obstacles, however, the recommendations contained in the *Principles* have been largely incorporated in the Model Act for Corporations that has been adopted in a majority of state corporation statutes. These duties are discussed at greater length in the sections that follow, in the context of the specific area they involve.

SOURCE OF CURRENT LEGALLY REQUIRED DUTIES OF AUDIT COMMITTEES

The majority of the current regulations affecting audit committees are issued by the SEC, which is the primary regulator of the U.S. securities markets. Accordingly, the SEC has principal responsibility for the regulation of accounting, financial reporting, external auditing, and related internal control systems of public U.S. corporations. The SEC is the primary enforcement agency for the securities laws that were enacted during the 1930s, including their many amendments, most recently the Sarbanes-Oxley Act of 2002.

The Securities Act of 1933 regulates the issuance of new securities to the public, while the Securities Exchange Act of 1934 regulates the purchase and sale of securities that are already in the hands of the public. As regulators of the securities markets, the SEC also approves rules issued by the stock exchanges, as self-regulatory organizations, that affect the companies that are listed on them.

With respect to accounting, the SEC oversees the work of the Financial Accounting Standards Board (FASB), which determines accounting principles that must be used by public companies in the United States. Concerning auditing, the SEC also oversees the activities of the Public Company Accounting Oversight Board (PCAOB), an independent board, which performs inspections of the quality of the audits performed by independent auditors and also sets auditing and ethics standards they must abide by in the audit of public companies. Regulations affecting audit committees have also arisen from other SEC regulations, such as those that were issued in 1999 as a result of the recommendations designed to improve audit committee effectiveness by the efforts of the Blue Ribbon Committee, a joint

[4] Id., Part 3A.03, pp. 115–116.

committee of the New York Stock Exchange and the National Association of Securities Dealers.[5]

In the post-Enron era, public company audit committees have been assigned more specific responsibilities relating to the oversight of financial disclosures and internal controls. In many companies, these committees have also been assigned responsibilities for overseeing risk management and compliance processes.

REPORT AND RECOMMENDATIONS OF THE 1999 BLUE RIBBON COMMITTEE ON IMPROVING THE EFFECTIVENESS OF CORPORATE AUDIT COMMITTEES

The New York Stock Exchange (NYSE) and National Association of Securities Dealers (NASD) jointly formed in 1998 a committee of well-known experts in the field of corporate governance to study audit committee aspects of corporate governance in public companies and, if necessary, develop appropriate recommendations for new regulations dealing with the audit committee oversight of financial reporting. The motivation for formation of the study was increasing concern expressed by the SEC that a crisis was developing in financial reporting. The SEC foresaw the coming bubble and subsequent collapse in the stock market that occurred several years later.

John C. Whitehead, former senior partner and co-chair of investment bankers Goldman Sachs, and Ira Millstein, world-renowned corporate governance expert and senior partner of the prominent law firm Weil Gotshal & Manges, were chosen to head up the effort. A panel of nine additional experts from industry, accounting, and financial institutions evaluated materials that were submitted by organizations and the public, held hearings, deliberated, and made a determination of the content of the final report. The study effort encompassed contributions from organizations representing the interests of financial and auditing firms, investment organizations, law firms, academia, and many other individuals of diverse backgrounds. As an aside, this author was thanked in the chairman's letter introducing the report as one of many who made a comment or provided some written contribution.

The work of the committee was accomplished on a fast-track schedule, so that a final report of recommendations for SEC implementation could be prepared, exposed for comment, and put into place within one year. The committee's output, *Report and Recommendations of the Blue Ribbon Committee on Improving the Effectiveness of Corporate Audit Committees* (*Blue Ribbon Committee Report*), was issued in 1999, well within the timetable that had been set. The report encompassed recommendations relating to external and internal auditors and senior and financial management as well as audit committees and boards of directors. A "three-legged stool" of responsibility was described in the report, including the responsibilities of

[5] NYSE and NASD, *Report and Recommendations of the Blue Ribbon Committee on Improving the Effectiveness of Audit Committees*, (New York: NYSE and NASD, 1999).

financial management including the internal auditor, the external auditor, and the audit committee.[6]

SUMMARY OF RECOMMENDATIONS

The 10 recommendations relating to audit committee responsibilities contained in the *Blue Ribbon Committee Report* are set forth next; Guiding Principles for Audit Committee Best Practices are presented in Chapter 5. The 10 Blue Ribbon Committee recommendations are:

1. *Independence*
   Members of the audit committee should be considered independent if they have no relationship to the corporation that may interfere with the exercise of their independence from management and the corporation.
2. *Independence*
   The NYSE and the NASD require listed companies with a market capitalization above $200 million have an audit committee comprised solely of independent directors. The NYSE and NASD maintain their current independence requirements as well as their respective definitions of independence for smaller companies.
3. *Financial Literacy*
   The NYSE and NASD require listed companies with a market capitalization above $200 million to have an audit committee comprised of a minimum of three directors, each of whom is financially literate.
4. *Audit Committee Structure and Process*
   The NYSE and NASD require the audit committee of each listed company to:
   (i) adopt a formal written charter that specifies the scope of the committee's responsibilities, and how it carries out those responsibilities, including structure, processes, and membership requirements, and
   (ii) review and reassess the adequacy of the audit committee charter on an annual basis.
5. *Audit Committee Structure and Process*
   The SEC should promulgate rules that require the audit committee for each reporting company to disclose in the company's proxy statement for its annual meeting of shareholders whether the audit committee has adopted a formal written charter, and if so, whether the audit committee satisfied its responsibilities during the prior year in compliance with its charter, which charter shall be disclosed at least triennially in the annual report to shareholders or proxy statement and in the next annual report to shareholders or proxy statement after any significant change.
6. *Audit Committee Relationships with Management, including the Internal Auditor, and with the Outside Auditors.*

[6] Id., p. 7.

That the listing rules for both the NYSE and NASD require that the audit committee charter for every listed company specify that the outside auditor is ultimately accountable to the board of directors and the audit committee, as representatives of shareholders, and that these shareholder representatives have the ultimate authority and responsibility to select, evaluate, and where appropriate, replace the outside auditor.

7. *Audit Committee Relationships with Management, including the Internal Auditor, and with the Outside Auditors*
   That the listing rules for both the NYSE and NASD should require that the audit committee charter for every listed company specify that the audit committee is responsible for ensuring its receipt from the outside auditors of a formal written statement delineating all relationships between the auditor and the company, consistent with Independence Standards Board Standard I, and that the audit committee is also responsible for actively engaging in a dialogue with the auditor with respect to any disclosed relationships or services which may impact the objectivity and independence of the auditor and for taking, or recommending that the full board take, appropriate action to ensure the independence of the outside auditor.
8. *Enhancing the Outside Auditors' Communication with the Audit Committee*
   That Generally Acceptable Auditing Standards (GAAS) should require that a company's outside auditor discuss with the audit committee the auditor's judgments about the quality, not just the acceptability, of the company's accounting principles as applied in its financial reporting; the discussion should include such issues as the clarity of the company's disclosures and degree of aggressiveness or conservatism of the company's accounting principles and underlying estimates and other significant decisions made by management in preparing the financial disclosure and reviewed by the outside auditors. The requirement should be written in a way to encourage open, frank discussion and to avoid boilerplate.
9. *Instituting Audit Committee Disclosure*
   That the SEC should require all reporting companies to include a letter from the audit committee in the company's annual report to shareholders and Form 10-K Annual Report disclosing whether or not, with respect to the prior fiscal year:
   (i) management has reviewed the audited financial statements with the audit committee, including a discussion of the quality of the accounting principles as applied and significant judgments affecting the company's financial statements;
   (ii) the outside auditors have discussed with the audit committee the outside auditors' judgments of the quality of those principles as applied and judgments referenced in (i) above under the circumstances;
   (iii) the members of the audit committee have discussed among themselves, without management or the outside auditors present, the information disclosed to the audit committee described in (i) and (ii) above; and
   (iv) the audit committee, in reliance on the review and discussions conducted with management and the outside auditors pursuant to (i) and (ii) above, believes that the company's financial statements are fairly presented in conformity with Generally Accepted Accounting Principles (GAAP) in all material respects.

10. *Mandating Auditor Interim Financial Review*
The SEC should require that a reporting company's outside auditor conduct an SAS 71 Interim Financial Review prior to the company's filing of its Form 10-Q.[7]

OVERVIEW OF CURRENTLY PRESCRIBED DUTIES AND RESPONSIBILITIES

The listings of public company audit committee duties and responsibilities under SEC rules and securities market regulations that follow originated from legislation, such as Sarbanes-Oxley, the *Blue Ribbon Committee Report*, or otherwise, and are set forth as presented in the 2007 *Director's Guidebook,* organized by area of responsibility involved. The legislative/regulatory source of these duties and responsibilities is covered later in this chapter. The more important duties are further discussed in subsequent chapters.

FORMAL WRITTEN CHARTER

Pursuant to SEC regulation, the major securities exchanges have mandated that audit committees of public companies develop a formal written charter that specifies the committee's duties and responsibilities as a condition of continued listing on the exchange. This charter must be reviewed annually and published at least once every three years in the proxy statement sent to shareowners.[8] Audit committee charters are discussed at greater length in Chapter 7.

PRINCIPAL RELATIONSHIP WITH EXTERNAL AUDIT FIRM

Sarbanes-Oxley has further clarified the widely held understanding that the external audit firm acts as a representative of the interests of corporate shareholders who have elected the board of directors to act on their behalf and through it the audit committee. In effect, the board of directors through the audit committee employs the external auditors to act on behalf of the interests of shareholders. Since performance of an audit requires close cooperation with members of management, however, external auditors must tactfully consider the possibly divergent interests of management and shareholders in all areas of the relationship with their client, the audit committee of the board of directors. Audit committees must recognize the sensitivity of their relationships with both management and the external audit firm.

---

[7] Id.

[8] NYSE, Inc., Listed Company Manual § 303A¶ 7(c)i. See www.nyse.com.

Specific duties required for audit committees that deal with the organization's external audit firm as set forth in the 2007 edition of the *Corporate Director's Guidebook* are:

- Select and engage the corporation's external auditor and determine, for each fiscal year, whether to continue that relationship;
- Review and approve annually the external auditor's fee arrangement and the proposed terms of its engagement, including the scope and plan of the audit;
- Approve, before each engagement, any additional audit-related or non-audit services to be provided by the audit firm, based on the committee's judgment as to whether the firm is an appropriate choice to provide such additional services and whether the engagement would impair the firm's independence.[9]

The language of the SEC Rule is even more descriptive of this area of responsibility. It clarifies that the audit committee is directly responsible for all aspects of the corporation's relationship with its external auditor, including the "appointment, compensation, retention, and oversight of the work."[10] It is quite clear that it is the audit committee, representing the corporation's shareowners, that is the client of the audit firm, and not management. Sarbanes-Oxley Section 301 adds to the 1934 Securities Exchange Act the notation that the registered public accounting firm "shall report directly to the audit committee."[11] While not legally required for not-for-profit organizations, this responsibility is becoming recognized as a best business practice.

The duty to approve in advance any engagement of the audit firm for further services beyond the annual audit was adopted to assure the fact and appearance of full independence of the firm from the corporation. Additional audit committee duties relating to the external audit firm deal with issues arising out of the annual audit and quarterly review of financial statements and financial and other disclosures; these are discussed later in this chapter.

RECEIPT OF CONFIDENTIAL AND OTHER INFORMATION

The 2007 edition of the *Corporate Director's Guidebook* sets forth further duties relating to the receipt of information from confidential sources, as required by Sarbanes-Oxley Section 301(4), and a general duty to serve as a sounding board for communications involving internal and external auditing. According to the *Guidebook*, audit committees are required to:

- Establish procedures to receive and respond to any complaints or concerns regarding the corporation's accounting, internal controls or auditing matters, including

[9] ABA, *Corporate Director's Guidebook,* 2007 p. 58.
[10] SEC Release No. 33-8220, *Standards Related to Listed Company Audit Committees,* April 23, 2003.
[11] Sarbanes-Oxley, § 301(2), P.L. 107–204.

procedures for the confidential and anonymous submission by employees of any such complaints or concerns;

- Serve as a channel of communication between the external auditor and the board and between the head of internal audit, if any, and the board.[12]

The first duty just noted, the confidential and anonymous receipt of accounting and related matters, is specifically set forth in Sarbanes-Oxley Section 301. The requirement for establishing a more generalized communications method for employees to report wrongdoing is set forth in the U.S. Sentencing Commission definition of an effective compliance and ethics program, including a requirement

> to have and publicize a system, which may include mechanisms that allow for anonymity or confidentiality, whereby the organization's employees and agents may report or seek guidance regarding potential or actual criminal conduct without fear of retaliation.[13]

Some industries, such as health care and defense procurement, have also developed more stringent requirements for having a confidential and anonymous method for reporting wrongdoing. Not all of the complaints are likely to involve matters of auditing, accounting, or internal controls, however. Those complaints may be directed to be dealt with by management; their disposition does not need to be overseen by the audit committee.

OVERSIGHT OF FINANCIAL AND OTHER DISCLOSURES

The 2007 edition of the *Corporate Director's Guidebook* next discusses duties that involve oversight of the preparation and dissemination of financial and other disclosures to the public. Audit committee members are charged with the important responsibility of assuring that the corporation's reports to the investing and general public are factual, comprehensive, and timely.

Exercise of these duties requires specific interaction with the external audit firm as well as with management. It should be noted that these audit committee responsibilities pertain to publicly held companies only. According to the *Guidebook*, audit committees are required to:

- Discuss the corporation's procedures for issuing quarterly and annual earnings press releases, as well as for providing financial information and earnings guidance to analysts, the financial press, and rating agencies;
- Review the corporation's annual and quarterly financial statements, and management certifications thereof, with management and the external auditor, and discuss

[12] ABA, *Corporate Director's Guidebook*, 2007 p. 59.

[13] U.S. Sentencing Commission, Sentencing Guidelines § 8B2.1(b)(5)(C).

with them the quality of management's accounting judgments in preparing the financial statements;

- Review the Management's Discussion and Analysis (MD&A) section in each periodic report prior to filing with the SEC and discuss with management and the external auditor any questions or issues that arise in connection with that review;
- Determine whether to recommend to the board that the audited annual financial statements be included in the corporation's annual report on Form 10-K to be filed with the SEC;
- Receive and consider any required communications from the external auditor as a result of its timely review of the quarterly financial statements.[14]

All of these duties are consistent with the mandate that the board of directors and its standing committees should provide oversight and guidance, but not become immersed in the details of the many business determinations made by management. Note that the wording of the first duty states the need to discuss the corporation's *procedures* used to make sure that all necessary diligence has been performed, not necessarily to review every judgment or outcome made by management.

For example, the final duty on the list does not contemplate that the audit committee should attempt to second-guess the propriety of accounting estimates that management has used. What the duty of discussing the quality of management's accounting judgments does require is that the audit committee must be satisfied that all accounting estimates are adequately supported by the facts, have been made with consistency over time and were done in good faith using supportable accounting principles, and have not been determined arbitrarily in order to achieve a predetermined level of earnings.

With respect to the duty to review the contents of the MD&A, it should be noted that the SEC has placed greater emphasis on this narrative disclosure in recent years. The disclosure should factually explain the reasons for changes in performance. See Chapter 8 for further discussion of how audit committees should carry out their responsibilities relating to the oversight of financial reporting and disclosures.

OVERSIGHT OF INTERNAL CONTROLS

The 2007 edition of the *Corporate Director's Guidebook* next discusses required audit committee duties that involve oversight of a public corporation's internal controls over financial reporting and risk management processes. The duties dealing with the quality of internal control and assessment of internal controls over

---

[14] ABA, *Corporate Director's Guidebook*, 2007, p. 59.

financial reporting and external auditor attestation on that assessment are requirements arising from Sarbanes-Oxley Section 404 and apply only to publicly held corporations.

As a best business practice, however, audit committees of all companies, including not-for-profits are likely to be just as concerned with oversight of all aspects of internal controls and not just the legally required focus for public companies on the controls over external financial reporting. The controls involving the effectiveness and efficiency of operations and compliance with policies, laws, and regulations are also critical to success. According to the *Guidebook*, public company audit committees are required to:

- Consider, in consultation with the external auditor and the senior internal auditing executive, if any, the adequacy of the corporation's internal controls, which, among other things, must be designed to provide reasonable assurance that the corporation's books and records are accurate, that its assets are safeguarded, and that the publicly reported financial statements prepared by management are presented fairly in accordance with generally accepted accounting principles;
- Review management's annual assessment of the effectiveness of internal control over financial reporting, and the external auditor's audit of internal control over financial reporting.[15]

The important subject of audit committee responsibilities relating to the oversight of internal controls is discussed at greater length in Chapter 11.

OVERSIGHT OF REQUIRED ANNUAL ASSESSMENT OF INTERNAL CONTROL OVER FINANCIAL REPORTING

As noted, Sarbanes-Oxley Section 404 requires the management of public companies to undertake an annual assessment of the effectiveness of internal control over financial reporting. This assessment must be included in the corporation's annual report to the SEC on Form 10-K and attested to by the company's external auditor. Both the SEC and the PCAOB have attempted to be responsive to the groundswell of criticism that the costs of compliance with Sarbanes-Oxley Section 404 have been much too high, far more than expected, and appeared to many to be greater than that necessary to conduct an effective audit of internal control over financial reporting. The high costs were thought to affect smaller public companies especially adversely.

In response to these concerns, the SEC has twice postponed for smaller public companies the effective date for publishing an annual management assessment of internal controls over financial reporting and the related external auditor attestation. The requirement date for the first annual management assessment and report on

[15] ABA, *Corporate Director's Guidebook*, 2007, pp. 59–60.

internal control over financial reporting for smaller public companies was finally set for fiscal years ended after December 15, 2007. The requirement for the first external auditor attestation on management's assertion was delayed until one year later.[16] Discussion continues on the benefits of further postponements.

During the postponement period, the SEC exposed draft guidance for public comment and later issued final rules for public companies to use in their assessment of internal control over financial reporting, called Interpretive Guidance. At the same time, the PCAOB developed a new auditing standard to replace Auditing Standard (AS) No. 2, exposed it for public comment, and on May 24, 2007, issued a new audit standard, AS No. 5, for internal control over financial reporting. The final SEC Interpretive Guidance and AS No. 5 are discussed in Chapter 11.

OVERSIGHT OF RISK MANAGEMENT AND COMPLIANCE PROCESSES

The 2007 *Corporate Director's Guidebook* next discusses required audit committee duties that involve oversight of a corporation's risk management and compliance processes. Although mandatory only for public companies, these duties are considered a best practice for privately held and not-for-profit organizations as well. The *Guidebook* states:

- Meet periodically with management to review the corporation's major risk exposures and discuss the steps management has taken to monitor and control such exposures, such as risk management programs, and procedures and policies addressing legal compliance.[17]

The language concerning legal compliance appears to be based on attorney concerns of the American Bar Association committee and may be more in the nature of best practice recommendations than the other requirements. Responsibilities dealing with oversight of methods used for risk assessment and risk management also arise from NYSE Listed Company Rule 303A.07(D).[18]

The importance of risk assessment to the successful and economical compliance with Sarbanes-Oxley Section 404 internal control reporting and related audit has become increasingly clear in recent years. Both the SEC and PCAOB have advised management and external auditors, respectively, to take a top-down and risk-based approach. The subject of audit committee responsibilities relating to risk

---

[16] SEC Release No. 33-8670, *Internal Control Over Financial Reporting in Exchange Act Periodic Reports of Non-Accelerated Filers and Newly Public Companies*, December 15, 2006, and reaffirmed in SEC Release No. 33-8809, *Amendments to Rules Regarding Management's Report on Internal Control Over Financial Reporting*, June 20, 2007.

[17] ABA, *Corporate Director's Guidebook*, 2007, p. 60.

[18] NYSE, Inc., Listed Company Manual § 303A¶ 7(D). See www.nyse.com.

management is discussed at greater length in Chapter 10. Chapters 5 and 12 further discuss how audit committees should carry out their responsibilities relating to oversight of ethics and compliance programs. Also, Chapter 9 contains further discussion of how internal auditing can be a valuable resource to the audit committee in areas of governance, risk management, and internal control.

ADDITIONAL DUTIES FOR PUBLIC COMPANY AUDIT COMMITTEES

The next group of audit committee duties from the 2007 edition of the *Corporate Director's Guidebook* is limited to publicly held corporations. Audit committees are required to:

- Review and approve the annual report of the audit committee to shareholders required to included in a public company's annual meeting proxy statement;
- Review and approve any related person transactions between the corporation and its officers or directors, or their family members or enterprises they control.[19]

The second responsibility arises from the listing rules of Nasdaq.

DUTY TO MAINTAIN COMPETENCE

The final audit committee duty from the 2007 *Corporate Director's Guidebook* is also a best practice. According to the *Guidebook*, audit committees should:

- Conduct an annual self-examination.[20]

This requirement parallels the requirement for the full board of directors to monitor the quality of its performance, so that individual directors as well as the committee as a whole may continually strive for improvement in performance.

Audit committees must schedule a sufficient number of meetings, allow enough time during them, and have done sufficient planning and study of materials in advance of those meetings to assure that all of these duties are accomplished successfully. The annual self-evaluation is an important aspect of the need to assure the full board that the audit committee has successfully met all of its responsibilities.

LEGISLATIVE/REGULATORY SOURCES OF SELECTED AUDIT COMMITTEE RESPONSIBILITIES

The provisions of Sarbanes-Oxley Section 301, "Public Company Audit Committees," of the Sarbanes-Oxley Act of 2002 concerning the structure of audit committees are discussed next. Additional provisions of Sarbanes-Oxley that relate to

[19] ABA, *Corporate Director's Guidebook*, 2007, pp. 59–60.
[20] Id.

responsibilities of audit committees are contained in Section 302, "Corporate Responsibility for Financial Reports," and Section 404, "Management Assessment of Internal Controls." These issues are further discussed in Chapter 11. The provisions of Section 406, "Disclosure of Code of Ethics for Senior Financial Officers," are discussed in Chapter 12.

AUDIT COMMITTEE RESPONSIBILITIES INCLUDED IN SARBANES-OXLEY SECTION 301

Section 301 of Sarbanes-Oxley sets forth important audit committee responsibilities. These include the directive that audit committees are directly responsible for relationships with the external auditor, the need to set up and maintain a system for receiving confidential complaints by employees and others, the authority to engage advisors, and appropriate funding.[21]

> (2) *Responsibilities Relating to Registered Public Accounting Firms.*
> The audit committee of each issuer, in its capacity as a committee of the board of directors, shall be directly responsible for the appointment, compensation, and oversight of the work of any registered public accounting firm employed by that issuer (including resolution of disagreements between management and the auditor regarding financial reporting) for the purpose of preparing or issuing an audit report or related work, and each such registered public accounting firm shall report directly to the audit committee.
>
> (3) *Independence.* This portion of Section 301 is discussed in Chapter 6.
>
> (4) *Complaints.* Each audit committee shall establish procedures for
>
> (A) The receipt, retention, and treatment of complaints received by the issuer regarding accounting, internal accounting controls, or auditing matters; and
> (B) The confidential, anonymous submission by employees of the issuer of concerns regarding questionable accounting or auditing matters.
>
> (5) *Authority to Engage Advisers.* Each audit committee shall have the authority to engage independent counsel and other advisers, as it determines necessary to carry out its duties.
>
> (6) *Funding.* Each issuer shall provide for appropriate funding, as determined by the audit committee, in its capacity as a committee of the board of directors, for payment of compensation
>
> (A) to the registered public accounting firm employed by the issuer for the purpose of rendering or issuing an audit report; and
> (B) to any advisers employed by the audit committee under paragraph (5).[22]

[21] Sarbanes-Oxley § 301, P.L. 107–204.
[22] Id.

SELECTED RESPONSIBILITIES SET FORTH BY THE NEW YORK STOCK EXCHANGE

The responsibilities that the NYSE requires listed companies to assume are set forth in Section 7 of Rule 303A in the NYSE Listed Company Manual.[23] The rule clearly states that these responsibilities are the sole responsibility of the audit committee and cannot be allocated to a different committee. In addition to or clarifying the duties that are set forth in legislation, these requirements include:

a. The audit committee must have a minimum of three members (contained in Rule 303A.07A).

This requirement is explained more fully in the commentary to the NYSE rule:

> Because of the audit committee's demanding role and responsibilities, and the time commitment attendant to committee membership, each prospective audit committee member should evaluate carefully the existing demands on his or her time before accepting this important assignment. Additionally, if an audit committee member simultaneously serves on the audit committees of more than three public companies, and the listed company does not limit the number of audit committees on which its audit committee members serve to three or less, then in each case, the board must determine that such simultaneous service would not impair the ability of such member to effectively serve on the listed company's audit committee and disclose such determination in the listed company's annual proxy statement or, if the company does not file an annual proxy statement, in the company's annual report on Form 10-K filed with the SEC.[24]

b. All audit committee members must satisfy the requirements for independence set out in Rule 303A.02. (contained in Rule 303A.07b). This subject is also discussed in Chapter 6.

c. The audit committee must have a written charter that addresses: (contained in Rule 303A.07c):

- (i) The committee's purpose—which at a minimum must be to:
  - (A) Assist the board oversight of
    - (1) The integrity of the company's financial statements,
    - (2) The company's compliance with legal and regulatory requirements,
    - (3) The independent auditor's qualifications and independence, and
    - (4) The performance of the company's internal audit function and independent auditors; and
  - (B) Prepare an audit committee report as required by the SEC to be included in the company's annual proxy statement;

---

[23] NYSE, Inc., *Listed Company Manual* § 303A¶ 7.
[24] Id.

(ii) An annual performance evaluation of the audit committee; and

(iii) The duties and responsibilities of the audit committee—which, at a minimum, must include those set out in Rule 10A of the Securities Exchange Act, as well as to:

(A) At least annually, obtain and review a report by the independent auditor describing: the firm's internal quality-control procedures; any material issues raised by the most recent internal quality-control review, or peer review, of the firm, or by any inquiry or investigation by governmental or professional authorities, within the preceding five years, respecting one or more independent audits carried out by the firm, and any steps taken to deal with any such issues; and (to assess the auditor's independence) all relationships between the independent auditor and the company.

This requirement is explained more fully in the Commentary to the NYSE Rule:

> After reviewing the foregoing report and the independent auditor's work throughout the year, the audit committee will be in a position to evaluate the auditor's qualifications, performance and independence. This evaluation should include the review and evaluation of the lead partner of the independent auditor. In making its evaluation, the audit committee should take into account the opinions of management and the listed company's internal auditors (or other personnel responsible for the internal audit function). In addition to assuring the regular rotation of the lead audit partner as required by law, the audit committee should further consider whether, in order to assure continuing auditor independence, there should be regular rotation of the audit firm itself. The audit committee should present its conclusions with respect to the independent auditor to the full board.[25]

(B) Meet to review and discuss the listed company's annual audited financial statements and quarterly financial statements with management and the independent auditor, including reviewing the company's specific disclosures under "Management's Discussion and Analysis of Financial Condition and Results of Operations." This subject is discussed further in Chapter 8.

(C) Discuss the listed company's earnings press releases as well as financial information and earnings guidance provided to analysts and rating agencies. This subject is discussed further in Chapter 8.

(D) Discuss policies with respect to risk assessment and risk management. This subject is discussed further in Chapter 10.

(E) Meet separately, periodically, with management, with internal auditors (or other personnel responsible for the internal audit function),

[25] NYSE, Inc., Listed Company Manual § 303A¶ 7(c)iii(A). See www.nyse.com.

and with independent auditors. This subject is discussed further in Chapter 9.

(F) Review with the independent auditor any audit problems or difficulties and management's response. This subject is discussed further in Chapter 8.

(G) Set clear hiring policies for employees or former employees of the independent auditors; and

(H) Report regularly to the board of directors.

The subject of the audit committee's charter is further discussed in Chapter 7.

SELECTED RESPONSIBILITIES SET FORTH BY NASDAQ

The responsibilities that the Nasdaq Stock Market requires listed companies to assume are set forth in Section (d) of Rule 4350 of the Nasdaq manual titled "Qualitative Listing Requirements for Nasdaq Issuers Except for Limited Partnerships."[26]

(d) Audit Committee

(1) *Audit Committee Charter*. Each Issuer must certify that it has adopted a formal written audit committee charter and that the audit committee has reviewed and reassessed the adequacy of the formal written charter on an annual basis. The charter must specify:

(A) the scope of the audit committee's responsibilities, and how it carries out those responsibilities, including structure, processes, and membership requirements;

(B) the audit committee's responsibility for ensuring its receipt from the outside auditors of a formal written statement delineating all relationships between the auditor and the company, consistent with Independence Standards Board Standard 1, and the audit committee's responsibility for actively engaging in a dialogue with the auditor with respect to any disclosed relationships or services that may impact the objectivity and independence of the auditor and for taking, or recommending that the full board take, appropriate action to oversee the independence of the outside auditor; and

(C) the committee's purpose of overseeing the accounting and financial reporting processes of the issuer and the audits of the financial statements of the issuer;

(D) the specific audit committee responsibilities and authority set forth in Rule 4350(d)(3).

(2) *Audit Committee Composition*. (This topic is also discussed in Chapter 6 of this book).

(A) Each issuer must have, and certify that it has and will continue to have, an audit committee of at least three members, each of whom must:

---

[26] NASDAQ Manual Online, Section 4350 (d) at www.complinet.com/nasdaq/display/display.html?rbid=1705&element_id=13.

(i) be independent as defined under Rule 4200(a)(15);
(ii) meet the criteria for independence set forth in Rule 10A-3(b)(1) under the Act (subject to the exemptions provided in Rule 10A-3(c));
(iii) not have participated in the preparation of the financial statements of the company or any current subsidiary of the company at any time during the past three years; and
(iv) be able to read and understand fundamental financial statements, including a company's balance sheet, income statement, and cash flow statement. Additionally, each issuer must certify that it has, and will continue to have, at least one member of the audit committee who has past employment experience in finance or accounting, requisite professional certification in accounting, or any other comparable experience or background which results in the individual's financial sophistication, including being or having been a chief executive officer, chief financial officer or other senior officer with financial oversight responsibilities.

(B) Notwithstanding paragraph (2)(A)(i), one director who:

(i) is not independent as defined in Rule 4200
(ii) meets the criteria set forth in Section 10A(m)(3) under the Act and the rules thereunder; and
(iii) is not a current officer or employee or a Family Member of such officer or employee, may be appointed to the audit committee, if the board, under exceptional and limited circumstances, determines that membership on the committee by the individual is required by the best interests of the company and its shareholders, and the board discloses, in the next annual proxy statement subsequent to such determination (or, if the issuer does not file a proxy, in its Form 10-K or 20-F), the nature of the relationship and the reasons for that determination. A member appointed under this exception may not serve longer than two years and may not chair the audit committee.

(3) *Audit Committee Responsibilities and Authority* The audit committee must have the specific audit committee responsibilities and authority necessary to comply with Rule 10A-3(b)(2), (3), (4) and (5) under the Act (subject to the exemptions provided in Rule 10A-3(c)), concerning responsibilities relating to:

(i) registered public accounting firms,
(ii) complaints relating to accounting, internal accounting controls or auditing matters,
(iii) authority to engage advisors, and
(iv) funding as determined by the audit committee.

Audit committees for investment companies must also establish procedures for the confidential, anonymous submission of concerns regarding questionable accounting or auditing matters by employees of the investment advisor, administrator, principal underwriter, or any other provider of accounting-related services for the investment company as well as employees of the investment company.

KEY POINTS IN CHAPTER 4

1. Legally required duties of the audit committee have expanded significantly since the passage of Sarbanes-Oxley. Additionally, the qualifications required for audit committee membership have been upgraded.
2. One of the most important duties involves interactions with the external auditors. On behalf of the full board, the audit committee is responsible for all interactions with the organization's external audit firm. This involves the initial selection, annual review of the firm's performance, evaluation of the scope of the audit, and a determination of the firm's compensation and whether the relationship should continue in the future.
3. To preserve independence, the audit committee should approve in advance any additional nonaudit engagements with the audit firm.
4. Audit committees of public companies must annually review their written charter to be sure it accurately reflects the committee's duties. The charter must be published in the company's proxy statement at least once every three years.
5. Public company audit committee reports must include a report of their activities in their organization's annual proxy statement.
6. The audit committee should oversee processes and discuss with management and the external auditor that all significant areas of judgment and other matters of application of accounting principles involving preparation of financial information, guidance to financial analysts, press releases, and other public disclosures's are appropriate, complete, and proper. The committee should specifically recommend that financial statements are appropriate to be included in annual reports to the SEC.
7. Oversight of the organization's internal auditing function and risk assessment and management program are an essential audit committee responsibility.
8. The audit committee should oversee internal control processes and discuss with management its evaluation of the effectiveness of internal controls. The audit committee of public companies must discuss with the external auditor its attestation on management's opinion on internal controls over financial reporting.
9. Unless the company has appointed another board standing committee to oversee ethics and compliance programs, the audit committee should oversee the effectiveness of the operation of the organization's confidential reporting system as well as other compliance systems.
10. The audit committee should meet periodically with management to review the corporation's major risk exposures and oversee the operation of the organization's risk management programs, including those having to do with the reduction of present and future risks from litigation.
11. The audit committee should conduct an annual self-examination of its effectiveness and engage in activities designed to make improvements.

Appendix 4A

FEI Corporate Governance Checklist

This portion of the FEI checklist involves the audit committee.

FEI Corporate Governance Checklist as Adapted and Revised from NYSE Corporate Governance Rule 303A

1. Listed companies must have a majority of independent directors.
2. In order to tighten the definition of "independent director" for the purposes of these standards:
   a. No director qualifies as "independent" unless the board of directors affirmatively determines that the director has no material relationship with the listed company. Companies must disclose these determinations.
   b. No director who is a former employee of the listed company can be "independent" until 5 years after the employment has ended.
   c. No director who is, or in the past 5 years has been, affiliated with a present or former auditor of the company can be "independent" until 5 years after the end of the auditing relationship.
   d. No director can be "independent" if he or she is, or in the past 5 years has been, part of an interlocking directorate in which an executive officer of the listed company serves on the compensation committee of another company that concurrently employs the director.
   e. Directors with immediate family members in the foregoing categories are likewise subject to the 5-year "cooling off" provisions for purposes of determining "independence."
3. To empower non-management directors to serve as a more effective check on management, the non-management directors of each company must meet at regularly scheduled sessions without management.
4. Add to the "independence" requirement for audit committee membership the requirement that director's fees are the only compensation a committee member may receive from the company.
5. Audit committee relationships:
   a. The board must increase the authority and responsibility of the audit committee, including granting it the sole authority to hire and fire independent auditors, and to approve any significant non-audit relationship with the independent auditors.

b. The audit committee must have a written charter that addresses the committee's purpose, its duties and responsibilities, and an annual performance evaluation of the audit committee.
c. Each listed company must have an internal audit function.

6. The duties and responsibilities of the audit committee must be, at a minimum, to:
   a. Retain and terminate the company's independent auditors.
   b. At least annually, obtain and review a report by the independent auditor. The report should describe: the firm's internal quality-control procedures; any material issues raised by the most recent internal quality-control review, or peer review, of the firm, within the last five years, dealing with one or more independent audits carried out by the firm, and any steps taken to deal with any such issues; and (to assess the auditor's independence) all relationships between the independent auditor and the company.
   c. Discuss the annual audited financial statements and quarterly financial statements with management and the independent auditor, including the company's MD&A disclosures.
   d. Discuss earnings press releases, as well as financial information and earnings guidance provided to analysts and rating agencies.
   e. As appropriate, obtain advice and assistance from outside legal, accounting, or other advisors.
   f. Discuss policies with respect to risk assessment and management.
   g. Meet separately, periodically, with management, with internal auditors, and with independent auditors.
   h. Review with the independent auditor any audit problems or difficulties and management's response.
   i. Set clear hiring policies for employees or former employees of the independent auditors.
   j. Report regularly to the board of directors.

Source: © 2007. Financial Executives International (FEI). Reprinted with permission from the Web site of FEI, 200 Campus Drive, Florham Park, NJ 07932-0674. 973.765.1000; www.financialexecutives.org.

Chapter 5

Overview of Additional Duties of Audit Committees Considered to Be Best Practices

In response to the governance failures in publicly held corporations that have occurred, much has been written on the subject of governance, including the key positioning and responsibilities of audit committees. Chapter 4 covered the duties of audit committees that are prescribed by law, regulation, or rule. A body of additional duties has emerged that authoritative bodies generally consider to constitute best practices for audit committees in well-run organizations, publicly held, private, and not-for-profit. These are based on decided court cases and the published conclusions of governance thought leaders.

This chapter outlines audit committee duties and responsibilities that have arisen from sources beyond legal and regulatory mandates. Several of these subjects are discussed at greater length in later chapters.

RECOMMENDATIONS OF THE BUSINESS ROUNDTABLE

One of the prominent organizations concerned with corporate governance is the Business Roundtable, an association of chief executive officers of leading U.S. companies with $4.5 trillion in annual revenues and more than 10 million employees. Member companies comprise nearly a third of the total value of the U.S. stock markets and represent over 40% of all corporate income taxes paid. The Roundtable has published a number of studies on the subject of corporate governance.

The 2005 version of the Business Roundtable *Principles of Corporate Governance*[1] contains these recommendations for audit committees of large publicly owned companies.

Characteristics of Audit Committees and Members

- Every publicly owned corporation should have an audit committee of at least three members, who should all be independent directors.

[1] Business Roundtable, Principles of Corporate Governance, 2005, a White Paper by Business Roundtable, November 2005 at http://64.203.97.43/pdf/CorporateGovPrinciples.pdf. Used with permission.

- Audit committees typically consist of three to five members.
- Audit committee members should meet minimum financial literacy standards, and at least one member of the audit committee should be an audit committee financial expert.
- Consideration should be given to whether it is appropriate to limit the number of public company audit committees on which a corporation's audit committee members may serve.

Audit Committee Responsibilities Concerning the Outside Auditor

- The audit committee is responsible for supervising the corporation's relationship with its outside auditor. In performing this responsibility, the primary functions of the audit committee include:
  1. Retaining the auditor and approving in advance the terms of the annual audit engagement.
  2. Overseeing the independence of the outside auditor. The audit committee should implement a policy covering the hiring of personnel who previously worked for the corporation's outside auditor.

Audit Committee Responsibilities for Overseeing Financial Reporting Processes

- The audit committee should review and discuss the corporation's annual financial statements with management and the outside auditor and should review the corporation's quarterly financial statements and related earnings releases prior to issuance;
- The audit committee should review and discuss with management and the outside auditor the corporation's critical accounting policies, the quality of accounting judgments and estimates made by management, and any material written communications between the outside auditor and management.

Audit Committee Responsibilities for Internal Controls, Ethics and Compliance

- The audit committee should understand and be familiar with the corporation's system of internal controls over financial reporting and its disclosure controls and procedures.
- On a periodic basis, the committee should review with both the internal and outside auditors, as well as management, the corporation's procedures for maintaining and evaluating the effectiveness of those systems.
- The committee should be promptly notified of any significant deficiencies or material weaknesses in internal controls and kept informed about the steps and timetable for correcting them.
- Unless the full board or another committee does so, the audit committee should oversee the corporation's program that addresses compliance with ethical and legal standards and important corporate policies, including the corporation's code of conduct and the mechanisms it has in place for employees to report compliance issues.

- In accordance with applicable legal requirements, the audit committee should establish procedures for receiving and handling complaints and concerns related to accounting, internal accounting controls, and auditing issues, and the committee should evaluate these procedures periodically and revise them as appropriate.
- The committee should be briefed regularly on the status of compliance issues, including concerns submitted through the committee's procedures for handing accounting and related concerns, and it should receive prompt notification of any significant compliance issues.

Audit Committee Responsibilities for Risk and Internal Auditing

- The audit committee should understand the corporation's risk profile and oversee its risk assessment and risk management practices.
- The audit committee should oversee the corporation's internal audit function, including reviewing the scope of the internal audit plan, reports submitted by the internal audit staff and management's response, and the appointment and replacement of the senior internal auditing executive.

General

- Audit committee meetings should be held frequently enough to allow the committee to monitor the corporation's financial reporting appropriately.
- The committee should meet privately with each of the internal and outside auditors and management on a regular basis, and in any event at least quarterly, and communicate with them between meetings as necessary.
- The audit committee also should hold private sessions with the corporation's chief legal officer on a regular basis to facilitate the communication of concerns regarding legal compliance matters and significant legal contingencies.[2]

RECOMMENDATIONS OF THE CONFERENCE BOARD

Another of the prominent research organizations concerned with corporate governance issues is the Conference Board. It calls itself the world's preeminent business membership and research organization and provides issues-oriented research and senior executive peer-to-peer conferences. The Conference Board's *Corporate Governance Handbook* from 2007 contains guidance on a number of audit committee issues that are cited elsewhere in this volume. The section on audit committee practices is introduced in this way:

> The audit committee plays a critical role in management oversight. The combination of requirements imposed by the Sarbanes-Oxley Act, SEC regulations, and stock exchange listing standards had dramatically increased the number and scope of the

[2] Id. pp. 17–20.

committee's responsibilities. Traditionally, audit committees focused on ensuring the accuracy of financial statements prepared by senior managers. But in today's environment, audit committees are also concerned with the retention and performance of external auditors, the effectiveness of internal controls, compliance with codes of ethics, and the anonymity of whistle-blowing procedures for accounting-related issues.[3]

GUIDING PRINCIPLES OF THE BLUE RIBBON COMMITTEE

In addition to the 10 recommendations for changes in the regulations governing audit committees that were published in the 1999 *Report and Recommendations of the Blue Ribbon Committee on Improving the Effectiveness of Corporate Audit Committees*[4] that were presented in Chapter 4, the committee also developed and published "Guiding Principles for Audit Committee Best Practices." The committee intended the principles to serve as building blocks for devising company-specific process and practices. The principles cover five subjects:

1. The audit committee's key role in monitoring the other component parts of the audit process.
2. Independent communication and information flow between the audit committee and the internal auditor.
3. Independent communication and information flow between the audit committee and the outside auditors.
4. Candid discussions with management, the internal auditor, and outside auditors regarding issues implicating judgment and impacting quality.
5. Diligent and knowledgeable audit committee membership.[5]

EIGHT HABITS OF HIGHLY EFFECTIVE AUDIT COMMITTEES

Another source of guidance for audit committees is the American Institute of Certified Public Accountants (AICPA). The AICPA has established an Audit Committee Effectiveness Center. The center's mission statement notes that audit committees are a key element of the governance process of every organization and that "the battle for financial statement integrity and reliability depends on balancing the

[3] Conference Board, *Corporate Governance Handbook 2007: Legal Standards and Board Practices*, Research Report R-1045-07-RR, (New York: Conference Board, 2007) p. 60.

[4] NYSE and NASD, *Report and Recommendations of the Blue Ribbon Committee on Improving the Effectiveness of Audit Committees,* 1999. (New York: NYSE and NASD, 1999).

[5] Id., pp. 37–44.

pressures of multiple stakeholders, including management, regulators, investors and the public interest."[6]

The eight habits of highly effective audit committees were laid out in an article in the *Journal of Accountancy*, the AICPA's membership magazine.[7]

1. Creating the audit committee charter is the first step that highly effective audit committees need to take. Defining the mission, together with identification of the authority, functions, and responsibilities of the committee along with the skills and experience of its members, provides the road map for committee actions.
2. The next step is the specification of critical success factors as competencies that audit committee members need to function effectively and discharge their responsibilities.
3. Committees should identify committee core values that reflect those of the organization and establish and follow written procedures fostering open communication, active participation, and equitable dispute resolution.
4. The chair should reserve the right to invite any group or individual to an audit committee meeting. Good working relationships with senior management and other members of the board facilitates success for the committee's agenda.
5. It is important to ensure that all members actively participate in setting the committee agenda and are engaged in all significant deliberations. Avoiding conducting committee business between meetings facilitates this goal.
6. Formulating decision-making processes for resolving stalemates will enable the committee to make progress on solving difficult issues.
7. At the beginning of each meeting, it is helpful to review the highlights from the previous meeting.
8. Summarizing decisions and information gained during the meeting at its conclusion helps to focus attention on accomplishments.

BEST PRACTICES RELATED TO AUDITING AND INTERNAL CONTROL

In addition to the duties for audit committees that are legally required, the 2007 edition of the *Corporate Director's Guidebook* sets forth additional duties and responsibilities that audit committees should undertake as matters of good corporate governance practice. Many audit committees have undertaken many of these responsibilities, and they are rapidly being considered to represent best business practice. Those relating to matters of internal control and auditing suggest that audit committees should:

---

[6] AICPA Web site, www.aicpa.org/audcommctr/homepage.htm.

[7] John F. Morrow and Joan Pastor, "Eight Habits of Highly Effective Audit Committees," *Journal of Accountancy* (September 2007), pp. 46–51.

1. Establish a direct or dotted-line reporting relationship with the internal auditor, as the committee should have appropriate input in hiring and firing the head of internal audit, evaluating performance, and approving the internal audit plans and budget for the internal audit group;
2. Review the external auditor's management letter and management's responses thereto (the auditor's letter comments on any control deficiencies observed during the course of the audit and makes other recommendations arising from the audit).[8]

As to the first duty, more and more audit committees are performing oversight of the plans and work programs of their organization's internal auditing functions. This is true whether internal auditing is being performed entirely in-house, in combination with outside consultants, or outsourced to an external party. Regardless of how internal auditing is staffed, it is clear that there should be an internal head of internal auditing or chief audit executive (CAE), and this person should be a senior executive and have frequent interaction with the audit committee.

Paragraph 120 of PCAOB Audit Standard (AS) No. 2 states that one of the factors determining the objectivity of a function like internal auditing is whether it "has direct access and reports regularly to the board of directors or the audit committee." Paragraph 121 of that Standard notes the importance of adherence to the *International Professional Standards for the Practice of Internal Auditing* of the Institute of Internal Auditors as a measure of the competency and objectivity of an internal auditing activity.

Although this specific language has been replaced as a part of the downsized replacement standard of AS No. 2 in AS No. 5, the concepts are still believed to be relevant. AS No. 5 was issued by the PCAOB and approved by the SEC in 2007. On the subject of the objectivity and competence of internal auditors providing assistance to the external auditor, AS No. 5 refers to AICPA Statement on Auditing Standards (SAS) No. 65, codified in auditing standard AU Section 322, which describes considerations for external auditors to use in determining the objectivity of internal auditing:

- Whether the internal auditor [chief audit executive] reports to an officer of sufficient status to ensure broad audit coverage and adequate consideration of, and action on, the findings and recommendations of the internal auditors.
- Whether [internal auditing] has direct access and reports regularly to the board or audit committee, or the owner-manager.
- Whether the board of directors, audit committee, or owner manager oversees employment decisions related to the internal auditor [Chief Audit Executive].[9]
- Whether policies exist to protect the objectivity of individual internal auditors:

[8] American Bar Association, *Corporate Director's Guidebook, Fifth Edition* (Chicago: ABA Committee on Corporate Laws, 2007), p. 60.

[9] AICPA, Statement on Auditing Standards (SAS) No. 65, codified in AU §322.10

- Prohibiting auditors from auditing areas where relatives are employed in important or audit-sensitive positions.
- Prohibiting internal auditors from auditing areas where they were recently assigned or are scheduled to be assigned on completion of responsibilities in the internal audit function.[10]

Concerning competence, AICPA SAS No. 65 notes that the external auditor may use information from a recent external quality review of internal auditing and also whether the internal auditors follow professional internal auditing standards as criteria in assessing competence as well as objectivity.[11]

In addition to the duties noted in this section, audit committees have undertaken other responsibilities. These include meeting privately in executive session with internal auditors and with external auditors without management presence. It is important that these meetings be regularly scheduled to avoid signaling that something may be out of the ordinary when scheduling such a meeting.

The support of the audit committee is very important to the success of the internal audit function in an organization. As noted in an earlier chapter, the New York Stock Exchange (NYSE) requires that all listed corporations have an internal auditing function. Not only should the audit committee be involved in overseeing the work of internal auditing, it should participate in the same actions relating to engagement and retention for the CAE that it does for the external audit firm. Best business practices recommend that the CAE report functionally to the audit committee and administratively to the chief executive officer.

In addition, an important task of the audit committee is to review and follow up on internal control and other recommendations made by either internal or external auditors. The responsibilities are further discussed in Chapter 9, which outlines how internal auditing can be a valuable resource to the audit committee.

BEST PRACTICES RELATING TO PUBLIC DISCLOSURE OF FINANCIAL INFORMATION

In addition to the legally required duties audit committees have concerning financial disclosures, the 2007 edition of the *Corporate Director's Guidebook* contains best practice recommendations relating to the disclosure of financial and other information to the public. These recommendations suggest that audit committees should:

1. Meet periodically with the company's disclosure committee or its representatives, if the corporation has such a committee; and
2. If another committee does not do so, meet privately with the corporation's legal counsel or other key advisors from time to time to review the status of pending

[10] Id.

[11] AICPA, SAS No. 65, codified in AU §322.9.

> litigation, discuss possible loss contingencies, and review other legal concerns, including the corporation's procedures and policies addressing legal compliance and reduction of legal risk.[12]

The first of these best practices is relevant only to publicly held corporations; the final is relevant to private and not-for-profit organizations as well as publicly held corporations.

For public companies, these suggested responsibilities relate closely to the audit committee legal requirements discussed earlier that are designed to make sure that the corporation complies with the provisions of the securities laws. According to the SEC Web site, the 1933 Securities Act is often referred to as the "truth in securities" law and has two basic objectives:

- Require that investors receive financial and other significant information concerning securities being offered for public sale; and
- Prohibit deceit, misrepresentations, and other fraud in the sale of securities.[13]

The 1934 Securities Exchange Act regulates the purchase and sale of securities that are already in the hands of the public. It empowers the SEC to require periodic reporting of information, including audited financial statements by companies having publicly traded securities. It also "governs the disclosure in materials used to solicit shareholders' votes in annual or special meetings held for the election of directors and the approval of other corporate action. Information contained in proxy materials, must be filed with the SEC in advance of any solicitation to ensure compliance with the disclosure rules. [Proxy] solicitations, whether by management or shareholder groups, must disclose all important facts concerning the issues on which holders are asked to vote."[14]

Additional information concerning audit committee responsibilities dealing with financial statement preparation and financial and other disclosures is contained in Chapter 8. Legal compliance is also an aspect of the objectives of ethics and compliance programs discussed next.

AUDIT COMMITTEE OVERSIGHT OF ETHICS AND COMPLIANCE PROGRAMS

In corporations where the board has not assigned the responsibility to a separate governance or a separate compliance committee, audit committees have been designated to accomplish the board's oversight of the organization's compliance and

[12] ABA, *Corporate Director's Guidebook,* 2007. p. 60.
[13] www.sec.gov/about/laws.shtml.
[14] www.sec.gov/about/laws.shtml.

ethics program. The ethical climate of the organization is a critically important determinant of the effectiveness of internal control, and so the audit committee needs to be directly involved with ethics-related processes. An ethical climate in the organization is also critical to the effectiveness of compliance programs. Sarbanes-Oxley Section 406 requires public companies to disclose whether it has adopted a code of ethics for senior financial officers and, if not, the reason therefore.[15]

Further, the U.S. Sentencing Guidelines provide that mitigating circumstances, especially the existence of an effective ethics and compliance program, could substantially reduce penalties otherwise payable in the event of a criminal conviction. Additionally, Sarbanes-Oxley Section 301(4) requires the audit committee to set forth procedures for "the receipt, retention, and treatment of complaints received by the issuer regarding accounting, internal accounting controls, or auditing matters" and "the confidential, anonymous submission by employees of the issuer of concerns regarding questionable accounting or auditing matters."[16] The subject of a confidential reporting mechanism was discussed in Chapter 2 and is discussed further in Chapter 12.

Corporations in businesses with significant federal government involvement, such as health care providers and the defense industry, have special responsibilities to assure that ethics and compliance programs are fully effective. Many companies believe there should be synergy in combining in the audit committee the responsibility for oversight of all compliance and ethics-related matters, although other corporations have placed these responsibilities under the corporate secretary and the corporate counsel. Some organizations have designated a high-level ethics and compliance officer to administer ethics and compliance programs; others designate that individual as the compliance officer.

SARBANES-OXLEY REQUIRES DISCLOSURE OF CODE OF ETHICS

The Section 406 requirement for disclosing whether a corporation does have a code of ethics, or if not, why not, defines a "code of ethics" as such standards that are reasonably necessary to promote:

1. honest and ethical conduct, including the ethical handling of actual or apparent conflicts of interest between personal and professional relationships;
2. full, fair, accurate, timely, and understandable disclosure in the periodic reports required to be filed by the issuer; and
3. compliance with applicable governmental rules and regulations.[17]

---

[15] Sarbanes-Oxley § 406. P.L. 107–204.
[16] Sarbanes-Oxley § 301. P.L. 107–204.
[17] Sarbanes-Oxley § 406(c). P.L. 107–204.

STOCK EXCHANGE IMPLEMENTATION OF CODE REQUIREMENT

The New York Stock Exchange, with the approval of the SEC, has developed more specific guidance for companies that are listed on that exchange. These requirements actually do require a code of conduct or ethics. The Nasdaq has a similar requirement but has not set forth specific guidance as to its content. NYSE Listed Company Rule 303A.10 states:

> Listed companies must adopt and disclose a code of business conduct and ethics for directors, officers, and employees, and promptly disclose any waivers of the code for directors or executive officers.[18]

Additional discussion of requirements for codes of ethics and conduct in Sarbanes-Oxley and related NYSE listing rules is contained in Chapter 12.

REQUIREMENTS OF THE U.S. SENTENCING COMMISSION

The revisions to the U.S. Sentencing Guidelines that were submitted to Congress and enacted in 2004[19] substantially tightened the requirements for compliance and ethics programs that are designed to limit penalties for law violations that result in criminal convictions. The Sentencing Guidelines apply to virtually all organizations—corporations, partnerships, associations, unions, trusts, and pension funds—private as well as public and nonprofit as well as for-profit.

Under the 2004 amendment to the guidelines, organizations must promote an organizational culture that encourages ethical conduct and a commitment to compliance with the law. The amendment also requires boards of directors and executives to assume responsibility for the oversight of compliance and ethics programs. Effective oversight and management presumes active leadership in defining the content and operation of the program. According to the press release announcing the amendment, high-level officials including the board of directors as well as employees need to be trained in relevant legal standards and obligations and the organization must give compliance and ethics officers sufficient authority and resources.[20] The U.S. Sentencing Guidelines are further discussed in Chapter 12.

GUIDANCE FROM THE OPEN COMPLIANCE AND ETHICS GROUP

An organization known as the Open Compliance and Ethics Group (OCEG)[21] has researched and published *Foundation Guidelines v1* (the Red Book)[22] that sets

[18] NYSE, Inc., *Listed Company Manual* § 303A10.

[19] U.S. Sentencing Commission, Amendments to the Guidelines, pp. 76–78 www.ussc.gov/2004guid/2004cong.pdf (accessed January 2008).

[20] U.S. Sentencing Commission, "Sentencing Commission Toughens Requirements for Corporate Compliance and Ethics Programs," April 13, 2004. *2004 Federal Sentencing Guideline Manual*, §8B2.1. *Effective Compliance and Ethics Program.*

[21] www.oceg.org.

[22] OCEG, *Foundation Guidelines, v1*, 2007, www.oceg.org.

forth guidance about core processes dealing with governance, risk, and compliance. The framework is intended to allow organizations to integrate governance, compliance, risk management, and integrity into everyday business operations. OCEG has also published a draft set of guidelines for benchmarking the quality of compliance and ethics programs. The topics for which the OCEG *Measurement and Metrics Guide* provides guidelines and benchmarks include:

- Integrated governance, compliance, risk management, and ethics
- Mission, vision, values
- Compliance and ethics programs
- Whistleblower hotlines
- Codes of conduct/codes of ethics
- Compliance and ethics training programs

As of the date of writing this chapter, OCEG is engaged in an extensive beta test of this document.[23] Chapter 12 provides further guidance from the OCEG.

ADDITIONAL AUDIT COMMITTEE BEST PRACTICES

Together with the increasing emphasis on fuller disclosure of compensation for senior management, pressure has increased for greater oversight of other benefits provided to senior executives, such as use of private aircraft and other perquisites. The 2004 edition of the *Director's Guidebook* contained this best practice recommendation. It is still relevant, although it is not included in the 2007 edition.

> If another committee [of the board] does not do so, establish and review policies or guidelines for expense reimbursements, perquisites, and other benefits provided to senior executives, and be satisfied that the corporation has in place an effective process to monitor compliance with such policies or guidelines.[24]

In most cases, however, the audit committee has such a full plate of other responsibilities that oversight of topics so closely related to compensation is highly likely to fall elsewhere, probably in the purview of the compensation committee.

Because of the audit committee's responsibilities to monitor the corporation's exposure to risks, in many cases the audit committee has been, appropriately, designated to lead efforts to deal with crisis situations facing the corporation. These situations include the possibility of fraud or disaster that might otherwise require management support beyond that which can be provided by senior management. In

---

[23] OCEG, *Measurement and Metrics Guide*, 2007, www.oceg.org.

[24] American Bar Association, *Corporate Director's Guidebook, Fourth Edition,* 2004, quoted in *Business Lawyer* (May 2004), p. 1090.

other cases, however, a special committee could be appointed to make an internal investigation of a matter involving potential litigation.

KEY POINTS IN CHAPTER 5

1. Court cases have strengthened, extended, and documented the need for effective audit committee oversight of compliance, auditing, and risk management functions.
2. The recommendations of prominent groups mirror and extend the legal requirements that have been assigned to audit committees.
3. Because of its importance to effective internal controls and the desirability of complying with the provisions of the U.S. Sentencing Guidelines, audit committees should place considerable emphasis on their continuing oversight of the operation and effectiveness of the organization's ethics and compliance program.
4. Key audit committee functions include oversight of the development, updating, and implementation of an individualized code of conduct and ethics, plus oversight of the operation and effectiveness of a confidential reporting mechanism and receiving the information it obtains.
5. Information the audit committee receives from the confidential reporting helpline/hotline operated as a part of the organization's ethics and compliance program can be helpful in assessing and measuring the risks the organization faces.
6. The chief audit executive, the person in charge of the internal audit function in the organization, should report functionally to the audit committee. This enables internal auditing to have the status, resources, and focus necessary to accomplish all aspects of the mission it has been given in its charter. The audit committee should review and approve the annual internal audit plans, budget, and staffing. The preferred internal auditing reporting relationship for administrative purposes is the CEO of the organization.
7. Oversight functions performed by the audit committee regarding internal auditing should also include a review of the performance of the CAE similar to that done for the external auditing firm. The review should focus on the remuneration and the issue of replacement or retention of the individual.
8. The audit committee should receive reports of internal auditing findings and recommendations as well as reports of management's responses and follow-up action on implementating recommendations for changes in policies and processes.
9. The audit committee should also receive any comments by the external audit firm, including its management letter, indicating internal control deficiencies or any other comments. The committee should follow up with management regarding its approach to dealing with the issues that have been raised.

10. The audit committee or its chair should be directly involved in oversight of all processes leading to the publication of financial, internal control, and other information, including press releases of actual results and guidance concerning future prospects that are provided to securities analysts.
11. Whenever necessary, audit committees should not hesitate to employee external experts at the corporation's expense to help the committee in discharging their duties.
12. Audit committees should be prepared to assume additional responsibilities on an emergency basis in situations that require independence from management.

Chapter 6

Necessary Characteristics of Audit Committees and Their Members

The personal characteristics of its members and the guiding principles and practices that the committee uses are important to the effectiveness of an audit committee.

INTRODUCTION

Perhaps one of the most important characteristics of an effective audit committee is its ability to deal effectively with other oversight functions serving the organization, such as the internal and external auditors, while at the same time maintaining the collegiality and cooperative relationships that are necessary for effective board membership.

Audit committee members require several important personal characteristics in addition to those that are necessary to function as effective members of the board of directors. All members of the audit committee must be independent of the management of the organization in appearance as well as in fact so they can effectively accomplish the audit committee's oversight mission, with its many responsibilities. More important, audit committee members must act with independence and objectivity.

Use of a nominating committee that is composed of independent directors facilitates independence and maintenance of objectivity in the audit committee. Having an audit committee that is largely beholden to the chief executive, chief financial officer, or other member of senior management would likely be worse than having no audit committee at all. Other standing committees of the board, such as the compensation committee, have a mandate of independence and objectivity, so their actions are not clouded by conflict. In no other committee, however, is the importance of independence greater than in the audit committee.

The utilization of fundamental principles of good governance is especially important to the effective functioning of the audit committee. Effective communication between management and the external auditors and between management and the internal auditors assures that good judgment has been used. The audit committee must be especially diligent in its efforts to represent the interests of shareholders and other stakeholders. Of course, audit committee members must have considerable expertise in matters of finance and accounting.

IMPORTANT PERSONAL ATTRIBUTES OF MEMBERS

In addition to the personal characteristics required of effective board members, discussed in Chapter 3, relevant personal attributes of an effective audit committee member include:

- Courage to challenge, when
  - The director does not believe management is forthcoming or responses do not make sense
  - No other committee members share a director's concerns
- Extremely high level of integrity
- Healthy skepticism
- Inquisitiveness and independent judgment—asking the right questions and appropriately interpreting the answers
- Recognition of the committee's increasingly significant role
- Knowledge of the company's risks and controls and the ability to offer informed insight
- A broad perspective on the business that extends beyond financial and technical knowledge
- Ability to offer new perspectives and constructive suggestions[1]

The fourth edition of the *Corporate Director's Guidebook* states that "common sense, diligence, and an attitude of constructive skepticism are critical qualifications for an audit committee member."[2] It also points out that the continuing education of audit committee members in the rapidly changing financial environment is another important obligation in which members should willingly engage.

IMPORTANCE OF TOTAL INDEPENDENCE

As noted earlier, independence of management is a critically important characteristic for all members of an audit committee. The American Law Institute's *Principles of Corporate Governance* recommends that public company audit committees should consist of at least three members who are independent of management. Independence as defined in the *Principles* means the committee should be composed exclusively of directors "who are neither employed by the corporation nor were so employed within the two preceding years, including at least a majority of members who have no significant relationship with the corporation's senior executives."[3]

[1] Catherine Bromilow and Barbara Berlin, *Audit Committee Effectiveness—What Works Best, Third Edition* (Altamonte Springs, FL: Institute of Internal Auditors Research Foundation, 2005), p. 70.

[2] American Bar Association, *Corporate Director's Guidebook, Fourth Edition,* 2004, quoted in *Business Lawyer* (May 2004): 1089.

Securities and Exchange Commission (SEC) rules state that an audit committee member:

(1) Cannot accept directly or indirectly, any consulting, advisory, or other compensatory fee from the issuer [organization], other than in the member's capacity as a director; and

(2) Cannot be an "affiliated person" of the corporation, as defined in the securities laws (one that controls, is controlled by, or is under common control with) the [organization] or a subsidiary of that [organization].[4]

Former officers of the corporation and other affiliated persons are banned from audit committee membership for varying periods. The contents of Section 301 of the Sarbanes-Oxley Act of 2002 concerning independence and the specific independence rules of the New York Stock Exchange (NYSE) and Nasdaq stock markets are discussed next.

PORTION OF SECTION 301 OF SARBANES-OXLEY CONCERNING AUDIT COMMITTEE INDEPENDENCE

(3) *Independence*

(A) IN GENERAL. Each member of the audit committee of the issuer shall be a member of the board of directors of the issuer, and shall otherwise be independent.

(B) CRITERIA. In order to be considered to be independent for purposes of this paragraph, a member of an audit committee of an issuer may not, other than in his or her capacity as a member of the audit committee, the board of directors, or any other board committee

(i) accept any consulting, advisory, or other compensatory fee from the issuer; or

(ii) be an affiliated person of the issuer or any subsidiary thereof.[5]

NEW YORK STOCK EXCHANGE RULE ON INDEPENDENCE

Rule 303A.2 of the NYSE Listed Company Manual contains specific guidelines for determining whether a director is independent and therefore eligible to serve on an audit committee. This rule states:

---

[3] ALI, *Principles of Corporate Governance: Analysis and Recommendations* (St. Paul, MN: American Law Institute Publishers, 1994), Part 3.05, p. 103.

[4] Securities Exchange Act of 1934, as amended, Rule 10A-3(b)(1).

[5] Sarbanes-Oxley § 301. P.L. 107–204.

(a) No director qualifies as "independent" unless the board of directors affirmatively determines that the director has no material relationship with the listed company. Companies must disclose these determinations.

(b) In addition, a director is not independent if:

(i) The director is, or has been within the last three years, an employee of the listed company, or an immediate family member is or has been within the last three years, an executive officer of the listed company.

(ii) The director has received or an immediate family has received during any 12-month period within the last three years, more than $100,000 in direct compensation from the listed company, other than director and committee fees and pension or other forms of deferred compensation for prior service.

(iii) (A) The director or immediate family member is a current partner of a firm that is the company's internal or external auditor;

(B) The director is a current employee of such a firm;

(C) The director has an immediate family member who is a current employee of such a firm and who participates in the firm's audit, assurance, or tax compliance (but not tax planning) practice; or

(D) The director or an immediate family member was within the last three years (but is no longer) a partner or employee of such a firm and personally worked on the listed company's audit within that time.

(iv) The director or an immediate family member is, or has been within the last three years, employed as an executive officer of another company where any of the listed company's present executive officers at the same time serves or served on that company's compensation committee.

(v) The director is a current employee, or an immediate family member is a current executive officer, of a company that has made payments to, or received payments from, the listed company for property or services in an amount which, in any of the last three years, exceeds the greater of $1 million or 2% of such other company's consolidated gross revenues.[6]

NASDAQ RULE ON INDEPENDENCE

The Nasdaq rules are quite similar. Rule 4350(d)(2) of the Nasdaq Stock Market Manual sets forth the composition requirements for audit committee membership of listed corporations. It states the general rule:

(2) Audit Committee Composition

(A) Each issuer must have, and certify that it has and will continue to have, an audit committee of at least three members, each of whom must:

(i) be independent as defined under Rule 4200(a)(15);

(ii) meet the criteria for independence set forth in Rule 10A-3(b)(1) under the Act (subject to the exemptions provided in Rule 10A-3(c));

[6] NYSE, Inc., Listed Company Manual § 303A¶ 2. See www.nyse.com.

(iii) not have participated in the preparation of the financial statements of the company or any current subsidiary of the company at any time during the past three years; and

(iv) be able to read and understand fundamental financial statements, including a company's balance sheet, income statement, and cash flow statement. Additionally, each issuer must certify that it has, and will continue to have, at least one member of the audit committee who has past employment experience in finance or accounting, requisite professional certification in accounting, or any other comparable experience or background which results in the individual's financial sophistication, including being or having been a chief executive officer, chief financial officer or other senior officer with financial oversight responsibilities.

(B) Notwithstanding paragraph (2)(A)(i), one director who:

(i) is not independent as defined in Rule 4200;

(ii) meets the criteria set forth in Section 10A(m)(3) under the Act and the rules thereunder; and

(iii) is not a current officer or employee or a Family Member of such officer or employee, may be appointed to the audit committee, if the board, under exceptional and limited circumstances, determines that membership on the committee by the individual is required by the best interests of the company and its shareholders, and the board discloses, in the next annual proxy statement subsequent to such determination (or, if the issuer does not file a proxy, in its Form 10-K or 20-F), the nature of the relationship and the reasons for that determination. A member appointed under this exception may not serve longer than two years and may not chair the audit committee.[7]

FINANCIAL KNOWLEDGE NECESSARY

It is understandable that all audit committee members must be financially literate and have basic qualifications and experience relating to financial matters, as virtually all of the duties of audit committees deal with financial information, risks, and related controls. NYSE Rule 303A.07 states that audit committees must consist of at least three individuals, all of whom must be financially literate. The Nasdaq rule is set forth in the last section.

In addition to the requirement that all audit committee members be financial literate, at least one member of the audit committee must qualify as a "financial expert" as defined by the SEC and stock exchange rules. This means they must have "accounting or related financial management expertise." Although not required, industry specific knowledge is also becoming more critical to successful service on an audit committee.

[7] NASDAQ Manual Online, Rule 4350(d)(2) at www.complinet.com/nasdaq/display/display.html?rbid=1705&element_id=13.

Sarbanes-Oxley Section 407 provides factors to be considered by the stock exchanges in setting rules defining whether an individual can be considered a financial expert. These factors are whether a person, through education and experience as a public accountant or auditor, or a principal financial officer, controller, or principal accounting officer of an issuer, or from a position involving the performance of similar functions has:

1. An understanding of generally accepted accounting principles and financial statements;
2. Experience in:
   (a) The preparation or auditing of financial statements of generally comparable issuers; and
   (b) The application of such principles in connection with the accounting estimates, accruals, and reserves;
3. Experience with internal accounting controls; and
4. An understanding of audit committee functions.[8]

CRITERIA FOR ASSESSING AUDIT COMMITTEE EFFECTIVENESS

As noted in Chapter 4, one of the duties required by statute, regulation, or rule is that the committee conduct an annual self-evaluation of the effectiveness of the committee as a whole. Continuing improvement is a strong attribute of an effective audit committee.

Additionally, rating agencies consider audit committee effectiveness one of the factors in determining their opinion of the quality of governance of the organization. These factors affecting the external auditor's determination of the effectiveness of an entity's internal controls were set forth in Appendix E to the PCAOB Auditing Standard (AS) No. 2 (superseded by AS No. 5):

- Extent of direct and independent interaction with key members of financial management, including the chief financial officer and the chief accounting officer.
- Degree to which difficult questions are raised and pursued with management and the [external] auditor, including questions that indicate an understanding of the critical accounting policies and judgmental accounting estimates.
- Level of responsiveness to issues raised by the [external] auditor, including those required to be communicated by the auditor to the audit committee.[9]

[8] Sarbanes-Oxley Act, § 407. P.L. 107–204.

[9] Public Company Accounting Oversight Board Auditing Standard No. 2, "An Audit of Internal Control over Financial Reporting that is Integrated with an Audit of Financial Statements," Appendix E, ¶ E-68. See www.pcaobus.org.

This language no longer appears in the shorter and more concise AS No. 5 that superseded AS No. 2, but it is still believed to represent the principles of relevant guidance. The audit committee should be an active participant in the governance of the organization. AS No. 5 does state in paragraph 25 that because of the importance of the overall control environment to good internal control, the external auditor should consider "[w]hether the Board or audit committee understands and exercises oversight responsibility over financial reporting and internal control." Paragraph 27 states that the external auditor should evaluate "[t]he nature and extent of the oversight of the [period-end financial reporting] process by management, the board of directors, and the audit committee."[10]

Assessments of the performance of individual members of the audit committee facilitates counseling members whose performance is substandard or replacing them if they do not wish to expend the necessary effort. Experience or knowledge in a particular area can be obtained through continuing professional education or personal coaching. Effectiveness factors to be considered for individuals mirror many that apply to all board members. They are:

- A willingness to prepare for and participate in the necessary business of the committee
- Knowledge and insight of the organization and its mission
- Perhaps most important, an objective point of view and ability to communicate the substance of complex issues

Periodic assessment of the quality and completeness of the audit committee's fulfillment of the functions set forth in its charter is an effective method of assuring that all of the committee's responsibilities are being properly performed. As noted earlier, audit committees in public companies are required to publish an annual report on their activities.

A series of questions designed to facilitate the committee's evaluation of its performance is set forth in Appendix 6A. This evaluation tool was developed by the auditing and consulting firm Deloitte and covers in depth all phases of the audit committee's responsibilities.

KEY POINTS IN CHAPTER 6

1. In addition to the characteristics necessary for an effective board member, additional important attributes of audit committee members include:
   - Extremely high level of integrity and healthy skepticism

[10] Public Company Accounting Oversight Board, Auditing Standard No. 5, "An Audit of Internal Control over Financial Reporting that Is Integrated with an Audit of Financial Statements," ¶ 27. See www.pcaobus.org.

- Inquisitiveness and independent judgment—asking the right questions and appropriately interpreting the answers
- Knowledge of the company's risks and controls and the ability to offer informed insight
- A broad perspective on the business that extends beyond financial and technical knowledge

2. Total independence in both fact and appearance, as well as action, is perhaps the single most important characteristic of audit committee members.
3. Common sense, diligence, and an attitude of constructive skepticism are critical qualifications for an audit committee member.
4. The financial and accounting responsibilities of the audit committee dictate that all members of the committee must be financially literate and have financial and accounting expertise. At least one member of the committee must be designated as an expert, in accounting and auditing, and he or she must have gained the requisite knowledge through specialized education and experience.
5. Broad business experience is also very helpful in view of the breadth of responsibilities being assigned to audit committees.
6. Knowledge of the industries in which the organization operates is an important determinant of an effective member of the audit committee.
7. The quality of the oversight of financial reporting provided by the audit committee is a key determinant of the effectiveness of the entity's internal control over financial reporting. The external audit firm must evaluate the quality of financial reporting as a part of its audit of internal control over financial reporting.
8. Periodic evaluation of the performance of the audit committee as a whole is an effective method of assuring that it covers all necessary functions that are set forth in its charter.
9. Assessment of the performance of audit committee members and remediation of any shortcomings allows for continual improvement and effective performance of the committee as a whole.

Appendix 6A

Audit Committee Performance Evaluation Questionnaire

Each of the following questions should be answered in terms of a 5-point scale with 5 equivalent to "strongly agree" and 4 equivalent to "agree" with 2 equal to disagree and 1 equal to "strongly disagree." A score of 3 should be used for "neither agree nor disagree." Questions that are inapplicable or for which sufficient information is not available to form a conclusion should not be answered. Questions that are potentially inapplicable because they deal with matters of public corporations only should be indicated with a bold asterisk * at the end of the question.

Composition and Quality

1. Potential audit committee members are identified with explicit consideration being given to the candidate's qualifications for serving on the audit committee.
2. Sources acting independent of management (e.g., independent board members assisted by an outside search firm) have been utilized to identify qualified audit committee members.
3. Audit committee members have the appropriate qualifications to meet the objectives of the audit committee's charter, including appropriate financial literacy.
4. Audit committee members have differing perspectives due to a diversity of experiences and backgrounds.
5. The audit committee demonstrates integrity, credibility, trustworthiness, willingness to actively participate, ability to constructively handle conflict, possession of interpersonal skills, and proactiveness.
6. The audit committee demonstrates appropriate industry knowledge.
7. Members of the audit committee meet all applicable independence requirements.
8. The audit committee reviews its charter annually to determine whether its responsibilities are adequately described and recommends any changes to the board for approval.
9. The audit committee monitors compliance with corporate governance regulations and guidelines.
10. The audit committee has participated in a continuing education program to enhance its members' understanding of relevant auditing, accounting, regulatory, and industry issues.

11. New audit committee members are provided with an orientation program to educate them on the company, their responsibilities, and the company's financial reporting and accounting practices.
12. The leadership of the audit committee chair is effective.
13. The audit committee, in conjunction with the nominating committee (or its equivalent) as appropriate, creates a succession/rotation plan for audit committee members, including the audit committee chair.

Understanding the Business, Including Risks

14. The audit committee considers the pressures on management that may impact the quality of financial reporting (e.g., earnings targets, compensation plans, and performance measures).
15. The audit committee considers the significant risks faced by the company. Examples include (but are not limited to):

- Regulatory and legal requirements
- Concentrations (e.g., suppliers and customers)
- Market and competitive trends
- Financing/liquidity needs
- Financial exposures
- Business continuity
- Company reputation
- Financial strategy execution

16. The audit committee understands and approves the process implemented by management to effectively identify, assess, and respond to the organization's key risks.
17. The audit committee understands and approves management's fraud risk assessment and has an understanding of identified fraud risks.
18. Management provides the audit committee with reports that include benchmarking information (comparing the company's financial performance and ratios with industry competitors/peers) with explanations for areas that differ significantly.

Process and Procedures

19. The audit committee reports its proceedings and recommendations to the board after each committee meeting.
20. The audit committee dedicates appropriate time and resources to execute its responsibilities.
21. The audit committee participates in the development of a calendar to ensure that responsibilities are met.
22. Audit committee members have the option to influence their meeting agendas in order to address emerging issues.
23. Audit committee meetings are conducted in an effective manner, with time spent primarily on significant issues.

24. The audit committee chair encourages input on the meeting agenda from the committee, management, the internal auditor, the independent auditor, and the other board of directors.
25. The audit committee sets clear expectations and provides feedback to the full board concerning the competency of the organization's CFO and senior financial management.
26. The audit committee has input into the succession planning process for the CFO.
27. The agenda and related information (e.g., prior meeting minutes, press releases, financial statements, etc.) are circulated in advance of meetings to allow audit committee members sufficient time to study and understand the information.
28. The written materials provided to audit committee members are appropriately balanced (i.e., relevant and concise).
29. The audit committee meetings are held at least quarterly.
30. The audit committee maintains adequate minutes of each meeting.
31. The audit committee, together with the compensation committee, regularly reviews management incentive plans to consider whether the incentive process is appropriate.
32. The audit committee meets periodically with the company's disclosure committee (committee responsible for reviewing the company's disclosure procedures).
33. The audit committee respects the line between oversight and management of the financial reporting process.
34. Audit committee members come to meetings well prepared.

Communications and Information

35. The level of openness between the audit committee and relevant parties (other board members, management, internal audit, and external audit) is appropriate.
36. For matters that require specialized expertise, the audit committee engages external parties as appropriate.
37. The audit committee receives and analyzes information from management on significant industry trends, analyst estimates and variations from budget.
38. Audit committee members periodically visit company locations to conduct onsite meetings with key members of management.

Oversight of the Financial Reporting Process, Including Internal Controls

39. The audit committee considers the quality and appropriateness of financial accounting and reporting.
40. The audit committee considers the transparency of disclosures.
41. The audit committee reviews the company's significant accounting policies.
42. The audit committee has a process for the review of significant issues prior to quarterly and annual earnings releases (e.g., with management and the independent auditors).
43. The audit committee understands and approves the process used by management to identify and disclose related-party transactions.

44. The audit committee has a process to review earnings releases (including pro forma or non-GAAP [generally accepted accounting procedures] information, and other financial information or earnings guidance).

45. The audit committee has a process to review 10-Qs, 10-Ks (including management's discussion and analysis), proxies and other filings, as appropriate, before issuance and provides comments to management and independent auditors as applicable.*

46. The audit committee reviews the processes related to financial statement certifications made by the CEO and CFO.

47. The audit committee receives sufficient information to assess and understand management's process to evaluate the organization's system of internal controls (e.g., financial reporting and disclosure controls, operation controls, and compliance controls).

48. The audit committee oversees the organization's external financial reporting and internal control over financial reporting.

49. The audit committee understands and gives appropriate consideration to the internal control testing conducted by management, the internal auditors, and independent auditors to assess the process of detecting internal control issues or fraud.

50. The audit committee believes that management's scope of internal control testing adequately supports its internal control assessment (as required by Section 404 of the Sarbanes-Oxley Act).*

51. If management's assessment of internal controls resulted in the identification of significant deficiencies or material weaknesses, plans to address these issues are reviewed, evaluated and monitored by the audit committee.

52. The audit committee makes inquiries of the appropriate parties (independent auditor, internal auditor and management) on the depth of experience and sufficiency of the company's accounting and finance staff.

53. The audit committee reviews the management recommendation letters written by the auditors (external and internal) and monitors the process to determine that all significant matters raised are addressed.

54. The audit committee ensures that management takes action to achieve resolution when there are instances of repeat comments from auditors, particularly for those related to internal controls.

55. Adjustments to the financial statements that resulted from the audit process are reviewed by the audit committee, regardless of whether they were recorded by management.

56. The audit committee is consulted when management is seeking a second opinion on an accounting or auditing matter.

Oversight of Audit Functions

57. The audit committee understands the coordination of work between the auditors (external and internal).

58. The audit committee regularly reviews the adequacy of the internal audit function (e.g., the charter, audit plan, budget, compliance, and number, quality, and continuity of staff).

59. The audit committee oversees the role of the internal audit director from selection to termination (e.g., appointment, evaluation, compensation, and retention).

60. The audit committee provides feedback to the internal audit director at least annually.

61. The internal audit reporting lines established with the audit committee promote an atmosphere where significant issues that might involve management will be brought to the attention of the audit committee.

62. The audit committee appropriately considers internal audit reports, management's responses, and improvement actions.

63. The audit committee oversees the role of the independent auditors from selection to termination (e.g., appointment, oversight, evaluation, retention, and pre-approval of services).

64. The audit committee considers the external audit plan and provides recommendations as appropriate.

65. The audit committee reviews the appropriateness of the audit fees paid to the independent auditor.

66. The audit committee comprehensively reviews management's representation letters to the independent auditors (including making inquiries about any difficulties obtaining the representations).

67. The audit committee has an effective process to evaluate the independent auditor's qualifications and performance.

68. The audit committee pre-approves all services (audit and non-audit) provided by the independent auditor.

69. The audit committee considers the scope of non-audit services provided by the independent auditor in determining the auditor's independence.

70. The audit committee reviews other professional services that relate to financial reporting (e.g., consulting, legal and tax strategy services) provided by outside consultants.

71. The audit committee monitors the process to determine that the independent auditor's partners are rotated in accordance with applicable rules.

72. The audit committee has private executive sessions with management, internal audit, and external audit, which result in candid discussion of pertinent issues.

Overall Ethics and Compliance Culture

73. Audit committee members are notified of communications received from agencies (e.g., governmental or regulatory) relating to areas of alleged violations or areas of non-compliance.

74. The audit committee oversees management's procedures for enforcing the company's code of conduct.

75. The audit committee determines that there is a senior level person designated as specifically responsible for knowing and understanding relevant legal and regulatory requirements.

76. The audit committee oversees the process in place to address:

- the risks of noncompliance with applicable regulations
- conflicts of interest
- violations of the code of ethical conduct

77. The audit committee oversees the organization's whistleblower process and reviews the log of incoming calls.

78. The audit committee oversees procedures designed to prohibit retaliation against whistleblowers.

Monitoring Activities

79. An annual performance evaluation of the audit committee is conducted and the findings are presented to the full board.

80. Matters identified from the audit committee self-assessment that require follow-through are resolved.

81. The company provides the audit committee with sufficient funding to fulfill its objectives.

Overall Assessment

82. What is your overall evaluation of the performance of the audit committee? (Scale of 1 to 5, 5 being the highest).[1]

[1] Source: Deloitte, Audit Committee Performance Evaluation (March 2006).

Chapter 7

The Audit Committee and Its Charter

As noted in Chapter 4, the audit committee of a publicly held corporation is required to publish its charter in its proxy statement pursuant to the provisions of Item 306 of Regulation S-K, which requires a statement as to whether the board of directors has adopted a written charter for the audit committee and, if so, requires a copy of the written charter to be filed as an appendix to the corporation's proxy statement at least every three years.[1] It is also a very well recognized best business practice for the audit committees of privately held corporations and not-for-profit organizations to prepare a charter of their mission and responsibilities.

PURPOSE AND CONTENTS OF AN AUDIT COMMITTEE CHARTER

The audit committee's charter sets forth in writing the purpose of the committee as well as the specific duties and responsibilities it undertakes. The charter should express realistic guidelines of the actual functions to be performed by the audit committee. It should not be an aspirational public relations document. It should be a working document that truly reflects what the audit committee is and does.

This chapter serves as a review for the reader of the contents of the duties and responsibilities contained in previous chapters, since it provides the opportunity to see how several companies have expressed audit committee duties and the different emphases placed on each duty. Chapter 6 discussed the requirement for the audit committee to periodically assess its effectiveness. This is a mandate for publicly held corporations and a best practice for privately held and not-for-profit organizations.

Appendix 7A presents a sample audit committee charter prepared by the auditing and consulting firm Deloitte. This charter is based on Deloitte's analysis of Fortune 1000 corporate charters and review of relevant laws and regulations. The statutory or regulatory source of each item in the sample charter is inserted in brackets. Thus it is complete from a legal perspective but does not necessarily present all best business practices.

Appendix 7B presents another sample charter that contains exemplary language appropriate for the charter of an audit committee. It was prepared by

[1] Code of Federal Regulations 17 CFR 229.306.

PricewaterhouseCoopers and sponsored by the Institute of Internal Auditors Research Foundation.

Appendix 7C presents sample excerpts from various corporate audit committee charters that illustrate additional duties and responsibilities that have evolved as best business practices. These excerpts are taken from actual audit committee charters that were published in their company's proxy statement.

The charter of the audit committee of Schering-Plough Corporation is noteworthy because of the clarity and completeness of the committee's responsibilities to interact with and oversee the corporation's relationships with the external auditing firm. 13 of 20 responsibilities listed involve the corporation's external auditors.

The charter of the audit committee of Microsoft Corporation is noteworthy due to the extensive number and types of interactions the committee has with internal auditing. Ten of the 32 total responsibilities of the audit committee involve the company's internal audit function. In addition to oversight of various aspects of the internal audit function itself, the Microsoft audit committee involves the senior internal audit executive in discussions of financial reporting, including reports to the Securities and Exchange Commission, earnings releases to the public, and earnings guidance to financial analysts.

The charter of the audit committee of 3M Company is noteworthy for its emphasis on risk management and compliance. Not only does the audit committee evaluate the policies and practices in place to manage business risks and compliance with laws and regulations, but it also evaluates the company's business conduct policies.

The charter of the audit committee of Lowe's Companies, Inc. is noteworthy as it expresses audit committee involvement with internal auditing concerning the independent audit and code of ethics. It also contains specific details of the committee's oversight of the operations of internal auditing.

The charter of the audit committee of General Electric is noteworthy as it limits the number of audit committees of other corporations on which a GE audit committee member can serve.

The charter of the audit committee of Continental Airlines, Inc. is noteworthy as the committee has a responsibility to review expenses of senior officers as well as related-party transactions. The committee also has the responsibility for reviewing environmental policies, standards, and related performance reports from management.

KEY POINTS IN CHAPTER 7

1. The audit committee charter should set forth in writing the mission of the committee, its structure and composition, and the specific duties and responsibilities the committee undertakes to accomplish.
2. The charter of a standing committee of the board of directors, like the audit committee, specifies to investors and other stakeholders (or to the organization in case of privately held corporations and not-for-profit organizations) its

position in the organization and what responsibilities it has committed to undertake on behalf of stakeholders.

3. The audit committee charter also provides a written benchmark for periodic assessment of the accomplishments of the committee.
4. The charter should be reviewed annually to ensure that it remains relevant, current, and appropriate. Public companies are required to publish the charter of their audit committee in their proxy statement at least every three years, or more often if revised.
5. Creation of an appropriate charter is only one step in ensuring the effectiveness of an audit committee. Even more important is the committee's commitment to perform the listed duties and responsibilities in a thoroughly professional manner.
6. Although best business practices for audit committees continue to evolve, the charter of each audit committee should be structured to the needs of the organization. There is no one-size-fits-all.

Appendix 7A

Sample or Model Audit Committee Charter (Statutory and Regulatory Perspective)

I. Purpose

The audit committee is established by and among the board of directors for the primary purpose of assisting the board in:

- Overseeing the integrity of the company's financial statements [NYSE Corporate Governance Rule 7(c)(i)(A)] and the company's accounting and financial reporting processes and financial statement audits [Nasdaq Corporate Governance Rule 4350(d)(1)].
- Overseeing the company's compliance with legal and regulatory requirements [NYSE Corporate Governance Rule 7(c)(i)(A)].
- Overseeing the registered public accounting firm's (independent auditor's) qualifications and independence [NYSE Corporate Governance Rule 7(c)(i)(A) and Nasdaq Corporate Governance Rule 4350(d)(1)].
- Overseeing the performance of the company's independent auditor [NYSE Corporate Governance Rule 7(c)(i)(A) and Nasdaq Corporate Governance Rule 4350(d)(1)] and internal audit function [NYSE Corporate Governance Rule 7(c)(i)(A].
- Overseeing the company's systems of disclosure controls and procedures, internal controls over financial reporting, and compliance with ethical standards adopted by the company.

Consistent with this function, the audit committee should encourage continuous improvement of, and should foster adherence to, the company's policies, procedures, and practices at all levels. The audit committee should also provide for open communication among the independent auditor, financial and senior management, the internal audit function, and the board of directors.

- The audit committee has the authority to obtain advice and assistance from outside legal, accounting, or other advisors as necessary to perform its duties and responsibilities [Sarbanes-Oxley Act Section 301, NYSE Corporate Governance Rule 6, and Nasdaq Corporate Governance Rule 4350(d)(3)]

  The company will provide appropriate funding, as determined by the audit committee, for compensation to the independent auditor, to any advisors that the audit committee chooses to engage, and for payment of ordinary administrative expenses of the audit committee that are necessary or appropriate in carrying out its duties [Sarbanes-Oxley Act Section 301, NYSE Corporate Governance Rule 6, and Nasdaq Corporate Governance Rule 4350(d)(3)].

The audit committee will primarily fulfill its responsibilities by carrying out the activities enumerated in Section III of this charter. The audit committee will report regularly to the board of directors regarding the execution of its duties and responsibilities [NYSE Corporate Governance Rule 7(c)(iii)(H)].

II. Composition and Meetings

The audit committee will comprise three or more directors as determined by the board. Each audit committee member will meet the applicable standards of independence and the determination of independence will be made by the board [Sarbanes-Oxley Act Section 301, NYSE Corporate Governance Rules 6 and 7(a) and (b), and Nasdaq Corporate Governance Rule 4350(d)(2)].

All members of the committee must comply with all financial-literacy requirements of the securities exchange(s) on which the company is listed. At least one member will qualify as an "audit committee financial expert" as defined by the SEC and determined by the board [Sarbanes-Oxley Act Section 407].

The members of the committee will be appointed by the board at the annual organizational meeting of the board to serve until their successors are elected. Unless a chairperson is elected by the full board, the members of the committee may designate a chairperson by majority vote.

The committee will meet at least quarterly, or more frequently as circumstances dictate. The committee chairperson will approve the agenda for the committee's meetings and any member may suggest items for consideration. Briefing materials will be provided to the committee as far in advance of meetings as practicable. Each regularly scheduled meeting will conclude with an executive session of the committee absent members of management. As part of its responsibility to foster open communication, the committee will meet frequently with management, the director of the internal audit function, and the independent auditor in separate executive sessions. [NYSE Corporate Governance Rule 7(c)(iii)(E)]. In addition, the committee will meet with the independent auditor and management to discuss the annual audited financial statements and quarterly financial statements, including the company's disclosures under "Management's Discussion and Analysis of

Financial Condition and Results of Operations" [NYSE Corporate Governance Rule 7(c)(iii)(B)].

II. Responsibilities and Duties

To fulfill its responsibilities and duties, the audit committee will:

Documents/Reports/Accounting Information Review

1. Review this charter at least annually and recommend to the board of directors any necessary amendments [NYSE Corporate Governance Rules and Nasdaq Corporate Governance Rule 4350(d)(1)].
2. Meet with management and the independent auditor to review and discuss the company's annual financial statements [Item 306 of Regulation S-K] and quarterly financial statements (prior to the company's Form 10-Q filings or release of earnings), as well as all internal control reports (or summaries thereof). Review other relevant reports or financial information submitted by the company to any governmental body or the public, including management certifications as required by the Sarbanes-Oxley Act of 2002 [Sarbanes-Oxley Act Sections 302 and 906] and relevant reports rendered by the independent auditor (or summaries thereof).
3. Recommend to the board whether the financial statements should be included in the annual report on Form 10-K [Item 306 of Regulation S-K].
4. Discuss earnings press releases, including the type and presentation of information, paying particular attention to any pro forma or adjusted non-GAAP information. Such discussions may be in general terms (i.e., discussion of the types of information to be disclosed and the type of presentations to be made) [NYSE Corporate Governance Rule 7(c)(iii)(C) and general commentary to Rule 7(c)].
5. Discuss financial information on earnings guidance provided to analysts and ratings agencies. Such discussions may be in general terms (i.e., discussion of the types of information to be disclosed and the type of presentations to be made) [NYSE Corporate Governance Rule 7(c)(iii)(C) and general commentary to Rule 7(c)].
6. Review the regular internal reports to management (or summaries thereof) prepared by the internal audit function, as well as management's response.

Independent Auditor

7. Appoint (and recommend that the board submit for shareholder ratification, if applicable), compensate, retain, and oversee the work performed by the independent auditor for the purpose of preparing or issuing an audit report or related work. Review the performance and independence of the independent auditor and remove the independent auditor if circumstances warrant. The independent auditor will report directly to the audit committee and the audit

committee will oversee the resolution of disagreements between management and the independent auditor if they arise [Sarbanes-Oxley Act Section 301, NYSE Corporate Governance Rule 6, and Nasdaq Corporate Governance Rule 4350(d)(3)].

8. Consider whether the auditor's provision of permissible non-audit services is compatible with the auditor's independence. Discuss with the independent auditor the matters required to be discussed under Statement on Auditing Standards (SAS) No. 61, as amended by SAS No. 84 and SAS No. 90 [Item 306 of Regulation S-K].

9. Review with the independent auditor any problems or difficulties and management's response [NYSE Corporate Governance Rule 7(c)(iii)(F)].

10. Review the independent auditor's attestation and report on management's assessment of internal control over financial reporting [Sarbanes-Oxley Act Section 404].

11. Hold timely discussions with the independent auditor regarding the following:

- All critical accounting policies and practices [Sarbanes-Oxley Act Section 204].
- All alternative treatments of financial information within generally accepted accounting principles related to material items that have been discussed with management, ramification of the use of such alternative disclosures and treatments, and the treatment preferred by the independent auditor [Sarbanes-Oxley Act Section 204].
- Other written communications between the independent auditor and management, including, but not limited to, the management letter and schedule of unadjusted differences [Sarbanes-Oxley Act Section 204].

12. At least annually, obtain and review a report by the independent auditor describing:

- The independent auditor's internal quality-control procedures [NYSE Corporate Governance Rule 7(c)(iii)(A)].
- Any material issues raised by the most recent internal quality-control review or peer review, or by any inquiry or investigation conducted by governmental or professional authorities during the preceding five years with respect to independent audits carried out by the independent auditor, and any steps taken to deal with such issues [NYSE Corporate Governance Rule 7(c)(iii)(A)].
- All relationships between the independent auditor and the company [NYSE Corporate Governance Rule 7(c)(iii)(A)] addressing the matters set forth in Independence Standards Board Standard No. 1 [Item 306 of Regulation S-K].
- This report should be used to evaluate the independent auditor's qualifications, performance, and independence. Further, the committee will review the experience and qualifications of the lead partner each year and determine that all partner rotation requirements, as promulgated by applicable rules and regulations, are executed. The committee will also consider whether there

should be rotation of the independent auditor itself [Commentary to NYSE Corporate Governance Rule 7(c)(iii)(A)].

13. Actively engage in dialogue with the independent auditor with respect to any disclosed relationships or services that may affect the independence and objectivity of the auditor and take appropriate actions to oversee the independence of the outside auditor [Nasdaq Corporate Governance Rule 4350(d)(1)].
14. Review and pre-approve (which may be pursuant to pre-approval policies and procedures—detailed as to the particular services with the audit committee informed of each service [Regulation S-X, 2-01(c)(7)]) both audit and non-audit services to be provided by the independent auditor. The authority to grant pre-approvals may be delegated to one or more designated members of the audit committee, whose decisions will be presented to the full audit committee at its next regularly scheduled meeting [Sarbanes-Oxley Act Section 202].
15. Set policies, consistent with governing laws and regulations, for hiring personnel of the independent auditor [NYSE Corporate Governance Rule 7(c)(iii)(G)].

Financial Reporting Processes, Accounting Policies, and Internal Control Structure

16. In consultation with the independent auditor and the internal audit function, review the integrity of the company's financial reporting processes (both internal and external), and the internal control structure (including disclosure controls and procedures and internal control over financial reporting).
17. Receive and review any disclosure from the company's CEO or CFO made in connection with the certification of the company's quarterly and annual reports filed with the SEC of: a) significant deficiencies and material weaknesses in the design or operation of internal control over financial reporting which are reasonably likely to adversely affect the company's ability to record, process, summarize, and report financial data; and b) any fraud, whether or not material, that involves management or other employees who have a significant role in the company's internal controls [Sarbanes-Oxley Act Section 302].
18. Review major issues regarding accounting principles and financial statement presentations, including any significant changes in the company's selection or application of accounting principles; major issues as to the adequacy of the company's internal control; and any special audit steps adopted in light of material control deficiencies [General Commentary to NYSE Corporate Governance Rule 7(c)].
19. Review analyses prepared by management (and the independent auditor as noted in item 11 above) setting forth significant financial reporting issues and judgments made in connection with the preparation of the financial statements, including analyses of the effects of alternative GAAP methods on the financial statements [General Commentary to NYSE Corporate Governance Rule 7(c)].

20. Review the effect of regulatory and accounting initiatives, as well as off-balance-sheet structures, on the financial statements of the company [General Commentary to NYSE Corporate Governance Rule 7(c)].
21. Review and approve all related-party transactions, defined as those transactions required to be disclosed under Item 404 of Regulation S-K [Nasdaq Corporate Governance Rule 4350(h)].
22. Establish and oversee procedures for the receipt, retention, and treatment of complaints regarding accounting, internal accounting controls, or auditing matters, including procedures for confidential, anonymous submissions by company employees regarding questionable accounting or auditing matters [Sarbanes-Oxley Act Section 301, NYSE Corporate Governance Rule 6, and Nasdaq Corporate Governance Rule 4350(d)(3)].

Note: The statutory or regulatory source of each item in the sample charter is inserted in brackets.

Appendix 7B

Sample Audit Committee Charter from the Institute of Internal Auditors Research Foundation

PURPOSE

To assist the board of directors in fulfilling its oversight responsibilities for the financial reporting process, the system of internal control over financial reporting, the audit process, and the company's process for monitoring compliance with laws and regulations and the code of conduct.

AUTHORITY

The audit committee has authority to conduct or authorize investigations into any matters within its scope of responsibility. It is empowered to:

- Retain outside counsel, accountants, or others to advise the committee or assist in the conduct of an investigation.
- Seek any information it requires from employees—all of whom are directed to cooperate with the committee's requests—or external parties.
- Meet with company officers, external auditors, or outside counsel, as necessary.

COMPOSITION

The audit committee will consist of at least three and no more than six members of the board of directors. The board or its nominating committee will appoint committee members and the committee chair.

Each committee member will be both independent and financially literate, as defined by applicable regulation and the board of directors. At least one member shall have expertise in financial reporting.

MEETINGS

The committee will meet at least four times a year, with authority to convene additional meetings, as circumstances require. All committee members are expected to attend each meeting, in person or via tele- or video-conference. The committee will invite members of management, auditors or others to attend meetings and provide pertinent information, as necessary. It will hold private meetings with auditors (see below) and executive sessions. Meeting agendas will be prepared and provided in advance to members, along with appropriate briefing materials. Minutes will be prepared.

RESPONSIBILITIES

The committee will carry out the following responsibilities:

Financial Statements

- Review significant accounting and reporting issues, including complex or unusual transactions and highly judgmental areas, and recent professional and regulatory pronouncements, and understand their impact on the financial statements.
- Review with management and the external auditors the results of the audit, including any difficulties encountered.
- Review the annual financial statements, and consider whether they are complete, consistent with information known to committee members, and reflect appropriate accounting principles.
- Review other sections of the annual report and related regulatory filings before release and consider the accuracy and completeness of the information.
- Review with management and the external auditors all matters required to be communicated to the committee under generally accepted auditing standards.
- Understand how management develops interim financial information, and the nature and extent of internal and external auditor involvement.
- Review interim financial reports with management and the external auditors, before filing with regulators, and consider whether they are complete and consistent with the information known to committee members.

Internal Control

- Consider the effectiveness of the company's internal control over annual and interim financial reporting, including information technology security and control.
- Understand the scope of internal and external auditors' review of internal control over financial reporting, and obtain reports on significant findings and recommendations, together with management's responses.

Internal Audit

- Review with management and the internal audit director the charter, plans, activities, staffing, and organizational structure of the internal audit function.
- Ensure there are no unjustified restrictions or limitations, and review and concur in the appointment, replacement, or dismissal of the internal audit director.
- Review the effectiveness of the internal audit function, including compliance with The Institute of Internal Auditors' *Standards for the Professional Practice of Internal Auditing.*
- On a regular basis, meet separately with the director of internal auditing to discuss any matters that the committee or internal audit believes should be discussed privately.

External Audit

- Review the external auditors' proposed audit scope and approach, including coordination of audit effort with internal auditing.
- Review the performance of the external auditors, and exercise final approval on the appointment or discharge of the auditors.
- Review and confirm the independence of the external auditors by obtaining statements from the auditors on relationships between the auditors and the company, including nonaudit services, and discussing the relationships with the auditors.
- On a regular basis, meet separately with the external auditors to discuss any matters that the committee or auditors believe should be discussed privately.

Compliance

- Review the effectiveness of the system for monitoring compliance with laws and regulations and the results of management's investigation and follow-up (including disciplinary action) of any instances of noncompliance.
- Review the findings of any examinations by regulatory agencies, and any auditor observations.
- Review the process for communicating the code of conduct to company personnel, and for monitoring compliance therewith.
- Obtain regular updates from management and company legal counsel regarding compliance matters.

Reporting Responsibilities

- Regularly report to the board of directors about committee activities, issues, and related recommendations.

- Provide an open avenue of communication between internal auditing, the external auditors, and the board of directors.
- Report annually to the shareholders, describing the committee's composition, responsibilities, and how they were discharged, and any other information required by rule.
- Review any other reports the company issues that relate to committee responsibilities.

Other Responsibilities

- Perform other activities related to this charter as requested by the board of directors.
- Institute and oversee special investigations as needed.
- Review and assess the adequacy of the committee charter annually, requesting board approval for proposed changes.
- Confirm annually that all responsibilities outlined in this charter have been carried out.
- Evaluate the committee's and individual members' performance on a regular basis.

Source: PricewaterhouseCoopers, *Audit Committee Effectiveness—What Works Best, Second Edition*. The Institute of Internal Auditors Research Foundation, 2000.

Appendix 7C

Excerpts from Selected Audit Committee Charters

SCHERING-PLOUGH CORPORATION* AUDIT COMMITTEE CHARTER (EXCERPTS) (APPROVED BY BOARD OF DIRECTORS ON FEBRUARY 27, 2007)

The Schering-Plough audit committee charter expresses its responsibilities for oversight of the external auditing function in considerable detail (13 of 20 responsibilities):

Responsibilities:

In carrying out its purposes, the Committee's policies and procedures should remain flexible, so that it may be in a position to best react or respond to changing circumstances or conditions. While there is no "blueprint" to be followed by the Committee in carrying out its purposes, the following should be considered with the responsibilities of the Committee

1. **Select Independent Auditors.** Select the independent auditors annually.
2. **Matters Concerning the Independence of Independent Auditors.**

   Review and discuss with the independent auditors the written disclosures required by Independence Standards Board Standard No. 1 regarding their independence and, where appropriate, recommend that the Board take appropriate action in response to the disclosures to satisfy itself of the independence of the independent auditors.

   Ensure the rotation of the lead (or coordinating) audit partner having primary responsibility for the audit and the audit partner responsible for reviewing the audit as required by law.

   Set policies for the Company's hiring of employees or former employees of the independent auditor.

   Pre-approve all auditing services and permitted non-auditing services (including the fees and terms thereof) to be performed for the Company by its independent auditor. The Committee may form and delegate authority to subcommittees consisting of one or more members when appropriate, including the authority to grant pre-approvals of audit and permitted non-audit services, provided that decisions of such subcommittee to grant pre-approvals shall be presented to the full Committee at its next scheduled meeting.

*Source: Schering-Plough Corporation website, accessed December 2007 http://phx.corporate-ir.net/phoenix.zhtml?c=89839&p=IROL-govCommittee&Committee=291.

3. **Review Quality Control Process of Independent Auditor.** Obtain and review a report from the independent auditor at least annually regarding
   (a) The independent auditor's internal quality-control procedures,
   (b) Any material issues raised by the most recent internal quality-control review, or peer review, of the firm, or by any inquiry or investigation by governmental or professional authorities within the preceding five years respecting one or more independent audits carried out by the firm,
   (c) Any steps taken to deal with any such issues, and
   (d) All relationships between the independent auditor and the Company. Present the conclusions of its review with respect to the independent auditors to the Board.
4. **Review Audit Plan.** Review with the independent auditors their plans for, and scope of, their annual audit.
5. **Conduct of Audit.** Discuss with the independent auditors the matters required to be discussed by Statement on Auditing Standards Nos. 61, 89, and 90 relating to the conduct of the audit, including any difficulties encountered in the course of the audit work and management's response, any restrictions on the scope of activities or access to requested information, and any significant disagreements with management.
6. **Review Audit Results.** Review with the independent auditors the report of their annual audit, the accompanying management letter, if any, and the reports of their reviews of the Company's interim financial statements conducted in accordance with Statement on Auditing Standards No. 100.
7. **Review Annual Financial Statements.** Review and discuss with management and the independent auditors the audited financial statements and the disclosures to be made in management's discussion and analysis. Recommend to the Board whether the audited financial statements should be included in the 10-K.
9. **Review Quarterly Financial Statements.** Review and discuss with management and the independent auditor the quarterly financial statements and the disclosures to be made in the MD&A prior to filing the 10-Q. Discuss with the independent auditors their review of the quarterly financial statements.
10. **Financial Reporting Issues and Judgments; Related Matters.** Discuss with management and the independent auditor significant financial reporting issues and judgments made in connection with the preparation of the Company's financial statements, including any significant changes in the Company's selection or application of accounting principles, any major issues as to the adequacy of the Company's internal controls and any special steps adopted in light of material internal control deficiencies.

    Review and discuss quarterly reports from the independent auditors on:
   (a) All critical accounting policies and practices to be used.
   (b) All alternative treatments of financial information within generally accepted accounting principles that have been discussed with management, ramifications of the use of such alternative disclosures and treatments, and the treatment preferred by the independent auditor.
   (c) Other material written communications between the independent auditor and management, such as any management letter or schedule of unadjusted differences.
   (d) Reports and disclosures of any insider or affiliated party transactions.

Discuss with management and the independent auditor the effect of regulatory and accounting initiatives as well as off-balance sheet structures on the Company's financial statements.

Discuss with management and the independent auditor any correspondence or published report which raises material issues regarding the Company's financial statements or accounting policies that is issued by the U.S. Securities and Exchange Commission or the New York Stock Exchange or other governmental agencies.

13. **Review Systems of Internal Accounting Controls.** Review with management, the senior corporate auditing executive, and the independent auditors the adequacy of the Company's internal controls over financial reporting that could significantly affect the Company's financial statements.

    Review disclosures made to the Committee by the Company's CEO and CFO during their certification process for the Form 10-K and Form 10-Q about any significant deficiencies in the design or operation of internal controls over financial reporting or material weaknesses therein and any fraud involving management or other employees who have a significant role in the Company's internal control over financial reporting.

    Review and discuss with the Chief Financial Officer, the senior Corporate Audits executive and the independent accountants the Company's report on internal controls over financial reporting and the auditors attestation relating thereto, prior to such documents being included in the 10-K.
14. **Securities Exchange Act of 1934.** Obtain assurance from the independent auditor that Section 10A(b) of the Securities Exchange Act of 1934 has not been implicated.
15. **Prepare Proxy Statement Report.** Prepare the report of the Committee required by the rules of the SEC to be included in the Company's annual proxy statement. Review and discuss with management the proxy statement disclosures about the Committee and the independent auditors. Review and discuss with management internal controls over proxy statement disclosure that is incorporated by reference into the 10-K.
16. **Board Reports.** Regularly report its activities to the Board in such manner and at such times as it deems appropriate. The Committee shall review with the Board any issues that arise with respect to the quality or integrity of Schering-Plough's financial statements, compliance with legal or regulatory requirements, the performance and independence of the independent auditors or the performance of the corporate auditors.

MICROSOFT CORPORATION AUDIT COMMITTEE CHARTER

The Microsoft charter notes that the audit committee has an extensive number and types of interactions with internal auditing (10 of 32 responsibilities):

1. The agenda for Committee meetings will be prepared in consultation between the Committee chair (with input from the Committee members), Finance management, the senior internal audit employee designated by the Committee to act as its direct liaison (the "Internal Audit Executive"), and the independent auditor....

10. Review the responsibilities, functions, and performance of the Company's internal audit department.
11. Review and approve the appointment or change in the Internal Audit Executive. . . .
14. Inquire of management, the Internal Audit Executive, and the independent auditor about significant risks or exposures, review the Company's policies for risk assessment and risk management, and assess the steps management has taken to control such risk to the Company.
15. Review with Finance management, the independent auditor, and the Internal Audit Executive the audit scope and plan, and coordination of audit efforts to ensure completeness of coverage, reduction of redundant efforts, the effective use of audit resources, and the use of independent public accountants other than the appointed auditors of the Company.
16. Consider and review with Finance management, the independent auditor, and the Internal Audit Executive:

    (a) The Company's annual assessment of the effectiveness of its internal controls and the independent auditor's attestation and report about the Company's assessment.

    (b) The adequacy of the Company's internal controls, including computerized information system controls and security.

    (c) Any "material weakness" or "significant deficiency" in the design or operation of internal control over financial reporting, and any steps taken to resolve the issue.

    (d) Any related significant findings and recommendations of the independent auditor and internal audit together with management's responses.
21. Consider and review with Finance management and the Internal Audit Executive:

    (a) Significant findings by the independent auditor or the Internal Audit Executive during the year and management's responses.

    (b) Any difficulties encountered in the course of their audit work, including any restrictions on the scope of their work or access to required information.

    (c) Any changes required in planned scope of their audit plan.
22. Participate in a telephonic meeting among Finance management, the Internal Audit Executive and the independent auditor before each earnings release to discuss the earnings release, financial information, use of any non-GAAP information, and earnings guidance.
24. Review the periodic reports of the Company with Finance management, the Internal Audit Executive, and the independent auditor prior to filing of the reports with the SEC, including the disclosures under "Management's Discussion and Analysis of Financial Condition and Results of Operations."
30. Meet with the Internal Audit Executive in executive session to discuss any matters the Committee or the Internal Audit Executive believes should be discussed privately with the Audit Committee.[1]

---

[1] Microsoft Corporation Web site, accessed May 2007. www.microsoft.com/about/companyinformation/corporategovernance/committees/audit.mspx.

3M COMPANY AUDIT COMMITTEE CHARTER

The 3M charter articulates considerable committee involvement with issues of risk management and compliance:

4. Risk Management and Compliance

a. Discuss policies and procedures with respect to risk assessment and risk management, the Company's major risk exposures, and the steps management has taken to monitor and mitigate such exposures.

b. Review the effectiveness of the system for monitoring compliance with laws, regulations, and the Company's business conduct policies, and the results of management's investigation and follow-up on any fraudulent acts or accounting irregularities.

c. Periodically obtain reports from management regarding compliance.

d. Review with the Company's General Counsel legal matters that may have a material impact on the consolidated financial statements and any material reports or inquiries received from regulators or governmental agencies regarding compliance.

e. Establish procedures for (i) the receipt, retention, and treatment of complaints received by the Company regarding accounting, internal accounting controls, or auditing matters; and (ii) the confidential, anonymous submission by Company employees of concerns regarding questionable accounting or auditing matters. Review periodically with management and Internal Audit these procedures and any significant complaints received.[2]

LOWE'S COMPANIES, INC. AUDIT COMMITTEE CHARTER

The Lowe's charter expresses committee involvement with internal auditing concerning the independent audit and code of ethics and expresses specific details of committee oversight of Lowe's internal audit function.[3]

[Audit Committee Has the] Authority and Responsibility:

- To review the scope and general extent of the independent auditor's audit examination prior to the annual audit, taking into account the Vice President of Internal Audit's evaluation for the performance of the independent accountants, including the degree of audit coordination and overall audit coverage.
- To review and approve the appointment, annual performance appraisal or discharge of the Vice President of Internal Audit.
- To meet on an annual basis with the Vice President of Internal Audit to:
    - Review the Internal Audit department's scope, staffing, training/development, budget and audit schedule, including the risk assessment upon which the audit schedule was developed, as well as plans for reviews of the Company's information systems, procedures and controls;

[2] 3M Web site accessed, January 2008. http://media.corporate-ir.net/media_files/NYS/MMM/corpgov/2007/Audit0207.pdf.

[3] Lowe's Companies Inc. Web site, accessed May 2007, www.shareholder.com/lowes/audit_charter.cfm.

- Review and approve the initial audit plan and any significant subsequent changes to the plan, the results of internal audit activities, including the independence, objectivity and qualifications of the internal audit staff, and periodically review and approve the Internal Audit Department charter;
- Review management's monitoring of compliance with the Company's Code of Ethics, including disclosures of insider and affiliated party transactions.

GENERAL ELECTRIC CHARTER

8. Audit Committee Memberships

The committee has determined that in view of the increasing demands and responsibilities of the Audit Committee, members of the committee should not serve on more than two additional Audit Committees of other public companies, and the chair of the committee should not serve on more than one other Audit Committee of a public company. Existing relationships exceeding these limits may continue in place provided that the full board of directors determines that such relationships do not impair the member's ability to serve effectively on the committee.[4]

CONTINENTAL AIRLINES, INC. CHARTER

The Continental audit committee charter notes the committee's responsibilities for review of expenses of senior officers as well as related-party transactions. The committee also has the responsibility for reviewing environmental policies, standards, and performance reports from management.

12. The Committee shall (a) to the extent it determines appropriate, review from time to time, the expenses of the senior officers (and, if it so desires, any other officers) of the Company charged to the Company or any of its subsidiaries, and any transactions between the Company or any of its subsidiaries and any affiliate of the Company and (b) at least annually, review those related party transactions that are required to be disclosed in the Company's proxy statement. . . .
18. The Committee shall review the Company's environmental policies and standards, and such reports as it may request from management or environmental consultants or advisors, and shall periodically discuss with management and legal counsel any material environmental proceedings, claims or other contingencies and such other environmental matters affecting the Company or any of its subsidiaries as the Committee shall from time to time determine appropriate or as the Board may specifically direct.[5]

[4] General Electric Web site, accessed Jan 2008, http://www.ge.com/company/governance/board/audit_committe_charter07.pdf.

[5] Continental Airlines Web site, accessed Jan 2008, http://www.continental.com/web/en-US/content/company/investor/docs/continental_charterauditcte_2005_02_11_01.pdf.

Chapter 8

Audit Committee Oversight of Financial Statements and Financial Disclosures

Chapters 4 and 5 outlined the important responsibilities that audit committees are tasked with relating to the oversight of the quality of financial statements as well as of the financial reports and other disclosures that organizations make to the public or to banks, regulatory authorities, and others. This chapter provides further details concerning these responsibilities.

AUDIT COMMITTEE DUTIES TO OVERSEE FINANCIAL STATEMENT PREPARATION

Audit committee oversight should mainly involve a process review and not a review, rehash, and questioning of each and every accounting decision management has made. Directors are not expected to hover over management and second-guess decisions. The audit committee is entitled to rely on the expertise of its professional advisors, including the external audit firm that it has employed to assist and represent it.

As noted in Chapter 4, one of the duties set forth in the 2007 *Corporate Director's Guidebook* that deals with this subject is:

> Determine whether to recommend to the board that the audited annual financial statements be included in the corporation's annual report on Form 10-K to be filed with the SEC [Securities and Exchange Commission].[1]

Although every member of the board of directors is required to sign the corporation's Form 10-K Annual Report, other board members rely to a great extent on the deliberations of the audit committee. The wording of the duty to recommend the financial statements be included in SEC filings had to be carefully chosen so that it did not duplicate the wording of the external audit firm's opinion. Such an opinion would have required professional expertise and experience on the part of the audit committee and that was not what Congress intended. The duty only supposes that the directors have exercised proper oversight using due care, diligence,

[1] American Bar Association, *Corporate Director's Guidebook, Fifth Edition* (Chicago: ABA Committee on Corporate Laws, 2007), p. 59.

and loyalty, the duties discussed in previous chapters. The New York Stock Exchange (NYSE) rule explains audit committee responsibilities to keep the full board informed concerning audit committee activities.

Listing rule 303A.07(H) of the NYSE requires that audit committees "[r]eport regularly to the board of directors."[2]

The commentary to this rule explains:

> The audit committee should review with the full board any issues that arise with respect to the quality or integrity of the listed company's financial statements, the company's compliance with legal or regulatory requirements, the performance and independence of the company's independent auditors, or the performance of the internal audit function.[3]

Another provision in the 2007 *Corporate Director's Guidebook* dealing with audit committee oversight of financial statement preparation is that the committee

> Review and consider any required communications from the external auditor as a result of its timely review of the quarterly financial statements.[4]

Professional auditing standards—American Institute of Certified Public Accountants (AICPA) Statements on Auditing Standards (SAS) Nos. 71 and 90 codified in AICPA *Professional Standards* AU § 380, *Communication with Audit Committees* and AU § 722, *Interim Financial Information*—require the external auditor to communicate to the audit committee any instances where management failed to respond to the auditor's notification that the quarterly financial statements may not be presented in accordance with generally accepted accounting principles in all material respects.

Another audit committee financial reporting duty contained in the *Guidebook* is:

> Review the corporation's annual and quarterly financial statements, and management certifications thereof, with management and the external auditor, and discuss with them the quality of management's accounting judgments in preparing the financial statements.[5]

This requirement is discussed further in the section titled "External Auditor Requirements for Communication with the Audit Committee." It recognizes the fact that the application of generally accepted accounting principles (GAAP) requires the exercise of significant amounts of judgment. This particular requirement is based on the provisions of professional auditing standards (SAS Nos. 61, 89, and 90), codified in AICPA *Professional Standards* AU § 380, *Communication with Audit Committees*

[2] NYSE, Listed Company Manual, Rule 303A.7(c)iii(H).

[3] Id.

[4] ABA, *Corporate Director's Guidebook,* 2007 p. 59.

[5] Id., p. 59.

and AU § 722, *Interim Financial Information*. These standards require the external auditors to assist audit committees to satisfy themselves that accounting and disclosure judgments in the organization's financial statements have adequate support in terms of the facts as well as appropriate accounting principles.

A final commentary to NYSE Rule 303A.07(c) summarizes and explains the duties of audit committees within the context of the responsibilities of management and the external auditor.

> While the fundamental responsibility for the listed company's financial statements and disclosures rests with management and the independent auditor, the audit committee must review: (A) major issues regarding accounting principles and financial statement presentations, including any significant changes in the company's selection or application of accounting principles, and major issues as to the adequacy of the company's internal controls and any special audit steps adopted in light of material control deficiencies; (B) analyses prepared by management and/or the independent auditor setting forth significant financial reporting issues and judgments made in connection with the preparation of the financial statements, including analyses of the effects of alternative GAAP methods on the financial statements; (C) the effect of regulatory and accounting initiatives, as well as off-balance sheet structures, on the financial statements of the listed company; and (D) the type and presentation of information to be included in earnings press releases (paying particular attention to any use of "pro forma," or "adjusted" non-GAAP, information), as well as review any financial information and earnings guidance provided to analysts and rating agencies.[6]

AUDIT COMMITTEE DUTIES REGARDING FINANCIAL DISCLOSURES

The duties audit committees have been legally tasked to perform on the subject of oversight of financial disclosures are listed in the 2007 edition of the *Corporate Director's Guidebook*. Except for the final duty, they are relevant only to publicly held corporations. The first duty is:

> Discuss the corporation's procedures for issuing quarterly and annual earnings press releases, and for providing financial information and earnings guidance to analysts, the financial press, and rating agencies.[7]

This requirement is for audit committees to discuss the procedures that were followed; in other words, it is a process review, not a second-guessing of decisions with the benefit of hindsight. Discussions with the external audit firm will provide audit committee members with information about accounting principles that management

[6] NYSE, Listed Company Manual, Rule 303A.7(c)iii(H). See www.nyse.com.
[7] ABA, *Corporate Director's Guidebook*. 2007, p. 59.

has employed and background as to the quality of the underlying assumptions and estimates. This aspect of audit committee oversight is discussed later in this chapter.

NYSE listing requirements in Rule 303A.7 express the requirement that audit committees should:

> Discuss the listed company's earnings press releases, as well as financial information and earnings guidance provided to analysts and rating agencies.[8]

This requirement is explained in the commentary to the rule:

> The audit committee's responsibility to discuss earnings releases, as well as financial information and earnings guidance, may be done generally (i.e., discussion of the types of information to be disclosed and the type of presentation to be made). The audit committee need not discuss in advance each earnings release or each instance in which a listed company may provide earnings guidance.[9]

Audit committees should provide oversight only and not micromanage exactly what the organization says in its press releases of actual results or guidance as to future results; committees should only oversee the preparation and disclosure processes that the organization follows to be sure they are defensible.

The 2007 *Corporate Director's Guidebook* continues with another requirement for audit committee oversight of financial disclosures:

> Review the Management's Discussion and Analysis (MD&A) section in each periodic report prior to filing with the SEC and discuss with management and the external auditor any questions or issues that arise in connection with that review.[10]

In this case, the audit committee is tasked to read the disclosures to be sure that they are factual, complete, and not misleading. The corporation's legal counsel as well as the external auditors will be helpful to the audit committee in assuring that all SEC requirements have been complied with. Audit committee members should understand the rationale for any judgmental items in the MD&A disclosures contained in the corporation's annual report to the SEC on Form 10-K.

AUDIT COMMITTEE DISCLOSURE DUTIES CONSIDERED BEST PRACTICES

Chapter 5 provided an overview of additional best practice recommendations from the 2007 edition of the *Corporate Director's Guidebook* relating to disclosure of financial and other information to the public:

[8] NYSE, Listed Company Manual, Rule 303A.7(c)iii(C). See www.nyse.com.
[9] Id.
[10] ABA, *Corporate Director's Guidebook* 2007, p. 59.

- Meet periodically with the corporation's disclosure committee or its representatives, if the corporation has such a committee;
- If another committee [of the board] does not do so, meet privately with the corporation's legal counsel from time to time to review the status of pending litigation, discuss possible loss contingencies and review other legal concerns, including the corporation's procedures and policies addressing legal compliance and reduction of legal risk.[11]

The first of these duties pertains only to publicly held corporations, whereas the next duty applies to all corporations. Establishment of a disclosure committee is a recommendation arising from requirements contained in Sarbanes-Oxley Section 302, which are discussed further in Chapter 11.

EXTERNAL AUDITOR REQUIREMENTS FOR COMMUNICATION WITH THE AUDIT COMMITTEE

The requirements for the external auditor to communicate significant matters to the audit committee and discuss their importance is set forth in professional auditing standards as contained in SAS Nos. 61, 89, and 90—codified in AICPA *Professional Standards* AU § 380, *Communication with Audit Committees* and AU § 722, *Interim Financial Information*. These pronouncements were issued as an outcome of the 1999 *Report and Recommendations of the Blue Ribbon Committee on the Improvement of Corporate Audit Committees*. They are designed to assist audit committees in the oversight deliberations.

These requirements, together with those concerning audit committee charters, were set out in SEC Release No. 34-42266, "Audit Committee Disclosure." Sarbanes-Oxley Section 204 also discusses the quality of financial reporting (codified in Section 10A(k) of the 1934 act) by requiring external auditors to:

> . . . report to the audit committee of the issuer
>
> (1) all critical accounting policies and practices to be used;
>
> (2) all alternative treatments of financial information within generally accepted accounting principles that have been discussed with management officials of the issuer, ramifications of the use of such alternative disclosures and treatments, and the treatment preferred by the registered public accounting firm; and
>
> (3) other material written communications between the registered public accounting firm and the management of the issuer, such as any management letter or schedule of unadjusted differences.[12]

---

[11] Id., p. 60.

[12] Sarbanes-Oxley § 204, P.L. 107–204.

The major issues that the external auditor (registered public accounting firm) are required to communicate to the audit committee are designed to enhance the committee's ability to effectively oversee the proper preparation of financial statements, the disclosures they contain, and other financial information communicated outside the organization. It should also be emphasized again that audit committee oversight is not synonymous with reperforming all of the processes required to prepare the financial statements in the first place nor second-guessing all of the accounting judgments made by management. Rather, oversight should involve making sure that all of those decisions were adequately supported by the facts and by applicable accounting principles, in other words, that appropriate due process had been followed.

SAS Nos. 61, 89, and 90, codified in AICPA *Professional Standards* AU § 380, *Communication with Audit Committees* and AU § 722, *Interim Financial Information* discuss a number of issues that audit committee members need to make sure they understand. The audit committee's designated expert should be helpful in making sure that this happens, but all committee members should participate in the discussion of issues including:

1. *Significant accounting policies.* The external auditor needs to be sure the audit committee is informed about the selection and any changes in significant accounting policies and their application. Also, the auditor should determine that the committee is informed about the methods used to account for significant unusual transactions and also the effect of applying significant accounting policies in areas where there is controversy or lack of authoritative guidance or consensus.
2. *Management judgments and accounting estimates.* The external auditor needs to make sure that the audit committee is informed about the process used by management in formulating particularly sensitive accounting estimates and about the basis for the auditor's conclusions regarding the reasonableness of those estimates.
3. *Audit adjustments.* The external auditor should inform the audit committee about any adjustments (a proposed correction of the financial statements that may not have been detected except through the auditing procedures performed) that could have a significant effect on the financial statements. Information should be provided concerning both adjustments that were and were not recorded, and should include items that could potentially cause future financial statements to be materially misstated.
4. *Judgments about the quality of accounting principles.* The external auditor should engage in an open and frank discussion with the audit committee concerning the auditor's judgments about the quality, not just the acceptability, of the accounting principles that the corporation has applied in its financial statements. Management should be a participant in these discussions. The requirements specifically refer to the qualitative characteristics that financial statements should demonstrate, including representational faithfulness, verifiability,

and neutrality. Specific items that should be included in such discussions are the selection of new or changes to accounting policies or their application, estimates, judgments, and uncertainties, unusual transactions, and practices related to specific financial statement items. Also included should be issues relating to the timing of transactions and the period in which they are recorded.

5. *Other information in documents containing audited financial statements.* The external auditor should make sure the audit committee understands the responsibilities that the audit examination includes with respect to such items.
6. *Disagreements with management.* Disagreement on matters of disclosure or application of accounting principles should be presented to audit committee even if they have been satisfactorily resolved.
7. *Difficulties encountered in performing the audit.* The external auditor should inform the audit committee of any significant problems encountered. These include unreasonable delays in providing needed information or setting an unreasonable timetable for completion of the audit.[13]

SUMMARY OF AUDIT COMMITTEE RESPONSIBILITIES FOR OVERSIGHT OF FINANCIAL STATEMENTS AND FINANCIAL REPORTING

A helpful listing of the detailed nature of the audit committee's oversight of financial statement preparation and financial reporting responsibilities is contained in the third edition of *Audit Committee Effectiveness—What Works Best*, prepared by PricewaterhouseCoopers and published by the Institute of Internal Auditors Research Foundation:

- Understand the processes used in developing the financial statements and be comfortable the supporting information systems are reliable.
- Assess management's degree of aggressiveness or conservatism in preparing the financial statements.
- Review significant accounting and reporting developments and issues, including recent regulatory pronouncements, and understand their impact on the financial statements.
- Assess the quality of accounting principles and the appropriateness of significant accounting policies, considering alternative treatments of generally accepted accounting principles (GAAP).
- Understand and be comfortable with management's assessment of materiality, both quantitative and qualitative, for financial statement purposes.
- Understand management's process for developing significant estimates and the impact of those estimates on the financial statements.

[13] AICPA *Professional Standards*, § AU380.07 to § AU380.16.

- Understand significant risks, including fraud risks, and plans to mitigate the risks.
- Discuss with internal and external auditors their audit plans to address significant risks and the audit results.
- Consider management's handling of proposed audit adjustments identified by the external auditors.
- Resolve disagreements between management and the external auditors.
- Recommend to the board whether the financial statements should be incorporated into the company's regulatory filings.[14]

KEY POINTS IN CHAPTER 8

1. Oversight of financial statement preparation and resulting reporting of financial results to investors, creditors, and the public at large is one of the most important duties of the full board and hence of the audit committee.
2. Audit committees need to become thoroughly familiar with the accounting policies selected by management, how they have been applied, and also any available alternative treatment methods.
3. Audit committees must become satisfied that not only are the accounting principles adopted by management acceptable in terms of generally accepted accounting principles, but also whether they have been applied in a quality fashion in terms of the context of the organization and its operations.
4. Professional auditing standards require that the external audit firm fully inform the audit committee about specified issues and events, including auditor adjustments whether made or not, any disagreements with management and how they were resolved, and the process and support for accounting estimates that were made. The external auditors must also communicate the quality of accounting, not just its acceptability.
5. Although audit committees are entitled to rely on information provided by internal and external auditors, members should be satisfied that they thoroughly understand the full impact and all of the nuances of the communications they receive from their auditors, and should raise questions in their executive sessions with the auditors.
6. The audit committee has a responsibility to oversee the broad parameters of the scope of the audit by the external audit firm. The audit committee should receive significant audit findings and follow up on those findings and recommendations made by the firm together with management's responses.
7. In public companies, audit committee responsibilities for financial reporting go well beyond merely the contents of the financial statements to include guidance to Wall Street financial analysts, the contents of press releases of summary data,

[14] PricewaterhouseCoopers, *Audit Committee Effectiveness—What Works Best, Third Edition* (Altamonte Springs, FL: Institute of Internal Auditors Research Foundation, 2005), p. 1.

and management's discussion and analysis of the financial statements contained in Form 10-K. The reporting of nonfinancial data is assuming increased importance.

8. Audit committees are expected to oversee management's processes in making financial statement determinations but not to become deeply involved with helping to make each and every accounting decision or exercising hindsight.

Chapter 9

The Audit Committee and Internal Auditing

The relationships between the audit committee and internal auditing should be bilateral and symbiotic. The mission of internal auditing varies in different organizations and should be based on IIA professional standards and tailor-made to the circumstances of the culture, management style, and operational focus of the organization it serves. According to the Institute of Internal Auditors (IIA), the membership organization of internal auditors, internal auditing should be broad in scope and "add value and improve an organization's operations."[1] Its increasing professionalism and greater visibility in first-class, well-managed organizations behooves all audit committees to regularly evaluate the contribution internal auditing is making in their organization.

INTRODUCTION

One of the more significant indicators of the effectiveness of an organization's governance is the contribution made by internal auditing as a resource to the board of directors and a monitor of the effectiveness of all governance processes. At the same time, a key success factor for internal auditing in an organization is the support provided by the audit committee and board. The audit committee assures that proper resources are allocated to the activity and determines the breadth and scope of practices that internal auditing utilizes in the areas of risk management, control, and governance. Thus, the two entities can cause symbiotic benefits for each other.

Another indication of the importance of internal auditing to an organization's governance is the attitudes of credit rating agencies. In their creditworthiness evaluation decisions, these service organizations are placing increasing importance on the quality of an organization's corporate governance and pay attention to the interactions of the audit committee and internal auditing. Exemplifying this trend, Moody's Investors Service, in October 2006, published a Special Comment on audit committee oversight of internal auditing. The comment notes: "Moody's views the audit committee's oversight of internal auditing as critical to the running of an institution."[2]

[1] Institute of Internal Auditors, *The Professional Practices Framework* (Altamonte Springs, FL: IIA 2007), p. xxix.

[2] Moody's, "Best Practices in Audit Committee Oversight of Internal Auditing," Special Comment (October 2006), p. 1.

INTERNAL AUDITING RESPONSIBILITIES

Guidance concerning the professional practice of internal auditing on a global basis is developed by the Institute of Internal Auditors, Inc. (IIA). This organization has promulgated a professional practice framework that includes a definition of internal auditing, a code of ethics, professional practice standards, and interpretive guidance, including position papers, practice advisories, and practice guides. After deliberation and public comment, this body's Internal Auditing Standards Board publishes the *International Standards for the Professional Practice of Internal Auditing*.

The definition of internal auditing set forth by the IIA is:

> Internal auditing is an independent, objective assurance and consulting activity designed to add value and improve an organization's operations. It helps an organization accomplish its objectives by bringing a systematic, disciplined approach to evaluate and improve the effectiveness of risk management, control, and governance processes.[3]

Internal auditing professional standards address the responsibilities of internal auditing in terms of risk management, control, and governance:

> ***Performance Standard 2110 – Risk Management***
>
> The internal audit activity [function] should assist the organization by identifying and evaluating significant exposures to risk and contributing to the improvement of risk management and control systems.[4]

The subject of risk management is further discussed in Chapter 10.

> ***Performance Standard 2120 – Control***
>
> The internal audit activity [function] should assist the organization in maintaining effective controls by evaluating their effectiveness and efficiency and by promoting continuous improvement.[5]

The subject of internal control is further discussed in Chapter 11.

> ***Performance Standard 2130 – Governance***
>
> The internal audit activity should assess and make appropriate recommendations for improving the governance process in its accomplishment of the following objectives:
>
> - Promoting appropriate ethics and values within the organization.
> - Ensuring effective organizational performance management and accountability

[3] IIA, *Professional Practices Framework*, 2007, p. xxxi.

[4] Id. p. 14.

[5] Id. p. 15.

- Effectively communicating risk and control information to appropriate areas of the organization.
- Effectively coordinating the activities of and communicating information among the board, external and internal auditors, and management.[6]

The subject of ethics-related initiatives is further discussed in Chapter 12.

GUIDANCE FOR AUDIT COMMITTEES IN INTERNAL AUDITING PROFESSIONAL STANDARDS

In order to accomplish the mission of internal auditing, professional guidance emphasizes the importance of various interactions of internal auditing with the audit committee. Practice Advisories are strongly recommended and endorsed by the IIA as interpretations of the professional Standards.

Practice Advisory 2060-2, *Relationship with the Audit Committee*, interprets the relevant internal auditing professional standard and discusses how it should be put into practice.[7] This document points out that audit committees and internal auditors have interlocking goals and explains in paragraph 3 that

> there are three areas of activities that are key to an effective relationship between the audit committee and the internal auditing function, chiefly through the Chief Audit Executive (CAE).
>
> - Assisting the audit committee to ensure that its charter, activities, and processes are appropriate to fulfill its responsibilities,
> - Ensuring that the charter, role, and activities of the internal audit function are clearly understood and responsive to the needs of the audit committee and the board, and
> - Maintaining open and effective communications with the audit committee and the chairperson.[8]

Other IIA Practice Advisories describe additional areas where specific practices designed to strengthen internal auditing are in order. One of these desirable practices is for the CAE to report on a functional basis directly to the audit committee. Paragraph 1 of Practice Advisory 1110-2, *Chief Audit Executive (CAE) Reporting Lines*, sets forth these aspects of functional reporting concerning the internal audit function that should be the responsibility of the audit committee:

- Approve the overall charter of the internal auditing function
- Approve the internal auditing risk assessment and related audit plan

[6] Id., p. 17.
[7] Id, p. 201.
[8] Id., p. 202.

- Receive communications from the Chief Audit Executive including private meetings with the CAE without management present.
- Approve all decisions regarding the appointment or removal of the CAE
- Approve the annual compensation and salary adjustment of the CAE
- Make appropriate inquiries of management and the CAE to determine whether there are scope or budgetary limitations that impede the ability of the internal auditing function to execute its responsibilities.[9]

Further, Practice Advisory 2060-2: *Relationship with the Audit Committee* suggests that the CAE can perform a number of activities to accomplish the desired role as trusted advisor to the audit committee. For example, the CAE can:

- Request that the committee review and approve the internal auditing charter on an annual basis.
- Review with the audit committee the functional and administrative reporting lines of internal auditing to the audit committee to ensure that the organizational structure in place allows adequate independence for internal auditors.
- Incorporate in the charter that the audit committee should review hiring decisions of the CAE, including appointment, compensation, evaluation, retention, and dismissal.
- Incorporate in the charter for the audit committee to review and approve proposals to outsource any internal audit activities.
- Assist the audit committee in evaluating the adequacy of the internal auditing personnel and budget, and the scope and results of the internal auditing activities, to ensure that there are no budgetary or scope limitations that impede the ability of the internal auditing activity to execute its responsibilities.
- Provide information on the coordination with and oversight of other control and monitoring functions (e.g., risk management, compliance, security, business continuity, legal, ethics, environmental, external audit).
- Report significant issues related to the processes for controlling the activities of the organization and its affiliates, including potential improvements to those processes, and provide information concerning such issues through resolution.
- Provide information on the status and results of the annual audit plan and the sufficiency of the activity's resources to senior management and the audit committee.
- Develop a flexible annual audit plan using an appropriate risk-based methodology, including any risks or control concerns identified by management, and submit that plan to the audit committee for review and approval as well as periodic updates.
- Report on the implementation of the annual audit plan, as approved, including as appropriate any special tasks or projects requested by management and the audit committee.

[9] Id., p. 70.

- Incorporate into the internal auditing charter the responsibility for internal auditing to report to the audit committee on a timely basis, any suspected fraud involving management or employees who are significantly involved in the internal controls of the company. Assist in the investigation of significant suspected fraudulent activities within the organization and notify management and the audit committee of the results.[10]

GUIDANCE PROVIDED BY CREDIT AGENCIES

Comments by the credit rating agency Moody's about the importance of audit committee oversight of internal auditing lists five central functions audit committees should perform:

1. Ensure the [internal] audit plan is sufficiently broad in scope and executed in a timely manner.
2. Ensure [internal] audit reports are actionable and implemented.
3. Enable an [internal] audit team that is independent, empowered, and sufficiently staffed and resourced.
4. Promote effective committee functioning, and staff the committee with sufficient expertise.
5. Promote an open, transparent relationship with the audit [function] and other control professionals.[11]

Effective governance results in lower costs of capital, as rating agencies include the quality of governance as a factor in determining an organization's creditworthiness and rating. It is interesting to note that these foundational internal auditing practices mirror items contained in the IIA's international professional standards and Practice Advisories.

The AICPA's *Audit Committee Toolkit* contains a description of the audit committee's relationship with the organization's internal auditors.[12] The description begins:

> It is in the best interest of all concerned for the audit committee and the internal auditing team (IAT) to maintain a strong positive relationship. The audit committee should view the IAT as its eyes and ears about what is going on within the company.

---

[10] Id., pp. 204–205.

[11] Moody's, *Best Practices in Audit Committee Oversight of Internal Audit,* p. 1, at www.moodys.com/moodys/cust/research/MDCdocs/09/2006000000426210.pdf?search=5&searchQuery=best+practices&click=1].

[12] AICPA, *The AICPA Audit Committee Toolkit* (New York: AICPA, 2004). Available at www.aicpa.org/acec. (Accessed Jan 2008).

> The audit committee chair and the CAE should have frequent contact between meetings of the audit committee. In fact, the CAE should have a "solid-line" reporting relationship to the audit committee, and the audit committee should be consulted before the CAE can be hired, fired, or reassigned.
>
> At every audit committee meeting, the committee should hold an executive session [without management presence] with the CAE. The IAT must recognize that it is an agent of the audit committee and not management.
>
> Discussions between the CAE and the audit committee should also address the competencies of the financial management team. The IAT is in the best position to determine whether the financial management team is able to address complex accounting issues on its own, or whether it relies too heavily on the independent auditor or other consultants for evaluation and decision-making.[13]

ASSESSMENT OF INTERNAL AUDITING QUALITY

IIA professional internal auditing standards require the periodic external evaluation of the quality of every internal audit function. IIA Professional Standard 1312 notes that external assessments should be conducted at least once every five years by a qualified, independent reviewer or review team from outside the organization. Accomplishing this task is important to provide assurance to the audit committee that internal auditing is successfully adding value to the organization by providing services designed to evaluate and improve the effectiveness of risk management, control, and governance processes.

The AICPA *Audit Committee Toolkit* also contains evaluation questions that audit committees can use to assess the quality of an internal audit function. A selection of these questions with some rephrasing includes:

a. Does the [function] appear to be using its time and resources effectively and efficiently?
b. Are the [function's] size and structure adequate to meet its established objectives?
c. Is the technical knowledge of the [personnel] sufficient?
d. Is expertise in auditing information systems available to address the organization's level of technology?
e. Are internal audit reports timely and sufficiently informative to allow appropriate action by management and audit committee?
f. Does management respond timely and appropriately to internal audit recommendations?

[13] Id. p. 93.

g. Does the scope of internal auditing extend to operational as well as financial areas?
h. If outsourced or co-sourced resources were utilized, were they effective and well coordinated with the overall internal audit plan for the year?
i. Was the involvement of the audit committee in setting the annual and long-range internal audit plan effective, so that efforts were concentrated in areas of greatest risk?
j. Did the internal audit function provide an expression of the effectiveness of the overall system of internal controls including ethics and compliance processes?
k. To what extent does the internal audit team keep itself informed of and involved in professional activities?
l. Has the charter of the internal audit function been reviewed to assure it is still relevant and complete?[14]

The AICPA has also developed audit committee toolkits designed for not-for-profit organizations and for governmental entities. These volumes contain additional questions specifically oriented to not-for-profit and governmental issues. The AICPA toolkit for for-profit corporations also contains a questionnaire dealing with internal control (see Chapter 11). Interestingly, this tool contains questions about internal auditing under the "Monitoring" heading:

> Does the internal auditing team have the right number of competent and experienced staff? Do they have access to the board of directors and audit committee? Is the reporting structure in place to ensure their objectivity and independence? Is the work of the internal auditing team appropriate to the organization's needs, and prioritized with the audit committee's direction?[15]

IMPORTANCE OF RESOURCE ALLOCATION BASED ON APPROVED RISK-BASED AUDIT PLAN

Permeating the internal auditing guidance to audit committees and key to the committee's effective oversight is the need to oversee the development of an effective risk-based audit plan and then monitor its fulfillment. Unfortunately, management may divert resources necessary for completion of the broad-scope internal auditing mission necessary to fulfill optimal governance measures to solve emergencies or deal with risks not foreseen when the internal auditing plan was developed and approved by the audit committee. The diversion of significant internal auditing resources to other projects could result in a serious weakness in the internal control structure and could open the committee to criticism.

[14] Id., pp. 95–98.
[15] Id., p. 70.

In the aftermath of Sarbanes-Oxley, internal audit functions in many organizations have been given major assignments to upgrade internal controls over financial reporting, without increasing internal auditing resources sufficiently to maintain previously established and approved audit plans. This has resulted in a number of internal auditing thought leaders expressing the necessity to "rebalance" priorities back toward more auditing based on professional standards rather than Sarbanes-Oxley compliance. A 2007 survey by Protiviti, a firm providing independent risk consulting and internal audit services, concluded that internal auditors are "streamlining their compliance efforts as a way to achieve rebalancing. Moreover, they are looking to reclaim personnel from the burdens of compliance activities, and reassign them to other vital tasks."[16]

PricewaterhouseCoopers (PwC), the international public accounting firm, has since 2005 annually performed a "State of the Profession" survey of internal auditing. In 2007, it included a consensus projection of the trends likely to shape the profession by 2012.[17] Factors likely to have a strong or very strong impact on internal auditing roles are: technology or continuous auditing; expanding risk management processes; the effects of globalization; and fraud, ethics, and compliance. The PwC report notes that internal auditing responsibilities for Sarbanes-Oxley compliance are expected to plateau or decline.[18]

The Ernst & Young 2007 Global Internal Audit Survey reports that more is being expected of internal auditors and a focus on compliance is "no longer enough,"[19] as they are being stretched to cover a much broader range of risks—including those related to fraud, major programs, contracts, and transactions. Although the internal auditing landscape has been dominated recently by Sarbanes-Oxley compliance, it "is now being challenged by pressures on resources and growing demands to help improve overall business performance."[20] The survey also found that finding people with the right specialist skills to help meet evolving and emerging risks is the biggest challenge facing internal audit leaders.[21]

---

[16] Protiviti, *Moving Internal Audit Back into Balance: A Post-Sarbanes-Oxley Survey, Second Edition,* (2007), p. 2. http://www.protiviti.com/downloads/PRO/pro-us/publications/IA_RebalSurvey_II.pdf. (Accessed Jan 2008)

[17] PricewaterhouseCoopers, *Internal Audit 2012: A Study Examining the Future of Internal Auditing and the Potential Decline of a Controls-Centric Approach,* PWC connected thinking, 2007. http://www.pwc.com/extweb/pwcpublications.nsf/docid/E5066FF9CA2ED6EC85257347007061F6 (Accessed Jan 2008).

[18] Id., p. 23.

[19] Ernst & Young Press Release, "Internal Auditors Facing Greater Expectations," October 11, 2007.

[20] Ernst & Young, *Global Internal Audit Survey – A Current State Analysis with Insights into Future Trends and Leading Practices*, 2007. Web site http://www.ey.com/global/Content.nsf/International/Business_Risk_-_Global_Internal_Audit_Survey_2007_-_Shifting_Internal_Audit_Landscape, p. 2. (Accessed Jan 2008).

[21] Id., p. 6.

KEY POINTS IN CHAPTER 9

1. Although not required by statute, audit committee oversight of the activities of internal auditing is increasingly recognized as a best practice for all organizations. The most important aspect of oversight is that the direct reporting line of the chief audit executive (CAE) should be functionally to the audit committee and administratively to the chief executive officer. A number of audit committee responsibilities resulting from this functional reporting relationship are set forth in internal auditing professional standards.
2. The audit committee should be directly involved with over seeing the annual internal auditing plan and personnel decisions regarding the performance of the CAE, and should ensure the internal audit function is properly structured, has been provided proper resources and has appropriate status within the organization to accomplish its mission.
3. The CAE should strive to become and remain a trusted advisor to the audit committee on subjects such as risk management, control, and governance.
4. As set forth in previous chapters, an effective, competent, independent, and adequately resourced internal audit function can be an extremely helpful facilitator of effective governance, particularly in areas where the audit committee has direct responsibility.
5. As an element of the organization's governance, internal auditing can also function as an important source of information and a resource to help the audit committee discharge its own duties. Audit committees should maintain awareness of the expanding expectations being made for internal auditing.
6. At the same time, effective relationships of the internal audit function and the CAE with various levels of management and the audit committee are critically important to the success of internal auditing. Internal auditing should not be viewed as an investigation, but rather an evaluation of process effectiveness and efficiency as well as a source of assistance to solve challenges in areas where it has expertise and experience.
7. Because the quality of internal auditing services provided to organizations varies as a result of many factors, a periodic external assessment of quality is important for audit committees to be satisfied they are effectively discharging their duties. An external assessment is also required by internal auditing professional standards.
8. Audit committees need to be sure the resources allocated to their internal audit functions are not overstretched by their attention to Sarbanes-Oxley Section 404 compliance, to the detriment of accomplishing more professionally oriented and risk-based internal auditing.

Chapter 10

The Audit Committee and Risk Management

INTRODUCTION

As outlined in Chapter 4, oversight of an entity's risk management processes is one of the newer but critically important responsibilities assigned to the audit committee. Analysis and proper management of business risks is the foundation of an efficient system of internal controls. Evaluation of risks is an important internal audit function and oversight of these functions is an important responsibility of audit committees.

LEGALLY REQUIRED DUTIES INVOLVING RISK MANAGEMENT

To ensure that the organization achieves its objectives, management needs to be sure that sound risk management processes are in place and are adequate and are effective. The board has the responsibility to oversee these processes. As noted in Chapter 4, the oversight of the organization's risk management processes has been added to the legally mandated responsibilities of audit committees. Although mandatory only for public companies, these duties are considered a best practice for privately held and not-for-profit organizations as well. The 2007 edition of the *Corporate Director's Guidebook* sets forth these responsibilities:

> Meet periodically with management to review the corporation's major risk exposures and discuss the steps management has taken to monitor and control such exposures, such as risk management programs, and procedures and policies addressing legal compliance.[1]

Audit committees of companies listed on the New York Stock Exchange (NYSE) have responsibilities dealing with oversight of methods an organization

[1] American Bar Association, *Corporate Director's Guidebook, Fifth Edition* (Chicago: ABA Committee on Corporate Laws, 2007), p. 60.

uses for risk assessment and risk management that arise from NYSE Listed Company Rule 303A.07(D). This rule states that the audit committee should "discuss policies with respect to risk assessment and risk management."[2]

The commentary to the rule explains this responsibility in more detail:

> While it is the job of the CEO and senior management to assess and manage the listed company's exposure to risk, the audit committee must discuss guidelines and policies to govern the process by which this is handled. The audit committee should discuss the listed company's major financial risk exposures and the steps management has taken to monitor and control such exposures. The audit committee is not required to be the sole body responsible for risk assessment and management, but, as stated above, the committee must discuss guidelines and policies to govern the process by which risk assessment and management is undertaken. Many companies, particularly financial companies, manage and assess their risk through mechanisms other than the audit committee. The processes these companies have in place should be reviewed in a general manner by the audit committee, but they need not be replaced by the audit committee.[3]

Although not undertaken by all organizations, this responsibility is generally considered to be a best business practice.

The term "risk" generally denotes a negative occurrence. While theoretically there can be negative risk, that is generally referred to as an opportunity rather than a risk. Opportunities discovered through the risk management process should be carefully considered to see how they could impact the organization's general strategy and achievement of objectives.

BEST PRACTICES IN RISK OVERSIGHT

The credit rating agency Moody's views audit committee oversight of risk management as a key aspect of running an organization, particularly a financial institution. Moody's believes that the board of directors [but usually delegated to the audit committee] has five central functions with respect to risk:

1. Approve the firm's risk appetite as a component of its strategy.
2. Understand and question the breadth of risks faced by the company.
3. Ensure robust oversight of risk at the board committee and senior management levels.
4. Promote a risk-focused culture and open communication across the organization.
5. Assign clear lines of accountability and encourage an effective risk management framework.[4]

---

[2] NYSE, Inc., Listed Company Manual § 303A¶ 7(D). At NYSE.com.

[3] Id.

[4] Moody's, *"Best Practices for a Board's Role in Risk Oversight,"* Special Comment, August 2006, at www.moodys.com/moodys/cust/research/mdcdocs/04/2005700000435561.pdf?search=5&searchquery=best%20practices&click=1. (Accessed January 2008).

In view of the increased attention being placed on the subject of risk management, these activities are very likely to become best business practices in all organizations. Responsibilities of the internal auditing function include risk management. (See Chapter 9).

PROCESS OF RISK MANAGEMENT

Risk is the possibility that an event might occur that would impact the successful achievement of one or more of the organization's objectives. Risk assessment involves the process of estimating the potential impact and the likelihood of occurrence of one or more business risks. As defined by the Institute of Internal Auditors, risk management is

> a process to identify, assesses, manage, and control potential events or situations to provide reasonable assurance regarding the achievement of the organization's objectives.[5]

Risk management includes four methods of dealing with the potential consequences of risk: risk acceptance, risk mitigation, risk avoidance, and risk transfer. Residual risk is the risk that remains after management has taken actions to reduce the impact and likelihood of an adverse event. Control activities are processes designed and undertaken to reduce the occurrence of a particular risk.

Risk acceptance is logically named. It means that the board of directors and senior management have both decided that it is acceptable for the organization to assume any consequences that might result from the existence of a particular residual risk and have decided not to take further preventive actions. This concept is also known as residual risk, as it represents risks that remain after management has instituted the actions described in the next paragraph.

Risk mitigation or reduction is defined as the process of instituting one or more direct actions to minimize the existence or consequences of a particular risk. For example, a requirement that two individuals review supporting documentation before signing checks that are drawn in excess of a specified amount tends to minimize the risk of unauthorized cash disbursements being made of a high amount.

Risk avoidance takes place when management decides to avoid strategies that have high risk, or takes actions that will otherwise eliminate or reduce risk exposure. Risk transfer results from a management decision to shift to another party the consequences of a specified risk for consideration, as in taking out an insurance contract. Transfer of risk to a third party also occurs when an organization engages in hedging activities using futures contracts.

---

[5] Institute of Internal Auditors, *The Professional Practices Framework* (Altamonte Springs, FL: IIA, 2007), p. 27.

Audit committees need to be aware of these concepts so as to evaluate how effective their organization is in utilizing the proper mix of strategies to manage its risks.

ENTERPRISE RISK MANAGEMENT

In recent years, there has been an emerging trend for organizations to manage their risks on an enterprise-wide basis, rather than by function or organizational unit. This practice is called enterprise risk management (ERM). It has been extensively adopted by banks and other financial institutions. Because cash is fungible, it makes sense to manage foreign exchange risks on an entity-wide basis, so that off-setting exposures in various divisions can be taken into account. Top companies have accomplished an entity-wide focus on risk management by either appointing a chief risk officer who has been given centralized responsibility for managing risk or by organizing a company-wide risk committee.

Approaching risk from a total-entity perspective has a number of advantages. First, it facilitates consideration of all business risks, whether they are financial, ethical, market-related, social, operational, or reputational. The fact that some risks arising in one area should be considered to be hedged in another is self-evident. The chief executive of a global enterprise was well known for musing that the sun is always shining somewhere on the company's operations. The ERM approach also encourages use of a uniform methodology for to dealing with risk, not individual methods in various business silos that do not provide the opportunity for analysis and comparison with methods used elsewhere in the organization.

Second, a reasoned approach to managing all risks in the same way maximizes the opportunity to categorize risks from the perspective of the total enterprise. Using the typical two-way analysis of risks where the horizontal represents likelihood and the vertical impact, it is easier to minimize the cost of controls of low impact and low likelihood risks.

There is no one-size-fits-all approach to managing risks on an enterprise-wide basis. Nevertheless, the Financial Executives Research Foundation's study of risk management lists four essential steps for effective risk management:

1. Identify the totality of risks the organization faces (all business risks, not just hazard risks or financial risks).
2. Analyze and measure the significance of each risk.
3. Evaluate the potential costs of the available alternative risk response strategies (accept, transfer, mitigate).
4. Determine whether risks are being either over-managed or under-managed.[6]

[6] Thomas Barton, William Shenker, and Paul Walker, *Making Enterprise Risk Management Pay Off* (Montvale, NJ: Financial Executives Research Foundation, 2001).

These comments about risk management are made from the perspective of a chief financial officer. The steps ensure that the risk management processes encompasses all business risks and that they have been systematically and carefully evaluated as to their size, content, and potential occurrence. Once all risks have been evaluated, management must consider the economics of alternative methods of dealing with them versus their expected cost of occurrence. Finally, the difference between the costs of occurrence and the costs of alternative risk response strategies provides an indication of whether risks are being properly managed.

COSO ERM INTEGRATED FRAMEWORK

In September 2004, the five-member Committee of Sponsoring Organizations of the Treadway Commission (COSO) issued a framework document on the subject of risk management, titled *Enterprise Risk Management—Integrated Framework.*[7] Published by COSO, this research study expands on COSO's earlier benchmark study of the framework of internal control. It also provides a more extensive and more robust focus on the broader subject of enterprise risk management (ERM). It incorporates by reference the entire contents of the 1992 COSO document on internal control, *Internal Control —Integrated Framework.*[8]

The 2004 COSO risk management framework defines ERM as

> a process, effected by an entity's board of directors, management and other personnel, applied in strategy setting and across the enterprise, designed to identify potential events that may affect the entity, and manage risk to be within its risk appetite, to provide reasonable assurance regarding the achievement of entity objectives.[9]

COSO's definition describes ERM as ongoing throughout an entity and effected by people at every level. It is applied in a strategy setting and applied across the enterprise, at every level and unit, and includes taking an entity-level portfolio view of risk. It is designed to identify potential events that, if they occur, would affect the entity. The most important objective of ERM is to manage risk and contain it within the organization's risk appetite. ERM is able to provide reasonable assurance to an entity's management and board of directors and is geared to achieve objectives in one or more separate but overlapping categories. This definition of ERM together with the next eight components describe the objectives and techniques for managing risk within an organization, so that the organization can achieve the goals it has set for itself.

---

[7] COSO, *Enterprise Risk Management—Integrated Framework: Executive Summary* (COSO, 2004). http://www.coso.org/publications.htm (Accessed January 2008).

[8] COSO, *Internal Control—Integrated Framework* (COSO, 1992). http://www.coso.org/publications.htm (Accessed January 2008).

[9] COSO, *Enterprise Risk Management*, 2004, p. 2.

According to COSO, there are eight components of enterprise risk management. The eight are:

1. *Internal environment.* The internal environment encompasses the tone of an organization and sets the basis for how risk is viewed and addressed by an entity's people, including risk management philosophy and risk appetite, integrity and ethical values, and the environment in which they operate.
2. *Objective setting.* Objectives must exist before management can identify potential events affecting their achievement. Enterprise risk management ensures that management has in place a process to set objectives and that the chosen objectives support and align with the entity's mission and are consistent with its risk appetite.
3. *Event identification.* Internal and external events affecting achievement of an entity's objectives must be identified, distinguishing between risks and opportunities. Opportunities are channeled back to management's strategy or objective-setting processes.
4. *Risk assessment.* Risks are analyzed, considering likelihood and impact, as a basis for determining how they should be managed. Risks are assessed on an inherent and residual basis.
5. *Risk response.* Management selects risk responses—avoiding, accepting, reducing, or sharing risk—developing a set of actions to align risks with the entity's risk tolerances and appetite.
6. *Control activities.* Policies and procedures are established and implemented to help ensure the risk responses are effectively carried out.
7. *Information and communication.* Relevant information is identified, captured, and communicated in a form and timeframe that enable people to carry out their responsibilities. Effective communication also occurs in a broader sense, flowing down, across, and up the entity.
8. *Monitoring.* The entirety of enterprise risk management is monitored and modifications made as necessary. Monitoring is accomplished through ongoing management activities, separate evaluations, or both.[10]

An ERM framework is geared to achieve an entity's objectives, set forth in four categories:

1. Strategic—high-level goals, aligned with and supporting its mission
2. Operations—effective and efficient use of its resources
3. Reporting—reliability of reporting
4. Compliance—compliance with applicable laws and regulations[11]

[10] Id., pp. 3–4.
[11] Id., p. 3.

These four objectives are discussed in the following paragraphs and may overlap but provide distinct goals that ERM is expected to achieve. COSO states that an additional category—safeguarding of resources—may be used by some entities. Because objectives relating to the last two objectives are within the control of the entity, ERM can be expected to provide reasonable assurance of achieving them. Achievement of strategic and operations objectives, however, is subject to events that are not always within the entity's control. Consequently, the role of ERM in these areas is to provide reasonable assurance that management and the board, in its oversight role, are made aware in a timely fashion of the extent the entity is moving toward achievement of the organization's planned objectives.[12]

Every organization has strategic risks, which can be defined as the failure to achieve goals that have been set. Well known, but not always adequately considered, is the fact that increased rewards are linked to increased risks. In the rush to achieve goals, it may be easy to approve strategies that involve greater risk than the enterprise has appetite for. Even when the board and senior management agree to forgo pursuit of risky business opportunities, lower-level managers may not be aware of such restrictions or may be otherwise motivated to ignore them while executing plans to reach approved financial goals. For instance, ERM provides an effective communications framework to assure that the entire organization is on the same page as far as risk acceptance is concerned.

ERM also provides the mechanism to survey potential operational risks to ascertain whether they are being managed appropriately at all levels of the organization. A partial listing of operational risks that audit committees should be sure their organization is considering includes:

- *Marketing risks.* These risks include consideration of political and economic risk in marketing in foreign countries and concentrations of most profitable business in a small number of products. Also, costs of recalling defective products make it more than just a legal compliance issue.
- *Process and production risks.* These risks involve consideration of safety issues, total quality processes, and logistical redundancy. The trend toward supplier consolidation into fewer vendors leaves few alternatives in the event of stoppages from whatever cause.
- *Crisis and business interruption risks.* These risks are usually categorized as high impact but low likelihood. They may be considered scaremongering and not always adequately considered. Organizations need to discuss candidly the possible occurrence of outlier events, both favorable and unfavorable, and possible responses to them. Using ERM to be prepared for and to avoid surprises is the essence of managing a modern organization. Risk management should enhance

---

[12] Id.

the trust and confidence of the board and senior management, something of far more long-term importance than merely protecting today's financial assets.

- *Information technology risks.* These risks have implications beyond legal compliance and can affect all phases of the business. Confidentiality and integrity of data as well as sufficient backup capability to assure continuous transaction processing is essential in today's environment of information technology importance. These risks are further discussed in Chapter 13.

Reporting risks are the subject of much of the audit committee's oversight responsibilities. Internal reporting of information for decision making is as important to organizational success as the required public reporting that is mandated by statute. ERM processes will ensure that no significant risk of high likelihood and impact is overlooked.

Legal and regulatory compliance risks run the gamut from employee issues such as equal opportunity, occupational health and safety, and health insurance, to environmental matters such as clean air, clean water, and disability access. Legal counsel can be helpful to the audit committee in determining whether current compliance activities are sufficient.

One reason an entity adopts enterprise-wide risk management processes is the harmonization of strategies to achieve a balance between risk and reward. This enables the efficient and effective deployment of resources. The COSO framework document suggests that utilizing ERM offers six benefit areas:

1. *Aligning risk appetite and strategy.* Management considers the entity's risk appetite in evaluating strategic alternatives, setting related objectives, and developing mechanisms to manage related risks.
2. *Enhancing risk response decisions.* Enterprise risk management provides the rigor to identify and select among alternative risk responses—risk avoidance, reduction, sharing, and acceptance.
3. *Reducing operational surprises and losses.* Entities gain enhanced capability to identify potential events and establish responses, reducing surprises and associated costs or losses.
4. *Identifying and managing multiple and cross-enterprise risks.* Every enterprise faces a myriad of risks affecting different parts of the organization, and enterprise risk management facilitates effective response to the interrelated impacts, and integrated responses to multiple risks.
5. *Seizing opportunities.* By considering a full range of potential events, management is positioned to identify and proactively realize opportunities.
6. *Improving deployment of capital.* Obtaining robust risk information allows management to effectively assess overall capital needs and enhance capital allocation.[13]

[13] Id., p. 1.

OTHER RISK MANAGEMENT FRAMEWORKS

Another holistic form of risk management is known as organization risk management (ORM). Unlike COSO's ERM, which has its source in finance, accounting, and auditing, ORM arose from more operational roots. Four factors drive this movement:

1. Operational processes, such as just in time, total quality improvement, and other cost-saving processes have stressed the desirability of holistic total-entity solutions.
2. Concerns over cost control have spilled over to include the awareness of the need to minimize the cost of risks.
3. The lack of management of risk on a coordinated basis has been blamed as a contributing factor for recent considerable losses. Enron comes to mind as an example.
4. The financial services industry has experienced severe consolidation, which has led to integration of banking, insurance, and securities companies, leading to thinking about risk from a broader perspective.

According to Peter C. Young and Steven C. Tippins, ORM is a general management function that seeks to assess and address the causes and effects of uncertainty and risk on an organization.[14] In principle, the purpose of ORM is to enable an organization to progress toward its goals in the most direct, economical, and effective way. Analysis of risks may be accomplished through use of the risk chain, which is made up of these links:

- *Environmental link.* This link refers to the general contextual conditions within which gain or loss events occur. They include all environments, social, legal, and operational.
- *Hazard/risk factor link.* This link relates to the conditions that exist within a given environment that elevate probabilities or potential magnitudes.
- *Exposure link.* This link isolates the actual loss exposures.
- *Peril/opportunity link.* This link analyzes the possibility that the risk might move from "potential" to "actual."
- *Outcome link.* This link is associated with the immediate and direct effects of an event.
- *Consequence link.* This link may not be relevant in all circumstances but exists as a reminder that the effects of an event may be long term and indirect.[15]

[14] Peter C. Young and Steven C. Tippins, *Managing Business Risk: An Organization-Wide Approach to Risk Management* (New York: American Management Association, 2001), p. 19.

[15] Id. pp. 84–91.

ROLE OF INTERNAL AUDITING IN RISK MANAGEMENT

An organization's internal audit function should be of considerable assistance to the audit committee in many ways. With respect to risk management, internal auditing professional standards have been taken from the Institute of Internal Auditors *Professional Practices Framework* and provide the following guidance:

> ***Performance Standard 2110.***
>
> The internal audit activity [function] should assist the organization by identifying and evaluating significant exposures to risk and contributing to the improvement of risk management and control systems.
>
> ***Implementation Standard 2110.A1.***
>
> The internal audit activity [function] should monitor and evaluate the effectiveness of the organization's risk management system.
>
> ***Implementation Standard 2110.A2.***
>
> The internal audit activity [function] should evaluate risk exposures relating to the organization's governance, operations, and information systems regarding the
>
> - Reliability and integrity of financial and operational information.
> - Effectiveness and efficiency of operations.
> - Safeguarding of assets.
> - Compliance with laws, regulations, and contracts.
>
> ***Implementation Standard 2110.C1.***
>
> During consulting engagements, internal auditors should address risk consistent with the engagement's objectives and be alert to the existence of other significant risks.
>
> ***Implementation Standard 2110.C2.***
>
> Internal auditors should incorporate knowledge of risks gained from consulting engagements into the process of identifying and evaluating significant risk exposures of the organization.[16]

Performing internal auditing services in accordance with these professional standards should provide information to the audit committee that will be helpful in their discharge of oversight responsibilities. Chapter 9 provides further discussion of the relationships of internal auditing with the audit committee.

[16] IIA, Professional Practices Framework, 2007, pp. 14–15.

KEY POINTS IN CHAPTER 10

1. The effective management of risks of all types is an important function of management and the organization as a whole. Effective risk management provides assurance that events are unlikely to occur that could prevent the organization from achieving its goals.
2. The audit committee should be involved in the oversight of risk management processes of risk assessment, risk mitigation, and risk transfer. The committee should also oversee the process of determining the organization's risk appetite.
3. The maintenance of an ethical culture within all levels of the organization is important to the management of risks and controls.
4. Audit committees have been assigned duties by the New York Stock Exchange to oversee the organization's risk processes. These duties are considered best practices for all organizations.
5. Audit committees need to understand the lexicon of risk, including residual risk, and the importance of estimating risk impact and likelihood.
6. The environments of risk involve more than just the physical environment with its hazards and perils. It includes social, political, and legal risks. A reputation built over decades can be lost in a very short time.
7. Use of an enterprise-wide perspective to assess and manage risks provides a number of advantages to the organization. They include:
   - Aligning risk appetite and strategy
   - Enhancing risk response decisions
   - Reducing operational surprises and losses
   - Identifying and managing multiple and cross-enterprise risks
   - Seizing opportunities
   - Improving deployment of capital
8. The COSO enterprise risk management framework contains eight components:
   (1) Internal environment
   (2) Objective setting
   (3) Event identification
   (4) Risk assessment
   (5) Risk response
   (6) Control activities
   (7) Information and communication
   (8) Monitoring
9. Other risk management frameworks contain similar concepts to those contained in ERM.
10. Internal auditing may provide significant assistance to the audit committee in its oversight of risk management processes.

Chapter 11

The Audit Committee and Internal Control

As discussed in previous chapters, among the more important responsibilities of the audit committee are oversight of internal controls and their annual evaluation together with the management of risks that lead to the necessity for controls. Risk management is discussed in Chapter 10.

AUDIT COMMITTEE DUTIES CONCERNING INTERNAL CONTROL

Chapter 4 discussed the fact that significant audit committee duties involve the oversight of internal control. The 2007 *Corporate Director's Guidebook* describes these duties in this way:

- Consider, in consultation with the external auditor and the senior internal auditing executive, if any, the adequacy of the corporation's internal controls, which, among other things, must be designed to provide reasonable assurance that the corporation's books and records are accurate, that its assets are safeguarded, and that the publicly reported financial statements prepared by management are presented fairly in accordance with generally accepted accounting principles;
- Review management's annual assessment of the effectiveness of internal control over financial reporting, and the external auditor's audit of internal control over financial reporting.[1]

This chapter outlines concepts of control and what actions the audit committee can take to implement its responsibilities related to risks and internal control. It also presents the source of the many duties audit committees have in this area.

CONCEPTS OF CONTROL

Internal control, as a concept, encompasses what an organization does in terms of its organization, management structure, and activities, to ensure that the risks faced by the entity will not materialize or significantly impede the organization in

[1] American Bar Association, *Corporate Director's Guidebook, Fifth Edition* (Chicago: ABA Committee on Corporate Law, 2007), pp. 59–60.

achieving its goals. The definition of internal control set forth by COSO in 1992 has achieved worldwide acceptance as a standard. It is broadly defined as:

> A process, effected by an entity's board of directors, management and other personnel, designed to provide reasonable assurance regarding the achievement of objectives in the following categories:
>
> - Effectiveness and efficiency of operations
> - Reliability of financial reporting
> - Compliance with applicable laws and regulations.[2]

COSO has set forth five components of internal control, each of which must be present and functioning effectively to conclude that internal control over operations is effective. The five components are:

- Control Environment
- Risk Assessment
- Control Activities
- Information and Communication
- Monitoring.[3]

The definition of control put forward by the Institute of Internal Auditors is:

> [a]ny action taken by management, the board [of directors], and other parties to manage risk and increase the likelihood that established objectives and goals will be achieved. Management plans, organizes, and directs the performance of sufficient actions to provide reasonable assurance that objectives and goals will be achieved.[4]

Thus, management has the responsibility to design, install, and maintain internal controls, and the audit committee is tasked to oversee these efforts. As noted in Chapter 9, the internal audit function can be very helpful in assisting the audit committee in discharging its responsibilities relating to internal control. Controls can be designed to be preventive, detective, or corrective in terms of application to risks. However, controls cannot assure success. Organization goals will be achieved only by selection of appropriate strategies by management with the approval of the board of directors together with skillful execution by management under the general oversight of the board.

---

[2] COSO, *Internal Control—Integrated Framework*, Executive Summary, September 1992, p. 1.

[3] Id., pp. 2–3.

[4] Institute of Internal Auditors, *The Professional Practices Framework* (Altamonte Springs, FL: IIA, 2007), p. 27.

SARBANES-OXLEY REQUIREMENTS FOR MANAGEMENT ASSESSMENT OF INTERNAL AND DISCLOSURE CONTROLS

Section 302 of the Sarbanes-Oxley Act of 2002, "Corporate Responsibility for Financial Reports," directs the Securities and Exchange Commission (SEC) to prescribe rules requiring every public company's chief executive officer and chief financial officer to certify the propriety of annual and quarterly reports filed with the SEC and the internal and disclosure controls involved in their preparation. The language of the certification must state:

(1) the signing officer has reviewed the report;
(2) based on the officer's knowledge, the report does not contain any untrue statement of a material fact or omit to state a material fact necessary in order to make the statements made, in light of the circumstances under which such statements were made, not misleading;
(3) based on such officer's knowledge, the financial statements and other financial information included in the report, fairly presents in all material respects the financial condition and results of operations of the issuer as of, and for, the periods presented in the report;
(4) the signing officers—

 (A) are responsible for establishing and maintaining internal controls;
 (B) have designed such internal controls to ensure that material information relating to the issuer and its consolidated subsidiaries is made known to such officers by others within those entities, particularly during the period in which the periodic reports are being prepared;
 (C) have evaluated the effectiveness of the issuer's internal controls as of a date within 90 days prior to the report; and
 (D) have presented in the report their conclusions about the effectiveness of their internal controls based on their evaluation as of that date;

(5) the signing officers have disclosed to the issuer's auditors and the audit committee of the board of directors (or persons fulfilling the equivalent function)—

 (A) all significant deficiencies in the design or operation of internal controls which could adversely affect the issuer's ability to record, process, summarize, and report financial data and have identified for the issuer's auditors any material weaknesses in internal controls; and
 (B) any fraud, whether or not material, that involves management or other employees who have a significant role in the issuer's internal controls; and

(6) the signing officers have indicated in the report whether or not there were significant changes in internal controls or in other factors that could significantly affect internal controls subsequent to the date of their evaluation, including any corrective actions with regard to significant deficiencies and material weaknesses.[5]

---

[5] Sarbanes-Oxley § 302(a), P.L. 107–204.

The requirements under Section 302 should not be considered to overlap those in Section 404 of Sarbanes-Oxley (discussed in the next section). The Section 302 requirements were designed to assure the public that senior management had carefully considered the contents of their organization's financial statements and other presentations and that the disclosures they contained were true, fair, and complete. Note that the requirements do not involve a context of disclosure in accordance with generally accepted accounting principles (GAAP) but rather more absolute standards of quality. Additionally, senior management is charged with knowing and disclosing to the audit committee any changes in controls, fraud involving management, and any significant deficiencies in internal controls over financial reporting.

SARBANES-OXLEY REQUIREMENTS FOR ASSESSMENT AND REPORTING ON INTERNAL CONTROLS AND EXTERNAL AUDIT ATTESTATION

The language of Sarbanes-Oxley Section 404, "Management Assessment of Internal Controls," states:

> (a) Rules Required—The [SEC] shall prescribe rules requiring each annual report [10-K and Annual Report to Shareowners] to contain an internal control report, which shall—
>
> 1. state the responsibility for management for establishing and maintaining an adequate internal control structure and procedures for financial reporting; and
> 2. contain an assessment, as of the end of the most recent fiscal year of the issuer, of the effectiveness of the internal control structure and procedures for financial reporting.
>
> (b) Internal Control Evaluation and Reporting—With respect to the internal control assessment required by subsection (a), each registered public accounting firm that prepares or issues the audit report for the issuer shall attest to, and report on, the assessment made by the management of the issuer. An attestation made under this subsection shall be made in accordance with standards for attestation engagements issued or adopted by the Board. Any such attestation shall not be the subject of a separate engagement.[6]

The certification requirements of Section 302 of Sarbanes-Oxley are published differently from those of Section 404. The Section 302 requirements result in structured paragraphs that are contained as exhibits to a public company's 10-K annual and 10-Q quarterly reports that are filed with the SEC. The Section 404 requirements result in a management assessment report and external auditor's opinion that

[6] Sarbanes-Oxley § 404, P.L. 107–204.

are set forth in the financial statements and external auditor report section of both the 10-K and the annual report to shareowners. The high visibility of the Section 404 management report and auditor opinion is part of the criticism that has arisen over the cost of compliance with this section of the act. Section 404 requirements were introduced in Chapter 4.

SEC INTERPRETIVE GUIDANCE TO MANAGEMENT ON ITS EVALUATION OF INTERNAL CONTROL

As noted, the high cost to companies of performing the internal control over financial reporting assessment required by Sarbanes-Oxley Section 404 resulted in the SEC issuing interpretive guidance designed to assist management to comply at more reasonable cost. SEC Release No. 33-8810, "Commission Guidance Regarding Management's Report on Internal Control over Financial Reporting Under Section 13(a) or 15(d) of the Securities Exchange Act of 1934," was issued on June 27, 2007.

This guidance aims to show management:

- How to vary evaluation approaches for gathering evidence based on risk assessments;
- How to use "daily interaction," self-assessment, and other ongoing monitoring activities as evidence in the evaluation;
- What is the purpose of documentation and how management has flexibility in approaches to documenting support for its assessment;
- Describe the significant flexibility for management to make judgments regarding what constitutes adequate evidence in low-risk areas; and
- To allow management and the auditor to have different testing approaches.[7]

The Interpretive Guidance is organized around two broad principles:

> The first principle is that management should evaluate whether it has implemented controls that adequately address the risk that a material misstatement of the financial statements would not be prevented or detected in a timely manner. The guidance describes a top-down, risk-based approach to this principle, including the role of entity-level controls in assessing financial reporting risks and the adequacy of controls. The guidance promotes efficiency by allowing management to focus on those controls that are needed to adequately address the risk of a material misstatement of its financial statements. The guidance does not require management to identify every control in a process or document the business processes impacting ICFR. Rather, management can focus its evaluation process and the documentation supporting the assessment on those controls that it determines adequately address the risk of a material misstatement of the financial statements. For example, if management determines that

[7] SEC Release No. 33-8810, "Commission Guidance Regarding Management's Report on Internal Control Over Financial Reporting Under Section 13(a) or 15(d) of the Securities Exchange Act of 1934," June 27, 2007, p. 4.

a risk of a material misstatement is adequately addressed by an entity-level control, no further evaluation of other controls is required.[8]

The second principle of the SEC Interpretive Guidance is:

Management's evaluation of evidence about the operation of its controls should be based on its assessment of risk. The guidance provides an approach for making risk-based judgments about the evidence needed for the evaluation. This allows management to align the nature and extent of its evaluation procedures with those areas of financial reporting that pose the highest risks to reliable financial reporting (that is, whether the financial statements are materially accurate). As a result, management may be able to use more efficient approaches to gathering evidence, such as self-assessments, in low-risk areas and perform more extensive testing in high-risk areas.[9]

The remainder of the SEC release covers these topics:

A. The Evaluation Process

1. Identifying Financial Reporting Risks and Controls
   a. Identifying Financial Reporting Risks
   b. Identifying Controls that Adequately Address Financial Reporting Risks
   c. Consideration of Entity-Level Controls
   d. Role of Information Technology General Controls
   e. Evidential Matter to Support the Assessment
2. Evaluating Evidence of the Operating Effectiveness of ICFR
   a. Determining the Evidence Needed to Support the Assessment
   b. Implementing Procedures to Evaluate Evidence of the Operation of ICFR
   c. Evidential Matter to Support the Assessment
3. Multiple Location Considerations

B. Reporting Considerations

1. Evaluation of Control Deficiencies
2. Expression of Assessment of Effectiveness of ICFR by Management
3. Disclosures about Material Weaknesses
4. Impact of a Restatement of Previously Issued Financial Statements on Management's Report on ICFR
5. Inability to Assess Certain Aspects of ICFR[10]

---

[8] Id., pp. 4–5.
[9] Id., p. 5.
[10] Id., p. 8.

PCAOB AUDIT STANDARD NO. 5

The guidance to external auditors regarding their attestation responsibilities relating to management's assessment and report under Sarbanes-Oxley have been issued by the Public Company Accounting Oversight Board (PCAOB). Audit Standard (AS) No. 5, "An Audit of Internal Control over Financial Reporting that Is Integrated with an Audit of Financial Statements" supersedes AS No. 2, issued in March 2004. The new standard was approved by the SEC on July 25, 2007, effective for years ended after November 15, 2007. The objective of the new guidance is to encourage external auditors to take a more top-down and risk-oriented approach and also to allow more use of testing by internal auditors and others in lieu of external audit work if the internal auditors and others are deemed to be competent and objective.

The PCAOB issued its adopting release for AS No. 5 on June 12, 2007.[11] It describes the accomplishments of the pronouncement in this way. The new standard:

- *Aligns* key terms and concepts with terms used in SEC rules and its interpretive guidance pronouncement to management. In addition to harmonizing terminology, the same definition of material weakness is used for both releases.
- *Emphasizes* the need for a top-down approach. The standard is structured around using a top-down approach to identify the most important controls to test. This approach follows the same principles that apply to the financial statement audit: The auditor determines the areas of focus through the identification of significant accounts and disclosures and relevant assertions.

Paragraph 21 of AS No. 5 defines what a top-down approach entails:

> A top-down approach begins at the financial statement level and with the auditor's understanding of the overall risks to internal control over financial reporting. The auditor then focuses on entity-level controls and works down to significant accounts and disclosures and their relevant assertions. This approach directs the auditor's attention to accounts, disclosures, and assertions that present a reasonable possibility of material misstatement to the financial statements and related disclosures. The auditor then verifies his or her understanding of the risks in the company's processes and selects for testing those controls that sufficiently address the assessed risk of misstatement to each relevant assertion. The auditor then verifies his or her understanding of the risks in the company's processes and selects for testing those controls that sufficiently address the assessed risk of misstatement to each relevant assertion.[12]

[11] Public Company Accounting Oversight Board, Release No. 2007-005A, June 12, 2007 at PCAOB Web site www.pcaobus.org.

[12] AS No. 5, "An Audit of Internal Control over Financial Reporting that Is Integrated with an Audit of Financial Statements," paragraph 21, at PCAOB Web site, www.pcaobus.org.

- *Explains* how different kinds of entity-level controls have different effects on the selection and testing of controls. For example, entity-level controls that monitor the operation of other controls in a precise manner may reduce or eliminate the need for testing of the underlying, process-level controls. The new standard allows auditors to tailor their top-down approach to the circumstances of individual companies by removing the requirement to specifically identify major classes of transactions and significant processes before identifying relevant assertions. If an entity-level control sufficiently addresses the assessed risk of misstatement, the auditor need not test additional controls relating to that risk. This flexibility should allow auditors to minimize testing and save resources.
- *Includes* a discussion of fraud risk and antifraud controls at the beginning of the standard to emphasize the importance of these matters in assessing risk.
- *Focuses* auditors on fulfilling the objectives that a properly performed walkthrough achieves rather than requiring performance of a walkthrough, which, under some circumstances, might lead to a checklist approach.
- *Emphasizes* that auditors need not scope the audit to find deficiencies that, individually or when aggregated with other deficiencies, do not constitute material weaknesses. The objective of the audit of internal control over financial reporting must be accomplished within the context of an audit of financial statements. It must not be a freestanding engagement to audit internal controls for the sake of determining their effectiveness and efficiency. At the same time, the standard retains the requirements to evaluate all deficiencies that are identified and communicate both material weaknesses and significant deficiencies, in writing, to the audit committee.
- *Allows* greater use of the work of corporate personnel to obtain evidence about the design and operating effectiveness of controls if the personnel are objective and competent. The former requirement that the external auditor be the principal gatherer of evidence is eliminated.[13]

The SEC press release[14] announcing the commission's approval of AS No. 5 noted four major changes from AS No. 2, the previous standard:

1. Auditing Standard No. 5 is less prescriptive.

   The mandatory requirements (i.e., the "shoulds") that exist in Auditing Standard No. 2 have been significantly reduced in Auditing Standard No. 5. That means the auditor can focus on performing tests in those areas where, in the auditor's judgment, it's actually necessary. Management and audit committees now can engage in a more meaningful dialogue with their auditors to ensure that auditors are

[13] PCAOB Release 2007-005A, pp. 5–14.

[14] SEC, Press Release 2007-144, July 24, 2007, "SEC Approves PCAOB Auditing Standard No. 5, Regarding Audits of Internal Control over Financial Reporting; Adopts Definition of Significant Deficiency."

focused on what matters—risk and materiality—and not on rote compliance with a rulebook. Auditing Standard No. 5 is less than half the length of Auditing Standard No. 2 and is easier to read.

2. Auditing Standard No. 5 makes the audit scalable—so it can change to fit the size and complexity of any company.

   There are notes throughout the new standard explaining how to apply the principles to smaller or less complex companies. Under the new standard, companies' control systems won't have to be designed to fit the audit standard, but rather to achieve the intended objective of improving the quality of financial statements.

3. Auditing Standard No. 5 directs auditors to focus on what matters most—and eliminates unnecessary procedures from the audit.

   It directs auditors to those areas that present the highest risk, such as the financial statement close process and controls designed to prevent fraud by management. It emphasizes that the auditor is not required to scope the audit to find deficiencies that don't constitute material weaknesses. It also allows auditors to use knowledge accumulated in previous years' audits to reduce testing.

4. Finally, Auditing Standard No. 5 includes a principles-based approach to determining when and to what extent the auditor can use the work of others.

A principles-based approach allows auditors to apply professional judgment in determining the extent to which they'll use the work of others. The new standard itself expressly permits auditors to use, in the internal control audit, testing and other internal control work performed by persons other than internal auditors. This principles-based approach is in fact based on the auditor's consideration of the objectivity and competence of those performing the work. These two factors are the most important considerations in the auditor's determination of when and to what extent the auditor can use the work of others.[15]

AICPA INTERNAL CONTROL GUIDANCE FOR AUDIT COMMITTEES

The AICPA has developed materials to assist the work of audit committees through its Audit Committee Effectiveness Center. These materials are described and made available through the AICPA Web site (www.aicpa.org/audcommctr/homepage.htm). Included among these materials are three audit committee toolkits designed to provide helpful but nonauthoritative guidance to three categories of organizations: not-for-profit, governmental, and all other.[16]

[15] Id.

[16] AICPA, *The AICPA Audit Committee Toolkit* (New York: AICPA, 2004). Also available at www.aicpa.org/acec.

The AICPA toolkits contain assessment questions audit committees can use to evaluate the effectiveness of their organization's internal control structure.[17] The toolkit questions are adapted from Volume 2 of *Internal Control—Integrated Framework* published in 1992 by COSO. The questions are arranged by category set forth by the COSO document. A selection of these questions with some rephrasing is presented in Appendix 11A.

KEY POINTS IN CHAPTER 11

(1) Audit committees have significant responsibilities for oversight of internal controls, and pursuant to Sarbanes-Oxley requirements, management's annual assessment of the effectiveness of internal control over financial reporting (ICFR).

(2) As part of its responsibilities to manage relationships with the external audit firm, the audit committee also has to deal with issues of the external auditor's audit of ICFR in connection with its audit of the financial statements.

(3) The Sarbanes-Oxley requirement for maintenance of proper disclosure controls also requires important audit committee oversight.

(4) COSO has provided the framework for internal control analysis and evaluation that has been widely accepted on a global basis. The COSO framework for risk management has extended this definition and modified some terms but has not altered its framework or applicability.

(5) Management's annual assessment of ICFR effectiveness can be more efficient and less costly due to SEC guidance to management issued in 2007.

(6) The changes in external auditing of ICFR because of changes brought about by PCAOB Audit Standard No. 5 should result in lower audit fees. AS No. 5 now requires a direct external audit opinion on ICFR as part of the normal financial statement audit but no longer requires an evaluation of assessment methods used by management.

(7) Effective internal control is importantly dependent on the effectiveness of ethics-related initiatives (discussed in Chapter 12) to bring about a strong ethical climate in the organization.

[17] Id., pp. 63–70.

Appendix 11A

Internal Control—A Tool for the Audit Committee

Purpose of This Tool: This tool focuses on the five interrelated components of an internal control system, as described in the *COSO Internal Control—Integrated Framework* publication.[1] The audit committee's role in the internal control structure of the company focuses on internal controls over financial reporting and the various systems (human resources, computing, and other) available to support that process, and this tool is created to facilitate that role. The audit committee needs to be assured that the controls are in place and operating effectively. This can be achieved through the committee's interaction with senior management, independent auditors, internal auditors, and other key members of the financial management team.

Instructions for Using This Tool: This tool is created around the five interrelated components of an internal control structure. Within each component is a series of questions that the audit committee should focus on to assure itself that controls are in place and functioning. These questions should be discussed in an open forum with the individuals that have a basis for responding to the questions. The audit committee should ask for detailed answers and examples from the management team, including key members of the financial management team, internal auditors, and independent auditors to assure itself that the system is operating as management represents. Evaluation of the internal control structure is not a one-time, but rather a continuous event for the audit committee—the audit committee should always have its eyes and ears open for potential weaknesses in internal control, and should continually probe the responsible parties regarding the operation of the system. These questions are written in a manner such that a "no response" indicates a weakness that must be addressed.

[1] The questions in this tool are adapted from "Evaluation Tools," Volume 2 of the *COSO* Internal Control—Integrated, *Framework,* 1992.

Control Environment—Tone at the Top	Yes	No	Not sure	Comments
Integrity and Ethical Values				
1. Does the organization have a comprehensive code of conduct, and/or other policies addressing acceptable business practice, conflicts of interest, and expected standards of ethical and moral behavior?	☐	☐	☐	
2. Is the code distributed to all employees?	☐	☐	☐	
3. Are all employees required to periodically acknowledge that they have read, understood, and complied with the code?	☐	☐	☐	
4. Does management demonstrate through actions its own commitment to the code of conduct?	☐	☐	☐	
5. Are dealings with . . . customers, suppliers, employees, and other parties based on honesty and fair business practices?	☐	☐	☐	
6. Does management take appropriate action in response to violations of the code of conduct?	☐	☐	☐	
7. Is management explicitly prohibited from overriding established controls? What controls are in place to provide reasonable assurance that controls are not overridden by management? Are deviations from this policy investigated and documented? Are violations (if any) and the results of investigations brought to the attention of the audit committee?	☐	☐	☐	
8. Is the organization proactive in reducing fraud opportunities by (1) identifying and measuring fraud risks, (2) taking steps to mitigate identified risks, (3) identifying a position within the organization to "own" the fraud prevention program, and (4) implementing and monitoring appropriate preventative and detective internal controls and other deterrent measures?	☐	☐	☐	
9. Does the company utilize an anonymous ethics and fraud hotline, and, if so, are procedures in place to investigate and report results to the audit committee?	☐	☐	☐	
Commitment to Competence				
1. Are the level of competence and the requisite knowledge and skills defined for each job in the accounting and internal audit organizations?	☐	☐	☐	
2. Does management make an effort to determine whether the accounting and internal audit organizations have adequate knowledge and skills to do their jobs?	☐	☐	☐	
Board of Directors and/or Audit Committee				
1. Are the audit committee's responsibilities defined in a charter? If so, is the charter updated annually and approved by the board of directors? (See also the tool "Audit Committee Charter Matrix," in this toolkit.)	☐	☐	☐	

Control Environment—Tone at the Top	Yes	No	Not sure	Comments
2. Are audit committee members independent of the company and of management? Do audit committee members have the knowledge, industry experience, and financial expertise to serve effectively in their role?	☐	☐	☐	
3. Are a sufficient number of meetings held, and are the meetings of sufficient length and depth to cover the agenda, and provide healthy discussion of issues?	☐	☐	☐	
4. Does the audit committee constructively challenge management's planned decisions, particularly in the area of financial reporting, and probe the evaluation of past results?	☐	☐	☐	
5. Are regular meetings held between the audit committee and the CFO, the CAE [the leader of internal audit team], other key members of the financial management and reporting team, and the independent auditors? Are executive sessions conducted on a regular basis? (See also the tool "Conducting an Audit Committee Executive Session: Guidelines and Questions," in this toolkit.)	☐	☐	☐	
6. Does the audit committee approve internal audit's annual audit plan?	☐	☐	☐	
7. Does the audit committee receive key information from management in sufficient time in advance of meetings to prepare for discussions at the meetings?	☐	☐	☐	
8. Does a process exist for informing audit committee members about significant issues on a timely basis and in a manner conducive to the audit committee having a full understanding of the issues and their implications?	☐	☐	☐	
9. Is the audit committee informed about personnel turnover in key functions including the audit team (both internal and the independent auditors), senior executives, and key personnel in the financial accounting and reporting teams? Are unusual employee turnover situations observed for patterns or other indicators of problems?	☐	☐	☐	
Management's Philosophy and Operating Style				
1. Is the accounting function viewed as a team of competent professionals bringing information, order, and controls to decision-making?	☐	☐	☐	
2. Is the selection of accounting principles made in the long-term best interest of the organization (as opposed to short-term maximization of income)?	☐	☐	☐	
3. Are valuable assets, including intellectual assets, protected from unauthorized access and use?	☐	☐	☐	
4. Do managers respond appropriately to unfavorable signals and reports?	☐	☐	☐	
5. Are estimates and budgets reasonable and achievable?	☐	☐	☐	

Control Environment—Tone at the Top	Yes	No	Not sure	Comments
Organizational Structure				
1. Is the organizational structure within the accounting function and the internal audit function appropriate for the size of the organization?	☐	☐	☐	
2. Are key managers in the accounting and internal audit functions given adequate definition of their responsibilities?	☐	☐	☐	
3. Do sufficient numbers of employees exist, particularly at the management levels in the accounting and internal audit functions, to allow those individuals to effectively carry out their responsibilities?	☐	☐	☐	
Control Environment—Assignment of Authority and Responsibility				
1. Is the authority delegated appropriate for the responsibilities assigned?	☐	☐	☐	
2. Are job descriptions in place for management and supervisory personnel in the accounting and internal audit functions?	☐	☐	☐	
3. Do senior managers get involved as needed to provide direction, address issues, correct problems, and/or implement improvements?	☐	☐	☐	
Human Resources Policies and Practices				
1. Are policies and procedures in place for hiring, training, promoting, and compensating employees in the accounting and internal audit functions?	☐	☐	☐	
2. Do employees understand that sub-standard performance will result in remedial action?	☐	☐	☐	
3. Is remedial or corrective action taken in response to departures from approved policies?	☐	☐	☐	
4. Do employees understand the performance criteria necessary for promotions and salary increases?	☐	☐	☐	
Risk Assessment				
1. Does the organization consider risks from external sources such as creditor demands, economic conditions, regulation, or labor relations [e.g., unions, etc.]?	☐	☐	☐	
2. Does the organization consider risks from internal sources such as key employees (retention and succession planning), financing and the availability of funding for key programs, competitive compensation and benefits, information systems security, and backup systems?	☐	☐	☐	
3. Is the risk of a misstatement of the financial statements considered, and are steps taken to mitigate that risk?	☐	☐	☐	
4. If applicable, are the risks associated with foreign/offshore operations considered, including their impact on the financial reporting process?	☐	☐	☐	

Control Environment—Tone at the Top	Yes	No	Not sure	Comments
Control Activities				
1. Does the organization have a process in place to ensure that controls as described in its policy and procedures manuals are applied as they are meant to be applied? Do the policy and procedures manuals document all important policies and procedures? Are these policies and procedures reviewed and updated on a regular basis? If so, by whom?	☐	☐	☐	
2. Do supervisory personnel review the functioning of controls? If so, how is that review conducted and what happens to the results? Is appropriate and timely follow-up action taken on exceptions?	☐	☐	☐	
Information and Communication				
1. Is a process in place to collect information from external sources, such as industry, economic, and regulatory information, that could have an impact on the business and/or the financial reporting process?	☐	☐	☐	
2. Are milestones to achieve financial reporting objectives monitored to ensure that timing deadlines are met?	☐	☐	☐	
3. Is necessary operational and financial information communicated to the right people in the organization on a timely basis and in a format that facilitates its use, including new or changed policies and procedures?	☐	☐	☐	
4. Is a process in place to respond to new information needs in the organization on a timely basis?	☐	☐	☐	
5. Is there a process in place to collect and document errors or complaints to analyze, determine cause, and eliminate a problem from recurring in the future?	☐	☐	☐	
6. Is a process established and communicated to officers, employees, and others, about how to communicate suspected instances of wrongdoing by the company or employees of the company? Further, does a process exist to ensure that anyone making such a report is protected from retaliation for making one?	☐	☐	☐	
Monitoring				
1. Do officers and employees understand their obligation to communicate observed weaknesses in design or compliance with the internal control structure of the organization to the appropriate supervisory or management personnel?	☐	☐	☐	
2. Are interactions with external stakeholders periodically evaluated to determine if they are indicative of a weakness in the internal control structure? (For example, consider the frequency of customer complaints about incorrect . . . [bills] .)	☐	☐	☐	

Control Environment—Tone at the Top	Yes	No	Not sure	Comments
3. Is there follow-up on recommendations from the internal and external auditors for improvements to the internal control system?	☐	☐	☐	
4. Are personnel asked to periodically state whether they understand and comply with the organization's code of conduct?	☐	☐	☐	
5. Are personnel required to sign off, indicating their performance of critical control activities such as performing reconciliations?	☐	☐	☐	
6. Does the internal audit team have the right number of competent and experienced staff? Do they have access to the board of directors and audit committee? Is the reporting structure in place to ensure their objectivity and independence? Is the work of the internal audit team appropriate to the organization's needs, and prioritized with the audit committee's direction?	☐	☐	☐	

Chapter 12

The Audit Committee and Ethics-Related Initiatives

Chapter 5 briefly described current requirements for listed corporations to have a code of conduct and mentioned that the U.S. Sentencing Guidelines strongly urge all organizations to install and maintain an effective ethics and compliance program. The importance of an ethical business culture is set forth in the Conference Board's *Corporate Governance Handbook 2007*:

> A culture of business integrity and a working environment prone to rigorous compliance with applicable laws and regulations originate at the top and flow down through all branches of the firm. As such, ethics and compliance practices are a crucial component of corporate governance programs and should take center stage in board agendas.[1]

While the corporate governance committee of the board may be responsible for oversight of ethic-related initiatives in large public corporations, the audit committee may have this responsibility in small and medium-size companies. This chapter outlines guidance about the necessary content that a code of conduct and ethics should have. Some guidance is contained in the New York Stock Exchange (NYSE) commentary to the requiring rule. Additionally, the chapter describes evaluation techniques that have been published by the Open Compliance and Ethics Group,[2] a nonprofit organization that uniquely seeks to help organizations drive performance by enhancing corporate culture and integrating governance, risk management, and compliance processes. Since the avoidance of fraud is one of the goals of an organization's ethics-related initiatives, fraud prevention and detection programs have found increased emphasis in many organizations.

SARBANES-OXLEY AND NYSE CODE OF CONDUCT AND ETHICS GUIDANCE

As noted in Chapter 4, Section 302 of Sarbanes-Oxley requires every public corporation to establish "whistleblower" processes for the anonymous submission of information without fear of retribution:

[1] Conference Board, *Corporate Governance Handbook 2007: Legal Standards and Board Practices*, Research Report R-1045-07-RR, p. 86 (New York: Conference Board, 2007).

[2] See oceg.org.

(4) *COMPLAINTS*. Each audit committee shall establish procedures for

(A) the receipt, retention, and treatment of complaints received by the issuer regarding accounting, internal accounting controls, or auditing matters; and

(B) the confidential, anonymous submission by employees of the issuer of concerns regarding questionable accounting or auditing matters.[3]

Chapter 4 also mentions the requirement in Sarbanes-Oxley Section 406 for disclosure whether the corporation has adopted a code of ethics for senior financial executives:

(a) CODE OF ETHICS DISCLOSURE.—The Commission shall issue rules to require each issuer, together with periodic reports required pursuant to section 13(a) or 15(d) of the Securities Exchange Act of 1934, to disclose whether or not, and if not, the reason therefore, such issuer has adopted a code of ethics for senior financial officers, applicable to its principal financial officer and comptroller or principal accounting officer, or persons performing similar functions.

(b) CHANGES IN CODES OF ETHICS.—The Commission shall revise its regulations concerning matters requiring prompt disclosure on Form 8–K (or any successor thereto) to require the immediate disclosure, by means of the filing of such form, dissemination by the Internet or by other electronic means, by any issuer of any change in or waiver of the code of ethics for senior financial officers.

(c) DEFINITION.—In this section, the term "code of ethics" means such standards as are reasonably necessary to promote—

(1) honest and ethical conduct, including the ethical handling of actual or apparent conflicts of interest between personal and professional relationships;

(2) full, fair, accurate, timely, and understandable disclosure in the periodic reports required to be filed by the issuer; and

(3) compliance with applicable governmental rules and regulations.[4]

The New York Stock Exchange has provided details of the necessary content of the required code of business conduct and ethics in a commentary to its Listing Rule 303A.10, the rule stating the requirement:

No code of business conduct and ethics can replace the thoughtful behavior of an ethical director, officer or employee. However, such a code can focus the board and management on areas of ethical risk, provide guidance to personnel to help them recognize and deal with ethical issues, provide mechanisms to report unethical conduct, and help to foster a culture of honesty and accountability.

Each code of business conduct and ethics must also contain compliance standards and procedures that will facilitate the effective operation of the code. These standards should ensure the prompt and consistent action against violations of the code.[5]

---

[3] Sarbanes-Oxley, § 302, P.L. 107–204.

[4] Sarbanes-Oxley § 406, P.L. 107–204.

[5] NYSE, Inc., Listed Company Manual § 303A¶ 10. See www.nyse.com.

In other words, each listed company may determine its own policies that address the objectives of the rule, but all listed companies should address these most important topics in their codes of conduct:

Conflicts of interest. A "conflict of interest" occurs when an individual's private interest interferes in any way—or even appears to interfere—with the interests of the corporation as a whole. A conflict situation can arise when an employee, officer or director takes actions or has interests that may make it difficult to perform his or her company work objectively and effectively. Conflicts of interest also arise when an employee, officer or director, or a member of his or her family, receives improper personal benefits as a result of his or her position in the company. Loans to, or guarantees of obligations of, such persons are of special concern. The listed company should have a policy prohibiting such conflicts of interest, and providing a means for employees, officers and directors to communicate potential conflicts to the listed company.

Corporate opportunities. Employees, officers and directors should be prohibited from (a) taking for themselves personally opportunities that are discovered through the use of corporate property, information or position; (b) using corporate property, information, or position for personal gain; and (c) competing with the company. Employees, officers and directors owe a duty to the company to advance its legitimate interests when the opportunity to do so arises.

Confidentiality. Employees, officers and directors should maintain the confidentiality of information entrusted to them by the listed company or its customers, except when disclosure is authorized or legally mandated. Confidential information includes all non-public information that might be of use to competitors, or harmful to the company or its customers, if disclosed.

Fair dealing. Each employee, officer and director should endeavor to deal fairly with the company's customers, suppliers, competitors and employees. None should take unfair advantage of anyone through manipulation, concealment, abuse of privileged information, misrepresentation of material facts, or any other unfair-dealing practice. Listed companies may write their codes in a manner that does not alter existing legal rights and obligations of companies and their employees, such as "at will" employment arrangements.

Protection and proper use of company assets. All employees, officers and directors should protect the company's assets and ensure their efficient use. Theft, carelessness and waste have a direct impact on the listed company's profitability. All company assets should be used for legitimate business purposes.

Compliance with laws, rules and regulations (including insider trading laws). The listed company should proactively promote compliance with laws, rules and regulations, including insider trading laws. Insider trading is both unethical and illegal, and should be dealt with decisively.

Encouraging the reporting of any illegal or unethical behavior. The listed company should proactively promote ethical behavior. The company should encourage employees to talk to supervisors, managers or other appropriate personnel when in doubt about the best course of action in a particular situation. Additionally, employees should report violations of laws, rules, regulations or the code of business conduct to appropriate personnel. To encourage employees to report such violations, the listed company must ensure that employees know that the company will not allow retaliation for reports made in good faith.[6]

U.S. SENTENCING GUIDELINES REQUIREMENTS

As noted in Chapter 5, provisions of the U.S. Sentencing Guidelines set forth in the Manual of the Sentencing Commission outline the parameters of an effective compliance and ethics system that can mitigate the severity of penalties otherwise determined. Chapter 8 of the Guidelines Manual includes the description of an effective ethics and compliance program, stating that an organization shall:

> (1) exercise due diligence to prevent and detect criminal conduct; and
>
> (2) otherwise promote an organizational culture that encourages ethical conduct and a commitment to compliance with the law.
>
> Such compliance and ethics program shall be reasonably designed, implemented, and enforced so that the program is generally effective in preventing and detecting criminal conduct. The failure to prevent or detect the instant offense does not necessarily mean that the program is not generally effective in preventing and detecting criminal conduct.[7]

The Sentencing Guidelines set forth seven minimum components that determine the framework of an effective compliance and ethics program. These are presented in Appendix 12A.

In the press release announcing the new standards for compliance and ethics programs, the Sentencing Commission noted the ground rules "put greater responsibility on boards of directors and executives," require companies to "demonstrate that they have identified areas of risk," "trained high-level as well as employees is relevant legal standards and obligations," and "given their compliance officers sufficient authority and resources to carry out their responsibilities."[8]

PREVENTING AND DETECTING FRAUD

One of the important objectives of ethics and compliance programs is the avoidance of losses associated with the fraudulent activities of officers and employees. The Association of Certified Fraud Examiners (ACFE) estimates that as much as six percent of the sales of U.S. corporations is lost due to various types of organizational fraud. Recent changes in auditing standards have also resulted in greater audit attention to the evaluation of fraud prevention and detection programs.

---

[6] Id.

[7] U.S. Sentencing Commission, 2007 Federal Sentencing Guidelines, Chapter 8B2.1.(a).

[8] U.S. Sentencing Commission News Release, "Commission Tightens Requirements for Corporate Compliance and Ethics Programs," May 3, 2004. See ussc.gov.

The Institute of Internal Auditors (IIA), the Association of Certified Fraud Examiners (ACFE), and the American Institute of Certified Public Accountants (AICPA) have developed five key elements of an effective antifraud program: governance, risk assessment, prevention, detection, and investigation and response.[9] The governance section of the guidance emphasizes the importance of going beyond compliance to a truly ethical culture. Directors, likely through the efforts of the audit committee, need to be sure that policies are in force that demonstrate strong governance and empower customers, employees, and vendors to meet high ethical standards which among other benefits, will deter fraud.

EXAMPLES OF CODES OF CONDUCT

The code of conduct of United Parcel Service (ticker symbol UPS) and that of Google, Inc. (ticker symbol GOOG) are presented as Appendixes 12B and 12C as examples of how corporations might differ in adopting codes to fulfill this Sarbanes-Oxley and stock exchange requirement. UPS is listed on the New York Stock Exchange and is thought of as a by-the-book kind of company, with a detailed manual of rules and routines – the "340 methods." On the other hand, GOOG is traded on Nasdaq and considered a more free-wheeling company. Every code of conduct and ethics should be individually developed and based on the core values of the specific organization. There is no one-size-fits-all best practice code of conduct and ethics. It is interesting to note differences in style.

The UPS code is organized into these sections:

1. Our Values and Management Philosophies
   - Asking Questions and Voicing Concerns
   - Retaliation
2. Our People
   - Equal Opportunity and Fair Treatment
   - Workplace Health and Safety
   - Drug and Alcohol Policy
   - Crisis Management and Workplace Violence Prevention
   - Conflicts of Interest
   - Gifts and Entertainment
   - Doing Business With the Company
   - Employee Ownership of the UPS Store
   - Employment Outside of UPS

[9] IIA, ACFE, AICPA, *Managing the Business Risk of Fraud: A Practical Guide*, 2008 (forthcoming). See http://www.theiia.org/recent-iia-news/?search=fraud&C=797&I=4449. (Accessed January 2008).

3. Our Customers
    - Doing Business With the Government
    - Antitrust/Fair Competition
    - Choosing Suppliers and Consultants
4. Our Shareowners
    - Insider Trading
    - Financial Performance
    - Investments
    - Records Management
    - Company Property and Services
    - Intellectual Property
    - Information Use and Security
    - Copyrighted Material
    - Trademarks
    - Confidential and Proprietary Information
5. Our Communities
    - Political Activities and Contributions
    - Transacting Transnational Business
    - Anti-Corruption Compliance
    - New Entity Procedure
    - Boycotts, Embargoes, and Restrictive Trade Practices
    - Government Controls for Transnational Shipments
    - Environmental Protection

The Google. Inc. code is organized in this way:

1. Serving Our Users
    - Usefulness
    - Honesty
    - Responsiveness
    - Taking Action
2. Respecting Each Other
    - Equal Opportunity Employment
    - Harassment and Discrimination
    - Drug and Alcohol Use
    - Weapons and Workplace Violence
    - Our Dog Policy

3. Avoiding Conflicts of Interest
   - Openness
   - Personal Investments
   - Gifts and Entertainment
   - Business Relationships
   - Friends and Relatives
4. Preserving Confidentiality
   - Confidential Information
   - Trademarks, Logos, and Copyrights
   - Google Partners
   - Competitors' Information
   - Outside Communication
5. Maintaining Books and Records
   - Business Transactions
   - Reporting Procedures
   - Reporting Irregularities
6. Protecting Google's Assets
   - Company Equipment
   - Computer and other Communications Resources
   - Need to Access and Monitor Communications on Google Facilities and Premises
   - Data Privacy
   - Third-Party Suppliers
   - Company Contracts
7. Obeying the Law
   - Improper Payments
   - Export Controls
   - Antitrust Laws
   - Insider Trading
8. Using Our Code

Although both the UPS and the Google codes are written in easy-to-understand language, there are clear differences. Neither is written in legalistic language, as legal-sounding codes are not believed to be effective. The UPS code, however, seems to have a greater emphasis on legal compliance, in that it makes frequent reference to appropriate sections of the UPS Corporate Compliance Web site and other relevant policy documents. In this way, readers can easily be made aware of and directed to the more legally-oriented requirements that their organization has published.

OCEG ETHICS AND COMPLIANCE EVALUATION TOOL

As another aspect of its efforts to bring ethics into mainstream American business, the Open Compliance and Ethics Group (OCEG) published a questionnaire, "Does the Company Get It?"[10] Audit committee members should consider the use of this assessment tool, which is useful in determining whether an organization has an effective process and culture in place to control and mitigate compliance- and ethics-related risks. Each question requests answers to: (1) why ask this question, (2) what are potential answers, and (3) what are red flags? The 20 questions are:

1. What does your organization say about compliance, ethics, and values in its formal mission and vision statement?...
2. How does your Board and management set the "tone at the top" and communicate compliance and ethics values, mission, and vision?...
3. How do you know if your employees and other stakeholders are "convinced" that the organization is serious about its compliance and ethics responsibilities?...
4. What is the scope of your compliance and ethics program and how does it integrate with your overall business strategy?...
5. How do you assess compliance and ethics risks and how does this process integrate with enterprise risk management (ERM)?...
6. What position in the organization provides oversight and leadership in the compliance/ethics function and where does this position fall in the organizational chart?...
7. What is the organizational structure of your compliance and ethics management team?
8. How are resources allocated for compliance and ethics management activities, both routinely and to address significant issues that arise?...
9. What does your Code of Conduct address and who receives it?...
10. How do you distribute your Code of Conduct and confirm that employees both receive and understand the Code and other policies?...
11. What is your process for updating policies/procedures?...
12. Can any requirements established by the Code of Conduct and other policies be waived or overridden and, if so, what is the process for doing so?...
13. How often, and by what methods, does your management communicate the values, mission, and vision of the compliance and ethics program to employees and other stakeholders?...

[10] OCEG, "Does the Company Get It?" (March 2004). See oceg.org.

14. Do you provide comprehensive training and conduct performance evaluations for each job role to ensure compliance and ethics responsibilities are understood and followed, and that necessary skills are learned and employed?...
15. How do employees, agents, and other stakeholders raise issues regarding compliance and ethics-related matters?...
16. How do you handle compliance and ethics issues that arise and scrutinize the sources of compliance failures?...
17. How consistently, and in what way, have you taken action against violators of the Code and Programs?...
18. What is the process for determining which issues are escalated to the Board and for informing the Board when issues are resolved?
19. What ongoing processes are in place to monitor the effectiveness of the compliance and ethics program?...
20. Does the organization engage an external law firm or consultant to audit compliance and ethics program elements?...[11]

ETHISPHERE COUNCIL EVALUATION CRITERIA

The Ethisphere Council is a consortium of organizations that believe that a more ethical business is a more profitable one. It was organized by Corpedia, Lexis-Nexis, Practicing Law Institute, and the National Association of Corporate Directors, both for-profit and not-for-profit organizations. The council's white paper on evaluating the effectiveness of a code of conduct (now available only to members) contains 43 elements organized into eight categories. Those categories, together with the weighting assigned by the council are:

Tone at the Top 17.5%
Readability and Tone 17.5%
Presentation and Style 12.5%
Non-Retaliation 10%
Public Availability 7.5%
Commitment 7.5%
Learning Aids 5%

Ethisphere notes five reasons why "ethics can be profitable":

1. *Ethical businesses are better at attracting and keeping customers.* Creating customer loyalty is an effective way of achieving this objective.
2. *Ethical businesses demand employee loyalty.* Running a respected ethical and responsible business gives your company that added advantage to attract and

[11] Id. For more information, see the OCEG Web site, www.oceg.org.

retain top talent, thereby reducing costs, decreasing turnover, and driving better margins.

3. *Ethical businesses attract institutional investors.* Many organizations see developing an ethical, responsible, and sustainable business as the key to attract, and, in many cases, diversify their institutional investor base.
4. *Ethics support easy brand extensions.* The ability to expand a brand and motivate an existing customer to purchase an additional product is one of the most significant profit drivers for any organization.
5. *Ethical business can minimize cost.* Having your business involved in an ethical scandal could lead to significant direct and indirect costs. Avoiding such scandals by having an infrastructure around ethics and responsible business is key.[12]

KEY POINTS IN CHAPTER 12

1. Assuming the organization has a strong ethical culture is a key responsibility of the board of directors. Monitoring programs designed to accomplish this objective are part of the responsibilities of the audit committees in a number of corporations, both public and private, for-profit and not-for-profit.
2. The provisions of the U.S. Sentencing Guidelines strongly motivate all organizations of every type to install and maintain an effective program of ethics and compliance.
3. Empirical evidence is growing that a culture of strong organizational ethics is key to the success of every ethics and compliance program.
4. The code of conduct of an organization should fit its values. There is not a one-size-fits-all answer to developing the appropriate code of ethics and conduct.
5. Prevention and detection of fraudulent activities is an important outcome of the presence of a strong ethical culture in the organization.

[12] Scott Lane, Business Integrity Proves Profitable, on Ethisphere Web site, www.ethisphere.com/category/expert. (Accessed December 2007).

Appendix 12A

Seven Minimum Components of an Effective Compliance and Ethics Program Under U.S. Sentencing Guidelines

(1) The organization shall establish standards and procedures to prevent and detect criminal conduct.

(2) (A) The organization's governing authority shall be knowledgeable about the content and operation of the compliance and ethics program and shall exercise reasonable oversight with respect to the implementation and effectiveness of the compliance and ethics program.

(B) High-level personnel of the organization shall ensure that the organization has an effective compliance and ethics program. Specific individual(s) within high-level personnel shall be assigned overall responsibility for the compliance and ethics program.

(C) Specific individual(s) within the organization shall be delegated day-to-day operational responsibility for the compliance and ethics program. Individual(s) with operational responsibility shall report periodically to high-level personnel and, as appropriate, to the governing authority, or an appropriate subgroup of the governing authority, on the effectiveness of the compliance and ethics program. To carry out such operational responsibility, such individual(s) shall be given adequate resources, appropriate authority, and direct access to the governing authority or an appropriate subgroup of the governing authority.

(3) The organization shall use reasonable efforts not to include within the substantial authority personnel of the organization any individual whom the organization knew, or should have known through the exercise of due diligence, has engaged in illegal activities or other conduct inconsistent with an effective compliance and ethics program.

(4) The organization shall take reasonable steps to communicate periodically and in a practical manner its standards and procedures, and other aspects of the compliance and ethics program... by conducting effective training programs and

otherwise disseminating information. [Included in the communication efforts should be all officers and employees and, as appropriate, the organization's agents.]

(5) The organization shall take reasonable steps—

(A) to ensure that the organization's compliance and ethics program is followed, including monitoring and auditing to detect criminal conduct;

(B) to evaluate periodically the effectiveness of the organization's compliance and ethics program; and

(C) to have and publicize a system, which may include mechanisms that allow for anonymity or confidentiality, whereby the organization's employees and agents may report or seek guidance regarding potential or actual criminal conduct without fear of retaliation.

(6) The organization's compliance and ethics program shall be promoted and enforced consistently throughout the organization through (A) appropriate incentives to perform in accordance with the compliance and ethics program; and (B) appropriate disciplinary measures for engaging in criminal conduct and for failing to take reasonable steps to prevent or detect criminal conduct.

(7) After criminal conduct has been detected, the organization shall take reasonable steps to respond appropriately to the criminal conduct and to prevent further similar criminal conduct, including making any necessary modifications to the organization's compliance and ethics program.

Source: 2007 Federal Sentencing Guidelines, Chapter 8B2.1.(b).

Appendix 12B

UPS Code of Business Conduct

UPS has a long-standing commitment to conduct our business in compliance with all applicable laws and regulations and in accordance with the highest ethical principles. The UPS Code of Business Conduct is one of many tools the UPS Business Conduct and Compliance Program provides our employees to assist them in meeting our legal and ethical obligations.

STATEMENT OF POLICY

We comply with the UPS Code of Business Conduct. We manage our business in compliance with all applicable laws and regulations of the countries in which we operate, and in accordance with our company's high standards of business conduct. All employees are expected to comply with the UPS Code of Business Conduct, which is essential to maintaining our reputation for honesty, quality, and integrity. It is also each employee's responsibility to report to the company any situation where our standards or the laws are being violated. Any employee disclosing, in good faith, violations or suspected violations of legal requirements or UPS business standards will not be subjected to retaliation or retribution. Likewise, failure to comply with the provisions of the UPS Code of Business Conduct will not be tolerated.

PREFACE

This UPS Code of Business Conduct sets forth standards of conduct for all of UPS. Throughout it, "UPS" is used to refer to the enterprise as a whole, to each person within it, and to any person who represents UPS or any part of the UPS organization.

Adherence to the Code is required of all employees and representatives of UPS. The Code is available in multiple languages on the Corporate Compliance Web site.

The Code provides information about our standards of integrity and explains our legal and ethical responsibilities. It does not address every specific situation or set forth a rule that will answer every question. Rather, it is intended to provide guidance on our responsibilities and to assist us in making the right decisions. Additional requirements are set forth in detail in various individual compliance programs developed by functions with appropriate expertise and training. It is our responsibility to understand which compliance programs apply to our area of responsibility and to manage the business accordingly.

The UPS Code of Business Conduct, Policy Book, and UPS Charter are complementary documents that work together to guide our objectives and explain our responsibilities to our four constituencies: people, customers, shareowners, and communities. To ensure a complete understanding, discussion of the Code, Policy Book, and UPS Charter at business meetings and other suitable occasions in encouraged.

Any employee of UPS, regardless of his or her position within the company, who violates our legal or ethical responsibilities, will be subject to appropriate discipline, which may include dismissal. Non-compliance with certain aspects of the Code and/or the Business Conduct and Compliance Program also may subject the individual offender and UPS to civil and/or criminal liability.

MIKE ESKEW'S MESSAGE: ON LEADING WITH INTEGRITY

Integrity has always been central to the way UPS does business.

As Jim Casey said in 1957, "We have become known to all who deal with us as people of integrity, and that priceless asset is more valuable than anything else we possess."

Of course, maintaining that priceless asset can never be taken for granted, as it is vital to our continued growth and success. As we continue to expand our operations around the globe, we must be even more vigilant in ensuring that our reputation is maintained in every country, community, and location where we do business.

As UPS employees and representatives, we have an obligation to make sure our daily decisions support the values and principles of the company.

But what does that mean exactly?

Certainly, it means managing the business to comply with the law and our ethical values. But our standard goes beyond the letter of the law. It also means we will conform to the spirit of what those regulations intend.

Simply put, it means our standard is to conduct business fairly, honestly, and ethically.

Today, as we continue to integrate deeper into our customers' supply chains, the level of trust between UPS and our customers extends deeper than ever.

In some ways, it takes us back to the company's roots. In those early days, Jim Casey asked retailers to trust that he would hold in confidence their individual customer lists. And he honored their trust.

More than ever in today's age of digital information sharing, we must protect customer interests as carefully as Jim did. We must treat each customer as if they were our only customer.

That means resisting any temptation to cut corners. Our success is owed to our people, who through the years, paid careful attention to integrity and demonstrated values that sustained customer relationships. Integrity also speaks to the way in which we treat our people, by creating an environment of trust and understanding.

Employees who get results at the cost of legal violations, or through dishonest dealings, do more than violate our standards. They undercut our ability to grow our business by undermining our reputation.

Compliance with our legal and ethical obligations is the responsibility of every employee and representative of UPS, as is the responsibility to report potential violations of those obligations. Reporting can be done directly through your supervisor or manager, through any other member of the management team by using the Open Door Policy, or by calling the UPS Help Line. It is important to come forward—if you are not comfortable with one method, another can be used.

In upholding our legal and ethical responsibilities, by conducting our business in compliance with the letter and spirit of those requirements, by using good judgment, and by respecting each other, UPS's legacy of leading with integrity will endure.

Leading with integrity is about creating a climate for success. It's about creating an environment where good people can make good decisions.

The UPS reputation has been earned over several generations. It is ours to benefit from and to uphold.

—Michael Eskew Chairman and Chief Executive Officer

OUR VALUES AND MANAGEMENT PHILOSOPHIES

For decades, UPS people have been motivated by commonly held principles and values that have allowed us to work toward mutual goals. These principles and values, originally established by our founders, remain as constant and as critical to our success as ever. The core of these values, which still inspires UPS employees today, is that UPS is a company of honesty, quality, and integrity.

This legacy is fundamental to our ability to attract and retain the best people, gain and keep the trust of our customers, create shareowner value, support the communities in which we operate, and protect our reputation.

It has always been, and continues to be, our policy to conduct business in compliance with all applicable laws and regulations and in accordance with the highest ethical standards. We expect—as we always have—that UPS employees, and the people acting on our behalf, will adhere to these principles.

ASKING QUESTIONS AND VOICING CONCERNS

This Code provides an overview of the legal and ethical responsibilities that we share. Each of us must uphold these responsibilities. The standards and expectations outlined here are intended as a guide for making the right choices. If any aspect of the Code is unclear to us, or if we have any questions or face dilemmas that are not addressed, this should be brought to the company's attention. If we become aware of a situation in which we believe our legal or ethical responsibilities are being violated or if we feel that we are being pressured to violate the law or our ethical responsibilities, it is our personal responsibility to communicate this concern to the company.

No employee will be disciplined, lose a job, or be retaliated against in any way for asking questions or voicing concerns about our legal or ethical obligations, when acting in good faith. "Good faith" does not mean an individual has to be right; but, it does mean believing information provided is truthful.

It is important that we communicate a question or concern through one of the many available channels.

We can speak with our direct manager or supervisor, or use the Open Door Policy to talk to someone else in management, including your Human Resources manager, or someone from the function with the expertise and responsibility to address the concern. Any of these people may have the information needed, or will be able to refer the question to another appropriate source.

Another communication channel to assist us is the UPS Help Line. We can contact the UPS Help Line when we have a concern or want to report a potential violation of our legal or ethical responsibilities. We may use whatever method of communication with which we feel most comfortable. The important thing is to get the needed guidance, to report what is known, and to get questions answered.

The UPS Help Line, which is answered by an outside vendor, is available to all employees, 24 hours a day, 7 days a week. Interpreters are available for language assistance. The UPS Help Line can be reached toll-free at 1-800-220-4126. Individual country codes can be found on the Corporate Compliance Web site and should be used for UPS Help Line calls made outside of North America.

Although callers are encouraged to identify themselves to assist the company in effectively addressing their concerns, callers may choose to remain anonymous, and that choice will be respected. The UPS Help Line is not equipped with caller ID, recorders, or other devices that can identify or trace the caller's number.

When the UPS Help Line is called, the person can expect that:

- A report will be forwarded to appropriate UPS management for follow-up.
- The concern will be addressed by members of management that may include representatives from Corporate Compliance, Human Resources, Corporate Legal, Security, or Internal Audit. If the inquiry is one that can be properly handled by someone in the region or district, it will be referred there for resolution. Each concern will be carefully evaluated before it is referred for investigation or resolution.
- The concern will be handled promptly, discreetly, and professionally.
- Discussions and inquiries will be kept in confidence to the extent appropriate or permitted by law.
- Certain follow-up information about how the concern was addressed may be obtained upon request.

Investigations into allegations of unethical or illegal conduct must be conducted confidentially and professionally. The UPS Guidelines for Investigation of Workplace Issues is available from Corporate Compliance for management who may conduct such an investigation.

Additional information can be found in the section titled "Retaliation" and on the Corporate Compliance Web site.

RETALIATION

Our commitment to integrity includes a responsibility to foster an environment that allows people to report violations without the fear of retaliation or retribution. No one should be discouraged from using any available channel within the organization. Even simple questioning of someone can lead to claims of retaliation, even though that was never the intent, as it may make a person feel that he or she did something wrong by choosing one method over another. People must be able to choose whichever method they are most comfortable with to communicate their concern.

Anyone who retaliates against another employee for reporting known or suspected violations of our legal or ethical obligations is in violation of the Code and subject to disciplinary action, up to and including dismissal. Retaliation also may be a violation of the law, and as such, could subject both the individual offender and UPS to legal liability.

Additionally, the same rules apply with regard to retaliation or retribution against employees related to company-sponsored solicitations, such as for charities or political action committees.

OUR PEOPLE

EQUAL OPPORTUNITY AND FAIR TREATMENT

We treat each individual fairly, and recruit, select, train, promote, and compensate based on merit, experience, and other work-related criteria. We comply with all laws governing fair employment and labor practices. We do not discriminate against any applicant for employment or any employee in any aspect of their employment at UPS because of age, race, religion, sex, disability, sexual orientation, military status, pregnancy, national origin, or veteran status.

Freedom from wrongful discrimination includes freedom from any form of discriminatory harassment. Prohibited harassment includes conduct that is intended to interfere or that has the effect of unreasonably interfering with a fellow employee's work performance or creating an environment that is intimidating, hostile, or offensive to the individual.

Additional information can be found in the UPS Professional Conduct and Anti-Harassment Policy available from Human Resources.

WORKPLACE HEALTH AND SAFETY

The health and safety of our people are of utmost importance to UPS, which is committed to protecting the health and well-being of each UPS employee. We strive to protect our people, customers, and the public from injury and illness through our Health and Safety programs. Government regulatory standards and employee input are used to develop comprehensive programs and work processes that are designed to promote safe workplaces and good health. We are all responsible for understanding and complying with UPS Health and Safety processes, procedures, and guidelines, as well as those issued by applicable regulatory authorities.

Employees are required to advise the company of any vehicle accident, workplace injury, instance of non-compliance, or any situation presenting a danger of injury. This information will assist in preventing injuries, and will ensure that appropriate medical attention is provided. Through investigation of such reports, we can identify contributing factors and determine if our policies and processes are effective and adequately communicated. When an unsafe condition, practice, or non-compliant action is identified, prompt and appropriate action must be taken to correct the condition and prevent it from happening again.

Additional information about Health and Safety issues is available from district, region, or Corporate Health and Safety.

DRUG AND ALCOHOL POLICY

It is our policy to maintain a drug-free and alcohol-free work environment. Use of alcohol and/or illegal drugs creates serious health and safety risks in the workplace. The use, sale, or possession of alcohol, illegal drugs, or other illegal substances is strictly prohibited while at work, on company property, or while on company business. This prohibition also includes illegal or improper use of controlled substances.

Reporting to work under the influence of any such substance is strictly prohibited. No one is permitted to go on duty or remain on duty if they possess or have the presence of an illegal or unauthorized controlled substance or alcohol in their system. Employees are not permitted to go on duty or remain on duty if they are impaired by the presence of an authorized controlled substance. In addition, we must comply with all laws and regulations regarding the use or possession of alcohol, illegal drugs, and controlled substances.

CRISIS MANAGEMENT AND WORKPLACE VIOLENCE PREVENTION

UPS is committed to a safe working environment, free of threats, intimidation and physical harm. Everyone has a right to work in a safe environment and shares the responsibility for assuring each other's safety. UPS has adopted a zero tolerance workplace violence policy. This means we will investigate and take appropriate action against any threat to a safe workplace.

UPS prohibits violent behavior including, but not limited to, physical assaults, fighting, threatening comments, intimidation, and the intentional or reckless destruction of company, employee, or customer property. Any comments or behavior that reasonably could be interpreted as an intent to do harm to people or property will be considered a threat. We also prohibit the unauthorized possession and/or use of weapons by any employee while at work, on company property, or while on company business.

Any employee who believes that he or she may be the target of violence or threats of violence, or is aware of violent or threatening conduct by, or directed at, a UPS employee that could result in injury to a person or the destruction of property, has a responsibility to immediately report the situation to his or her immediate supervisor or manager. If an employee is unable to or prefers not to contact an immediate supervisor or manager, the employee can call the UPS Help Line (see "Asking Questions and Voicing Concerns").

Additional information is available from your local Security Department.

CONFLICTS OF INTEREST

We are all expected to give our undivided business loyalty to UPS when conducting our job-related duties. Accordingly, we must be careful to avoid conflicts of interest—situations where our private interests conflict, or even appear to conflict, with the interests of UPS as a whole. Therefore, we should not place ourselves in situations that might force us inappropriately to choose between our own personal or financial interests and the interests of UPS.

Conflicts of interest can arise in many common areas, despite our best efforts to avoid them. However, such conflicts can generally be resolved by promptly notifying your manager of any actual, perceived, or potential conflict of interest situation. The manager can then provide guidance on how best to resolve the conflict. If needed, an employee also may contact Corporate Compliance for guidance.

Conflicts of interests also must be disclosed on the annual Business Ethics Questionnaire.

Additional information about conflicts of interest, including information about investments in other companies, is available in the sections of this Code titled "Investments" and "Political Activities and Contributions" and on the Corporate Compliance Web site.

GIFTS AND ENTERTAINMENT

All employees and representatives of UPS should understand the legal and ethical issues associated with gifts and entertainment and how they can affect our relationship and reputation with our customers, suppliers, and the general public. The decision to offer or to accept gifts or entertainment should be made only in compliance with legal requirements and ethical considerations, and with the involvement of a manager if unsure of the appropriate course.

The issue of gifts and gratuities may have legal implications when the government, or government entity is involved, and serious consequences can result from mishandling these relationships. Offering or accepting bribes and pay-offs is always prohibited.

Business gifts and entertainment are courtesies designed to build goodwill and sound working relationships among business partners. We do not, however, want to obtain business through improper means as to gain any special advantage in a relationship. Business gifts that compromise, or even appear to compromise, our ability to make objective and fair business decisions are inappropriate.

Solicitation of gifts is never appropriate, even for charitable purposes or UPS events. All gifts and entertainment, other than infrequent items of nominal value, must be disclosed to a manager.

The difference between appropriate and inappropriate gifts is not always easy to determine. The UPS Guidelines for Gifts and Gratuities should be reviewed to determine whether a gift is appropriate. Any doubt should be resolved in favor of not giving or receiving the gift.

Additional information is available in the UPS Guidelines for Gifts and Gratuities and in the UPS Anti-Corruption Compliance Program materials available on the Corporate Compliance Web site.

DOING BUSINESS WITH THE COMPANY

A conflict of interest could arise if an employee, a spouse, a relative, or a close personal friend, has a personal stake in a business that supplies or seeks to supply goods or services to UPS, is a UPS customer or potential customer, or competes with UPS. Accordingly, the following standards apply in such situations:

- If a UPS employee, spouse, relative, or close personal friend is an employee of, or has a significant interest in a business that provides or is seeking to provide goods or services to UPS, the UPS employee must not attempt to use his or her position with UPS to influence the bidding process or negotiation in any way. Similarly, the UPS employee must not use personal relationships to improperly influence dealings with a customer or a potential customer.
- If the position of a relative or friend who works for a competitor is such that a potential conflict of interest could arise, the UPS employee should seek guidance from a manager.

EMPLOYEE OWNERSHIP OF THE UPS STORE

As a general rule, a UPS employee, or a member of his or her immediate family, may own a Mail Boxes Etc. or The UPS Store franchise. It is, however, necessary to evaluate the possibility of any conflicts of interest. Ownership of a Mail Boxes Etc. or the UPS Store franchise by a UPS employee, or a member of his or her immediate family, does not necessarily create a conflict of interest. In each case, however, the UPS employee must ensure that undivided business loyalty to UPS is maintained. This requires obtaining all necessary approvals as described in the Guidelines for UPS Employee Ownership of The UPS Store.

Refer to the Guidelines for UPS Employee Ownership of The UPS Store on the Corporate Compliance Web site for additional information.

EMPLOYMENT OUTSIDE OF UPS

Although employment outside of UPS is not necessarily a conflict of interest, depending upon an individual's position with UPS and UPS's relationship with the other organization, a conflict could arise.

Outside employment also could be a conflict of interest if it causes, or might be perceived by others to cause, an employee to choose between that interest and the interests of UPS. If a situation arises, either through scheduling or other potential conflicts, our undivided business loyalty requires that we resolve the conflict in favor of UPS.

We should not, without approval of the Corporate Secretary, serve as directors or officers of, or consultants to, any organization that supplies goods or services to UPS, buys goods or services from UPS, or competes with UPS. If a position outside the Company could present a conflict of interest, discuss the situation with a manager.

Service as a director or officer of a non-profit organization does not require approval of the Corporate Secretary.

Any UPS employee, management or non-management, who has received approval to serve as a director or officer of, or consultant to, any for-profit organization that supplies goods or services to UPS, buys goods or services from UPS, or competes with UPS must complete the Business Ethics Questionnaire (BEQ) annually. The employee's manager is responsible for ensuring that the employee receives, completes, and returns the BEQ each year.

In some cases, UPS employees may be involved in outside businesses that are not UPS competitors or suppliers. These situations do not necessarily constitute a conflict of interest, but it is the employee's responsibility to ensure that these activities do not conflict with UPS's interests.

This requires keeping the two activities strictly separated by adhering to the following standards. A UPS employee:

- May not do work relating to other organizations on UPS time.
- May not use UPS equipment and supplies, or the time of any UPS personnel for outside work.
- May not promote products or services from an outside business to other UPS employees during working hours or on UPS property.
- May not attempt to sell products or services form an outside business to UPS.
- May not use his or her position in the company to promote an outside business.

OUR CUSTOMERS

We compete fairly and in accordance with the highest standards in all of our customer relationships. We want to earn business on the basis of superior services and products and competitive prices, not through improper, unethical, or questionable business practices.

Our credibility with our customers depends on our ability to fulfill our commitments. Any time we fail to live up to a commitment, hard-earned customer trust is damaged.

To preserve our customer relationships:

- We do not misrepresent our services or products in any sales or promotional efforts.
- We communicate clearly, so that our customers understand the terms of our business relationships, including contracts, performance criteria, schedules, prices, and responsibilities.
- We protect our customers' confidential information.
- We only make promises to customers that we believe we will be able to keep.

DOING BUSINESS WITH THE GOVERNMENT

Doing business with the government is not always the same as doing business with private parties. Activities that might be appropriate when working with private sector customers may be improper or even illegal—when a national or local government is our customer. For example, business courtesies or entertainment that might be acceptable when dealing with private parties—like paying for meals or drinks—may not be appropriate when working with government officials. In addition, due to complex legal requirements, some types of bid-related information, which might be proper in a transaction with a private party, may not be requested or received when dealing with governments or their officials.

Additional information is available on the Corporate Compliance Web site.

ANTITRUST/FAIR COMPETITION

UPS's policy is to compete vigorously, aggressively, and successfully in today's increasingly competitive business climate, and to do so at all times in compliance with all applicable antitrust and competition laws throughout the world. The antitrust laws of countries around the globe are designed to preserve a competitive economy and to promote fair and vigorous competition. We are all required to comply with these laws and regulations, which are explained in more detail in the UPS Guidelines for Antitrust/Competition Law Compliance.

These guidelines cover such areas as Dealing with Customers, Commercial Counters, Competitors, Suppliers/Vendors, Attending Trade Association Meetings,

Providing Subsidiary Services, Obtaining Information about Competitors, Mergers and Acquisitions, International Business, and Writing a Document.

Fair competition standards are a matter of law in virtually every country in which we operate. We are all required to comply with these laws and regulations. Those UPS employees who are involved in marketing, sales, purchasing, or contracts, or in discussions with competitors, have a particular responsibility to ensure that they understand our standards and the applicable competition laws.

All management employees are expected to become familiar with the UPS Guidelines for Antitrust/Competition Law Compliance, and how these responsibilities apply to their current positions.

Additional information about antitrust and fair competition laws can be found in the UPS Guidelines for Antitrust/Competition Law Compliance, available on the Corporate Compliance Web site.

CHOOSING SUPPLIERS AND CONSULTANTS

We strive to be fair in our choice of suppliers and consultants and are honest in all business interactions with them. We choose our suppliers and consultants based on appropriate criteria, such as qualifications, competitive price, and reputation. Anyone responsible for buying or leasing materials or services on behalf of UPS must conscientiously guard their objectivity.

We also should avoid any implication that UPS's continued purchase of goods or services from the supplier depends on the supplier purchasing goods or services from UPS. Doing so may not only violate our policies, but may also be a violation of antitrust or fair competition laws. UPS may properly require that goods it purchases be delivered via UPS, but it would not be proper for UPS to require that its suppliers use only UPS when shipping to its other non-UPS customers.

Nothing contained in this section is intended to limit or restrict encouraging our vendors and suppliers to use UPS services. It is recommended that appropriate UPS sales people be involved in such efforts.

We also expect our suppliers and consultants—and others who do business with us or on our behalf—to conduct their business on behalf of UPS in compliance with all applicable laws and regulations and in accordance with the highest ethical standards.

Additional information can be obtained from the Corporate Procurement Department.

OUR SHAREOWNERS

INSIDER TRADING

Buying or selling securities while in possession of material, non-public information (or "inside information") may violate U.S. and other securities laws.

Inside information is information that a reasonable investor would consider important in making investment decisions and that is non-public, or has been public only for a very short time.

Examples of inside information may include:

- Contracts or proposed contracts with customers or suppliers
- Proposed acquisitions, joint ventures, or divestitures. New products or services and regulatory approvals or disapprovals
- Financial performance

Insider trading is both unethical and illegal, and we should not trade in any stock or other securities on the basis of such inside information, including inside information we learned about an organization with which UPS does or might do business.

The same rules against using inside information apply when we give that information—to someone else, so that the individual can profit from that information by trading in stock or other securities.

UPS, like many public companies, has adopted specific trading restrictions to guard against insider trading. These restrictions are designed to protect the employees and UPS from liability associated with inappropriate use of inside information, and these restrictions apply to specified employees and those living in their household. Do not confuse the applicability of these trading restrictions with the broader prohibition on trading when in you possession of inside information.

Additional information can be found in the UPS Insider Trading Compliance Guidelines available on the Corporate Compliance Web site.

INVESTMENTS

Investments in an organization with which UPS does or may do business can raise important compliance issues relating to insider trading, conflicts of interest and misuse of confidential information. The standards in this section apply to any financial or ownership interest in any company with which UPS does business (including customers, suppliers, vendors, and service partners), as well as companies with which UPS may do business (including potential customers, suppliers, vendors, and service partners) and competitors of UPS.

Investment in such an organization is not allowed if a UPS employee has direct or indirect responsibility, or even appear to conflict, with the interests of UPS. This means a UPS employee should not have any financial or ownership interest in an organization if it could cause the employee, or might be perceived by others to cause the employee, to choose between that interest and the interests of UPS. Such an investment constitutes a conflict of interest that must be avoided. If there is question about whether such an investment is or is not appropriate, the employee should consult with a manager, review the UPS Insider Trading Compliance Guidelines, or contact Corporate Compliance or Corporate Legal.

RECORDS MANAGEMENT

Many of us create or prepare some type of information during our workday, such as financial reports, accounting records, business plans, environmental reports, injury and accident reports, expense reports, and time cards. People inside and outside UPS depend on these reports to be accurate, truthful, and properly maintained. These people include employees, government representatives, auditors, and the communities in which we operate. No one may deviate from our commitment to manage information accurately and truthfully. Our records are maintained for required periods as defined in the UPS Records Retention Schedule.

Additional information can be found in the UPS Records Management Guidelines available on the Corporate Compliance Web site.

COMPANY PROPERTY AND SERVICES

The use of company time, labor, supplies, equipment, tools, buildings, or other assets for personal benefit is prohibited. Employees are required to pay for personal use of UPS services. Company property used in the course of work with UPS remains the property of UPS and must be returned upon request by UPS or upon termination of employment.

Collectively, we have a responsibility for safeguarding and making proper and efficient use of UPS's property, including:

- Company time
- Cash, checks, drafts, and charge cards
- Land and buildings
- Vehicles
- Equipment, including fax machines, copiers, and telephones
- UPS uniforms
- Materials and supplies
- Computer hardware and software
- Information assets, including electronic data and intellectual property
- Scrap and obsolete equipment.

UPS property must not be used for any purpose not related to UPS business without prior authorization from the appropriate manager.

INTELLECTUAL PROPERTY

UPS depends on intellectual property, such as information, processes, and technology. Those tools are available at our disposal because of significant investments of time and company funds. If our intellectual property is not properly protected, it becomes available to others who have not made similar investments. This would cause us to lose our competitive advantage and compromise our ability to provide unique services to our customers.

UPS intellectual property includes confidential UPS business information, trade secret technology (such as computer software and systems), patented inventions and processes, trademarks, and copyrighted works.

It is the responsibility of every UPS employee or representative to help protect UPS intellectual property. It is the responsibility of UPS managers and supervisors to foster and maintain awareness of the importance of protecting the UPS intellectual property.

Additional information is available in the UPS Intellectual Property Protection Manual, available on the Corporate Compliance Web site.

INFORMATION USE AND SECURITY

We use information technology and engage in electronic communications to manage our business efficiently, and to comply with UPS policy and legal requirements. We comply with UPS business and security practices that protect confidential and/or proprietary information. We permit brief, limited personal communications that do not violate the law or other UPS policies, and that do not interfere with our business responsibilities.

UPS is committed to the use of advanced technologies in its business operations. These powerful tools, provided for business purposes, expand the information available to us and enhance our ability to communicate with each other, our business partners, vendors, and customers.

Additional information is available in the UPS Information Use and Security Compliance Manual and UPS Intellectual Property Protection Manual, available on the Corporate Compliance Web site.

COPYRIGHTED MATERIAL

We may not reproduce, distribute, or alter copyrighted materials owned by others without a valid license or prior permission of the copyright owner or its authorized agent. It is not always easy to determine if such permission exists, and we must confirm that appropriate permission exists before using such materials.

Copyrighted works include, but are not limited to, printed articles from publications, TV and radio programs, videotapes, music performances, printed photographs, digital photographs, training materials, manuals, documentation, software programs, databases, diskettes, CDs, and Web pages. In general, the laws that apply to printed materials are also applicable to audio, visual, and electronic media. Presentation slides, training materials, management models, or other materials prepared by outside consultants or organizations also may be copyrighted.

To avoid violations of copyright laws, all UPS employees and representatives must ensure that appropriate authorization is obtained prior to using or reproducing any materials. While UPS has obtained license or other forms of permission to use and reproduce copyrighted materials, any doubt with regard to whether use is authorized should be resolved in favor of not using or reproducing the materials.

Additional information is available in the UPS Information Use and Security Compliance Manual and UPS Intellectual Property Protection Manual, available on the Corporate Compliance Web site.

TRADEMARKS

In order to maintain our reputation and the value of the UPS brand, we must ensure proper use of our name and our trademarked images at all times. UPS owns a number of symbols, brand marks, and logos that identify various aspects of our company. It is important to reproduce these images accurately, because they also represent our company and help maintain the UPS image. Incorrect usage of our trademarks by UPS employees or others should be reported to Corporate Compliance or Corporate Legal.

UPS trademarks (marks used in connection with goods) and service marks (marks used in connection with a service) that have been registered with appropriate authorities worldwide should appear in print and other visual media with the appropriate registration notice.

Correct use of registration and common law notices in all print and visual communication helps protect UPS registered marks and unregistered marks. The procedures outlined on the UPS Brand Exchange Web site must be followed for correct usage of UPS marks, or contact UPS Brand Management with any questions.

CONFIDENTIAL AND PROPRIETARY INFORMATION

Information is a valuable corporate asset. Dissemination of information is critical to our success. However, much information about UPS's business activities is confidential or proprietary. Just as UPS values and protects it own confidential and proprietary information, it is our policy and practice to respect the confidential and proprietary information of others, including information we may have about our customers, suppliers, and employees.

Because the disclosure of confidential or proprietary information could seriously damage UPS's interests, safeguarding this information is the responsibility of all UPS employees and representatives. If we learn about proprietary or confidential information during the course of employment or relationship with UPS, we should be careful not to share it with others, including other employees, unless they need to know it for a legitimate business reason that will not violate any law, regulation, or UPS policy.

We may be asked to provide information about a customer to a job function or business, but depending upon the circumstances, this could be a violation of

Antitrust/Fair Competition, Privacy, or other laws, or our contractual commitments to the customer. If employees not usually privileged to the information as a part of their job responsibilities request that information, we should consult with a manager, Corporate Compliance, or Corporate Legal prior to divulging the requested information.

We should also guard against unintentionally disclosing proprietary or confidential information. Situations that could result in inadvertent disclosure of sensitive information include: discussing confidential or proprietary information in public—in restaurants, on elevators, or on airplanes; talking about it on public or mobile phones; working with sensitive information on laptop computers in public; or transmitting such information by insecure means. Our obligation to protect UPS's confidential and proprietary information continues even after you leave the company.

Additional information can be found in the UPS Privacy Policy, the UPS Guidelines for Antitrust/Competition Law Compliance, the UPS Trading Compliance Guidelines, the Guidelines for UPS Affiliate Information Sharing, the UPS Information Use and Security Compliance Manual and UPS Intellectual Property Protection Manual.

OUR COMMUNITIES

POLITICAL ACTIVITIES AND CONTRIBUTIONS

UPS encourages all UPS employees to be informed voters, but personal participation in the political process, including contributions of time or financial support, is completely voluntary.

Election laws in some countries prohibit campaign contributions by corporations, whether by direct or indirect use of company funds or resources. In accordance with these laws, UPS does not make direct contributions to any candidate for political office where national or local law makes such contributions illegal.

As private citizens, we may participate in the political process, including contributing to the candidates or political parties of our choice. However, such personal political activities or contributions must not involve or even appear to involve use of UPS's funds or resources. UPS's funds and resources include, but are not limited to, company time, facilities, office supplies, letterhead, phones, and fax machines. Employee work time also is considered a contribution by UPS. Therefore, we cannot be paid by the company for any time spent campaigning for a political party.

U.S. election laws provide for corporations to establish and maintain political action committees, which may lawfully make campaign contributions. UPS has established a political action committee in the United States called the UPS Political Action Committee (UPSPAC). Participation in and contributions to UPSPAC are entirely voluntary and are used only for political purposes. Any employee has the right to refuse to contribute to UPSPAC without reprisal.

UPS employees who hold or seek political office must do so on their own time, whether on vacation, unpaid leave, after hours, or on weekends. Where permitted by law, UPS requests that employees obtain permission for the Secretary of the Company prior to running for political office, in order to avoid a potential conflict of interest. Any UPS employee who runs for political office will be required to complete the Business Ethics Questionnaire (BEQ). Any UPS employee who holds such an office should contact Corporate Compliance.

Additional information is available from Public Affairs. Country-specific guidance is available through Corporate Compliance.

TRANSACTING TRANSNATIONAL BUSINESS

Transnational business is vital to UPS. The laws of both the United States, and other countries in which we operate, frequently affect our transnational business transactions. Among other things, these laws regulate UPS's interaction with foreign governments and their officials, restrictive trade practices, and import and export shipments. Antitrust laws, which are discussed in the "Antitrust/Fair Competition" section, also regulate many aspects of UPS's business outside of the United States. UPS is committed to conducting its business abroad in compliance with all applicable laws. All employees involved in UPS's transnational business should be familiar with and adhere to these requirements.

ANTI-CORRUPTION COMPLIANCE

As a U.S.-based corporation, UPS is subject to the U.S. anti-bribery laws that are enforceable worldwide and cover all UPS operations, including all businesses, agents, and joint ventures. Anti-bribery laws include the Foreign Corrupt Practices Act (FCPA) and all such laws of the countries in which we operate.

Broadly speaking, the FCPA prohibits a U.S.-based company or any of its worldwide businesses or affiliates from bribing—or offering, promising, or authorizing anything of value to—a foreign government official in order to obtain or retain business. We conduct our business in accordance with the FCPA, and every one of us, regardless of the country in which we work, must adhere to its requirements.

Under the FCPA as well as other anti-bribery laws, UPS, its employees, and its agents also are prohibited from doing indirectly what we are prohibited from doing directly—we cannot make any payment to a third party if all or any part of the payment will be given to a prohibited person. UPS could be held liable for such payments even if the company did not know, but should have known, that the payment was going to a prohibited person.

All management employees are expected to become familiar with the UPS Anti-Corruption Compliance Manual, and how these responsibilities apply to their current positions, and to review them whenever their position or responsibilities change.

NEW ENTITY PROCEDURE

UPS uses various business arrangements, including independent contractors, general sales agents, and joint ventures to conduct its operations worldwide.

New entity procedures have been developed to provide a uniform basis for evaluating potential businesses for these arrangements and to minimize the potential business and legal risks that may be created through these arrangements. The due diligence in completing the New Entity Request Information Worksheet is critical and mandatory. A new relationship must not be established until the information is properly evaluated and appropriate approvals are obtained.

Additional information can be found in the UPS Anti-Corruption Compliance Manual, available on the Corporate Compliance Web site.

BOYCOTTS, EMBARGOES, AND RESTRICTIVE TRADE PRACTICES

A boycott occurs when one person, group, or country refuses to do business with certain other people or countries. As a U.S.-based company, all UPS operations must comply with U.S. laws pertaining to boycotts. U.S. anti-boycott laws generally prohibit U.S. companies and their subsidiaries from participating in or cooperating with any international boycott, unless the boycott has been approved by the U.S. government. Economic sanctions or trade embargoes imposed or approved by the United States are examples of boycotts with which we must comply.

These anti-boycott laws also require U.S. companies and their worldwide subsidiaries to report any requests they receive to engage in a boycott.

We must be particularly alert for requests for information or contract terms that:

- Request information about any person's past, present, or prospective relationship with boycotted countries or blacklisted companies.
- Request information about any person's race, religion, gender or nationality.
- Request discrimination against individuals or companies on the basis of race, religion, gender or nationality.

All employees should report any such requests to Corporate Compliance, Corporate Legal, or their region's Legal Department.

GOVERNMENT CONTROLS FOR TRANSNATIONAL SHIPMENTS

All import and export shipments are subject to regulation by various government agencies, principally Customs, both in origin and destination countries. These laws are designed to ensure that imported products are properly admitted into the country to safeguard the public and domestic industries and to ensure the proper collection of duties, taxes, and fees. We are responsible for submitting accurate information about import shipments to Customs and other applicable government agencies.

Various governments administer programs restricting and/or limiting the export and import of goods. These restrictions include embargoed countries and designated nationals, businesses, and various other entities that have violated export laws or participated in activities deemed critical to the security of that country.

All UPS employees and representatives involved in the import and export of shipments on behalf of UPS and its customers should be familiar with and adhere to all procedures and documentation necessary to properly import or export shipments.

Additional information is available from Corporate Compliance.

ENVIRONMENTAL PROTECTION

We are committed to conducting our business in a manner that protects the environment. Our commitment to the environment goes beyond complying with environmental laws and includes a commitment to advancing programs that promote improvement of the environment. Everyone who is part of the UPS organization is expected to support our effort to maintain a leadership role in protecting the environment.

Through the Corporate Environmental Affairs Department, we have established a site- and activity-specific environmental compliance and pollution prevention programs to address our environmental responsibilities. We continually evaluate improved technology and seek opportunities to improve environmental performance.

Our environmental responsibilities include:

- Properly storing, handling, and disposing of hazardous and other waste.
- Managing wastewater and storm water in compliance with applicable regulations.
- Monitoring and maintaining the integrity of underground storage tanks.
- Complying with laws regarding clean air.
- Protecting against and appropriately responding to spills and releases.
- Seeking ways to minimize waste and prevent pollution.

In addition, we must provide timely, truthful, and accurate information required in connection with applications for environmental permits and other reports called for under permits or regulatory requirements.

Additional information is available from Corporate Plant Engineering.

TRANSPORTATION REGULATIONS

The handling and transportation of many items by UPS are regulated by various national and local government authorities. These regulations cover such items as hazardous materials/dangerous goods, pharmaceuticals, alcoholic beverages, and other special commodities.

We conduct our business in accordance with the requirements imposed by external authorities in a manner that protects the safety of our people, our customers, and the public in all modes of service. We establish standards and procedures related to the handling and transportation of these items and embed them into our everyday business processes. We are all responsible for complying with applicable governmental laws and regulations worldwide and for understanding and adhering to established UPS procedures related to these transportation issues.

UPS employees, representatives, and customers are expected to comply with all applicable governmental laws and regulations, and UPS-specific requirements.

Additional information on each of these programs is available from Corporate Compliance.

HOW TO SUGGEST CHANGES TO THE CODE OF BUSINESS CONDUCT

If you have any suggestions for changes to the UPS Code of Business Conduct, please submit them promptly, as indicated below, while they are fresh in your mind. This form is included for your convenience in submitting recommendations for changes. If you prefer, you may use your own words, stationary, and format.

To: Code of Business Conduct Review Corporate Compliance United Parcel Service Corporate Office Atlanta, GA

I recommend the following change(s) be made in the UPS Code of Business Conduct:

Section on page _____

Comments:

Suggested new wording:

The Code is not an express or implied contract of employment and does not create any contractual rights of any kind between UPS and its employees. In addition, all employees should understand that the Code does not modify their employment relationship, whether at will or governed by contract. This Code is intended to clarify each employee's existing obligation for proper conduct. UPS reserves the right to amend, alter, or terminate the Code or the policies at any time for any reason.

Source: UPS Web site—http://investor.shareholder.com/ups/governance/documentdisplay.cfm?DocumentID=563. (Accessed March 2008).

Appendix 12C

Google, Inc. Code of Conduct

PREFACE

Our informal corporate motto is "Don't be evil." We Googlers generally relate those words to the way we serve our users—as well we should. But being "a different kind of company" encompasses more than the products we make and the business we're building; it means making sure that our core values inform our conduct in all aspects of our lives as Google employees.

The Google Code of Conduct is the code by which we put those values into practice. This document is meant for public consumption, but its most important audience is within our own walls. This code isn't merely a set of rules for specific circumstances but an intentionally expansive statement of principles meant to inform all our actions; we expect all our employees, temporary workers, consultants, contractors, officers, and directors to study these principles and apply them to any and all circumstances which may arise.

The core message is simple: Being a Googler means holding yourself to the highest possible standard of ethical business conduct. This is a matter as much practical as ethical; we hire great people who work hard to build great products, but our most important asset by far is our reputation as a company that warrants our users' faith and trust. That trust is the foundation upon which our success and prosperity rests, and it must be re-earned every day, in every way, by every one of us.

So please do read this code, then read it again, and remember that as our company evolves, the Google Code of Conduct will evolve as well. Our core principles won't change, but the specifics might, so a year from now, please read it for a third time. And always bear in mind that each of us has a personal responsibility to incorporate, and to encourage other Googlers to incorporate, these principles into our work and our lives.

Table of Contents

SERVING OUR USERS

Google has always flourished by serving the interests of our users first and foremost. Our goal is to build products that organize the world's information and make it accessible to our users. Here are several principles that all Googlers should keep in mind as we work toward that goal.

USEFULNESS

Our products, features and services should make Google more useful for our users, whether they're simple search users or advertisers, large companies or small companies. We have many different types of users but one primary goal for serving them all. "Is this useful?" is the one question every Googler should keep in mind during every task, every day.

HONESTY

Our communications with our users should be appropriately clear and truthful. Our reputation as a company that our users can trust is our most valuable asset, and it is up to all of us to make sure that we nourish that reputation.

RESPONSIVENESS

Part of being useful and honest is being appropriately responsive: recognizing relevant user feedback when we see it, and doing something about it. We take pride in responding to communications from our users, whether in the form of comments, questions, problems, or compliments.

TAKING ACTION

Saying that Google, and the products and services we produce, should be useful, honest, and responsive is one thing; achieving that goal 100 percent of the time is, of course, quite another. That means that improving our work over time is largely contingent on the vigilance of our staff. Any time you feel our users aren't being well served, don't hesitate to bring it to the attention of the appropriate person. Googlers don't sit back and say nothing when the interests of our users are at stake. When you feel it's warranted, we encourage you to take a stand.

RESPECTING EACH OTHER

Google is committed to maintaining a supportive work environment in which all employees reach their fullest potential as participants in and contributors to our shared endeavor. To this end, every Googler is expected to do his or her utmost to promote a respectful workplace culture that is free of harassment, intimidation, bias, and discrimination of any kind. If you know of a situation in which you feel these conditions aren't being met, you should immediately report the facts of the situation to your supervisor or the Human Resources Department or both. The important thing is that you bring the matter to Google's attention promptly, so that any concern about discrimination or harassment can be investigated and addressed appropriately.

EQUAL OPPORTUNITY EMPLOYMENT

Google is an equal opportunity employer. Employment here is based solely upon one's individual merit and qualifications directly related to professional competence. We don't discriminate on the basis of race, color, religion, national origin, ancestry, pregnancy status, sex, age, marital status, disability, medical condition, sexual orientation, gender identity, or any other characteristics protected by law. We will also make all reasonable accommodations to meet our obligations under the Americans with Disabilities Act (ADA) and state disability laws.

HARASSMENT AND DISCRIMINATION

Google is committed to maintaining a workplace environment free from discrimination and harassment. In keeping with this policy, Google strictly prohibits unlawful discrimination or harassment of any kind, including discrimination or harassment on the basis of race, color, veteran status, religion, national origin, ancestry, pregnancy status, gender, sex, age, marital status, disability, medical condition, sexual orientation, gender identity, or any other characteristics protected by law.

We strictly prohibit all forms of unlawful harassment on the part of all employees, temporary workers, independent contractors, interns, and other professional service providers. We prohibit unlawful harassment in any form, including verbal, physical, or visual harassment.

Sexual harassment includes, but isn't limited to, making unwanted sexual advances and requests for sexual favors where (1) submission to such conduct is made an explicit or implicit term or condition of employment or (2) submission to or rejection of advances is used as the basis for employment decisions affecting an individual, including granting of employee benefits. Sexual harassment also includes unwanted conduct that has the purpose or effect of substantially interfering with an individual's work performance or creating an intimidating, hostile, or offensive working environment, even if it does not lead to tangible or economic job consequences.

If you believe you've been harassed by anyone with whom you come into contact at Google, you must immediately report the incident to your supervisor, Human Resources, or both. Similarly, supervisors and managers who know of any such incident must immediately report the harassment to Human Resources, which will promptly and thoroughly investigate any complaints and take appropriate corrective action when it is warranted. Employees who are found to have violated this Code are subject to discipline up to and including immediate discharge.

As with all other provisions of this Code, retaliation for reporting any incidents of discrimination or harassment or perceived discrimination or harassment, for making any complaints of discrimination or harassment, or participating in any investigation of incidents of discrimination or harassment or perceived discrimination or harassment is strictly prohibited. If a complaint of retaliation is substantiated, appropriate disciplinary action, which may include discharge, will be taken.

Too often one hears stories of employees who were harassed, often for long periods of time, but didn't feel comfortable coming forward. We want to make it entirely clear that Google is not, and never will be, the kind of company in which any employee should ever feel that way. If you feel there's a problem, please let us know about it immediately so that any concern of discrimination or harassment can be investigated and addressed promptly and appropriately.

DRUG AND ALCOHOL USE

Our position on substance abuse is quite simple: It is incompatible with our employee's health and safety, not to mention their chances of long-term success with this company. Employees who are under the influence of alcohol or drugs while on the job can endanger themselves and others and create serious disruptions. So, while any Googler who has cracked opened a beer at a Google-sponsored event, such as at a Friday afternoon TGIF, knows that the legal consumption of alcohol by adults isn't absolutely prohibited on the Google campus, moderation and personal responsibility are the touchstones that should govern the consumption of alcohol while on Google property/worksites, attending a Google-sponsored event, or on company business. Alcohol use that leads to impaired performance or inappropriate behavior, endangers the safety of anyone, or violates the law is strictly prohibited. With regard to drugs, Google strictly prohibits the use, manufacture, possession, purchase, sale or distribution of any illegal drug or controlled substance while on Google property/worksites, attending a Google-sponsored event, or performing company business.

In cases where an employee's manager has reasonable suspicion to believe that the employee is under the influence of drugs and/or alcohol and such influence may adversely affect the employee's job performance, safety, or the safety of others in the workplace, the employee's manager may request an alcohol and/or drug screening for the employee. A reasonable suspicion is based on objective symptoms such as factors relating to the employee's appearance, behavior, speech, etc.

As a condition of employment, Google requires each employee to abide by the terms of this policy and notify the company of any criminal drug statute conviction within five days of such conviction. Each employee will be provided a copy of this policy and will be required to acknowledge that they have reviewed this policy.

Employees who violate Google's substance abuse policy are subject to discipline up to and including termination and, in certain situations, may be subject to civil or criminal penalties.

WEAPONS AND WORKPLACE VIOLENCE

Google's commitment to providing all our employees with a completely safe work environment extends to any and all forms of weapons and workplace violence. Google will not tolerate any level of violence, or the threat of violence, in our workplace. Under no circumstances should any employee bring any sort of weapon to work or threaten violence of any kind; violations of this policy will result in appropriate disciplinary action, up to and including dismissal. As with other elements of this Code, if you become aware of any violation of Google's weapons and workplace violence policy, you should report it to the Human Resources department immediately. In the case of potential violence, contact Google Security at 650-623-5555.

OUR DOG POLICY

Google's respect and affection for our canine friends is an integral facet of our corporate culture.

We have nothing against cats, per se, but we're a dog company, so as a general rule we feel cats visiting our campus would be fairly stressed out.

AVOIDING CONFLICTS OF INTEREST

A conflict of interest occurs when, because of your role at Google, you are in a position to influence a decision or situation that may result in personal gain for you or your friends or family at the expense of the company or our users. All of us at Google should avoid situations that present actual or apparent conflicts of interest; it is our responsibility to act at all times with the best interests of Google and our users in mind. In no way should you personally profit from transactions based on your relationship with Google if it harms the company.

Being open and honest about the possibility of a given conflict of interest is the key to ensuring that it doesn't become a problem. If you're ever in doubt about whether a given action or decision would or wouldn't represent a conflict of interest, please consult your manager or Google's Compliance Program Management Office beforehand.

OPENNESS

You should consider it your responsibility to promptly disclose any interest you may have that could conflict with the interests of Google. For example, if one of your family members (including your parents, siblings, children, or in-laws) is or becomes a Google supplier, customer, partner, or competitor, that may not necessarily represent a conflict of interest, but, nonetheless, the right thing to do is to let your manager know about the situation immediately.

One way to consider whether a given action, relationship, gift, etc. constitutes a conflict of interest is to imagine you are at a company meeting. Could you justify your actions in front of your peers? The answer to that question should help you evaluate the situation.

PERSONAL INVESTMENTS

You should not invest, without approval from the Audit Committee of our Board of Directors, in a Google customer, supplier, partner, or competitor if it's at all likely that your investment could compromise the fulfillment of your responsibilities as a Googler. As a general rule, the greater your responsibilities at Google, the more they relate to the relationship between Google and the customer, supplier, partner, or competitor and the larger the amount of the desired investment, the more likely it is that you're doing something that actually or apparently conflicts with the company's interests. When in doubt about whether a personal investment creates an actual or apparent conflict of interest, you should always discuss the situation with your manager or Google's Compliance Program Management Office before making the investment.

GIFTS AND ENTERTAINMENT

You should not accept any significant gift, payment, or anything else of value from customers, vendors, consultants, partners, or anyone else doing business with Google if the gift would likely be perceived as unduly influencing your business decisions or otherwise creating an actual or apparent conflict of interest. Not all gifts and entertainment necessarily represent conflicts of interest; inexpensive "token" gifts, infrequent and moderate business meals and entertainment, and invitations to events like ball games, celebratory meals, and such can be considered ordinary aspects of many Googlers' business relationships, provided that they aren't excessive or create the appearance of impropriety. Accepting an invitation to a cocktail party thrown by an advertising partner, for instance, might be considered not only an acceptable business activity but a necessary one for an AdWords sales employee. Similarly, accepting a company T-shirt or coffee mug isn't likely to change your assessment of a potential business relationship. However, tickets to something like the Olympics, Super Bowl or World Cup, especially if travel and lodging are included, are in that "gray zone" where it is important to carefully think about the context. Always ask your manager for approval when accepting these and any other significant gifts and entertainment, and don't hesitate to raise any questions or concerns you may have with the Compliance Program Management Office. Gifts of cash or cash equivalents are never permitted.

You should also be appropriately cautious when giving gifts. Google competes for business on the merits of our products, services and people, and never through the offering of improper payments, including gifts or entertainment. In fact, it's worth remembering that many of the companies with whom you have professional dealings will have gifts-and-entertainment policies of their own—many more restrictive than Google's. Be sensitive with regard to any gift you're about to give, including invitations to events, and if you think the gift you're contemplating giving might fall into that "gray zone," it's probably worth checking with your business counterpart to be sure he or she isn't, even inadvertently, violating his or her own company's policy.

BUSINESS RELATIONSHIPS

Like many of the other situations described in this Code, business relationships that you pursue outside your work at Google require above all your good faith and common sense. As a rule, professional relationships with companies that compete with Google create at least the appearance of a conflict of interest and should be avoided. Accepting personal employment or fees of any kind from any Google supplier, customer, or partner can also create conflicts with your job responsibilities at Google, especially if your job responsibilities relate in any way to the relationship between the supplier, customer, or partner and Google. Before accepting personal employment or fees from a Google supplier, customer, or partner, you should review the arrangement with your manager and, if necessary, Google's Chief Compliance Officer.

Google employees, including our senior executives, sometimes get the opportunity to serve on other companies' boards. We aren't against this as a matter of principle, but a few words of caution are in order. For one, no Google employee should ever serve as a board member for a company that directly competes with Google. In addition, becoming a board member of a company that is a Google supplier, customer or partner can present greater potential conflict of interest issues than accepting personal employment or fees from such a company. Before you join the board of a Google supplier, customer or partner, you must make sure you receive prior approval from Google's Chief Compliance Officer or General Counsel. Additionally, Google officers must review any outside board memberships with the Chief Compliance Officer or General Counsel before accepting.

It's also important to point out that business opportunities discovered through your work at Google belong first and foremost to Google; you should not pursue such an opportunity yourself unless you first disclose it fully to and receive permission to pursue it from Google's Chief Compliance Officer or General Counsel.

FRIENDS AND RELATIVES

Similarly, business relationships with friends and relatives whose interests may conflict with Google's can easily leave you with the sort of conflict of interest that can be difficult to resolve happily. Our rule here is simple: you should not enter into a Google-related business relationship with a close relative, friend or significant other, or a business they manage or control, without first contacting our Chief Compliance Officer or General Counsel. This includes, but is not limited to, appointing him, her or the business as an auditor or outside counsel, or otherwise engaging him, her or the business as a vendor or supplier of goods or services to Google.

PRESERVING CONFIDENTIALITY

As we all know, our company's confidential and proprietary information is an invaluable asset that all Googlers must take great care to protect; company information that leaks prematurely into the press or to competitors can hurt product launches, eliminate our competitive advantage, and prove costly in any number of other ways. So our responsibilities in this arena extend beyond merely not revealing confidential Google material—they also include the proper labeling, securing, and disposal of confidential Google material; the safeguarding of confidential information that Google receives from third parties under nondisclosure agreements; and internal compliance with applicable intellectual property laws, such as those protecting patents, copyrights, trade secrets, and trademarks.

The key to exercising proper vigilance in safeguarding confidential Google material is to be sure you know the proper rules of conduct in advance. To whatever extent your particular job involves dealing with confidential information, please be sure you've read the following guidelines, and bear them in mind in the course of your business dealings.

Please remember that the consequences of disclosing confidential or proprietary information can be severe, including dismissal, civil lawsuits against you (by us or others) with significant claims for, among other things, monetary damages, and/or criminal prosecution.

CONFIDENTIAL GOOGLE INFORMATION

Google's "confidential information" may include financial information, product information, user information, etc. The first rule is pretty simple: it is your responsibility to exercise all due care to ensure that confidential company material stays that way. At times, however, some particular project or negotiation properly necessitates disclosing confidential information to a third party. Disclosure of confidential information should be on a "need to know" basis. When such instances arise, be sure to first contact the Legal Department so they can draft an appropriate nondisclosure agreement for the signature of all appropriate parties. In addition, please promptly report to our Legal Department any possible infringements of Google intellectual property.

There are, of course, "gray areas" in which you will need to apply your best judgment. Suppose, for instance, that a friend who works at a non-profit charitable organization asks you for advice about how to improve that site's Google search ranking? Using your Googler knowledge to give your friend site-optimization tips that he or she could have found in any number of books, articles and Web sites isn't likely to be problematic, but giving tips that aren't publicly known definitely would be. As always, your own judgment is likely to be your best barometer—make sure you use it.

Finally: it's a small world (especially here in Silicon Valley), and some of us will undoubtedly find ourselves involved in personal relationships with people employed by one of our competitors. In this case, as in most others, common sense applies: you shouldn't tell your significant other anything the company considers confidential, any more than you'd reveal that information to a stranger at a coffee shop (and you shouldn't solicit confidential information about the competing company, either).

TRADEMARKS, LOGOS AND COPYRIGHTS

The name Google Inc., the names of numerous Google products and services, and the various logos related to those products and services are all the company's intellectual property, and unauthorized use of them can do real damage to our company's public image. So it's important to remember that any use of Google logos and trademarks must be cleared in advance by our Marketing Director.

GOOGLE PARTNERS

Just as you should be careful not to disclose confidential Google information, it's equally important not to disclose any confidential third-party information with which you may be entrusted in the course of your work. You should take care not to accept any confidential information from third parties without first contacting our Legal Department so it can draft an appropriate nondisclosure agreement. Even after the agreement is signed, try only to accept as much information as is necessary to accomplish your business objectives. Also, please remember that you are personally responsible for reading the nondisclosure agreement and abiding by its restrictions.

You should also be sure that you obtain legal licenses for any third-party software you use in your work, and that you receive a publisher's consent or consult the Legal Department, before copying any publication or software in connection with your work with Google.

COMPETITORS' INFORMATION

The level of business ethics to which we aspire requires that we apply the same rules to our competitors' information as we do to our own, and that we treat our competitors as we hope they will treat us. We respect our competitors and, above all else, believe in fair play in all circumstances; we would no sooner use a competitor's confidential information to our advantage than we would wish them to use ours. So, although gathering publicly available information about competitors is certainly a legitimate part of business competition, you should not seek out our competitors' confidential information or seek to use it if it comes into your possession. The same goes for confidential information belonging to any of your former employers. If an opportunity arises to take advantage of competitors' confidential information, remember: don't be evil. We compete, but we don't cheat.

OUTSIDE COMMUNICATIONS

As a general rule, all Googlers know that we believe in being extremely careful about disclosing company information. It's almost always a bad idea to post discussions or information about Google on the Internet or anywhere else unless you're authorized to do so as part of your job. And you should never discuss the company with members of the media unless you've been explicitly authorized to do so by our public relations department.

MAINTAINING BOOKS AND RECORDS

Accurate financial reporting is a core aspect of corporate professionalism. Our goal at Google is, and will always be, accounting transparency and accuracy.

To meet this standard, we consider it essential to maintain detailed, accurate books, records, and accounts to accurately reflect our transactions and to provide full, fair, accurate, timely, and understandable disclosure in reports and documents that we file with or submit to the Securities and Exchange Commission and in other public communications. To make sure that we get this right, Google maintains a system of internal accounting controls to reinforce and verify our own compliance with these policies. Please be certain that, in the course of your work, you always stay in full compliance with any system of internal controls that is communicated to you by the CEO, CFO, General Counsel, Chief Compliance Officer, Finance Department, or head of your department, or that is generally communicated through the company's intranet site.

BUSINESS TRANSACTIONS

Your own job at Google may or may not involve significant record-keeping; but whenever appropriate, we're all responsible for helping to make sure that Google's books are accurate. When you're involved in business transactions, be sure that you're following company procedures for carrying out and reporting them, obtaining appropriate management authorization for them (for instance, making sure you have Finance Department and, where appropriate, Legal Department approval before entering into revenue-related contracts), and maintaining appropriate documentation for them.

REPORTING PROCEDURES

Whenever the occasion arises, you should do everything possible to cooperate with our accounting/finance team, external auditors, and legal counsel by giving them candid, thorough information to ensure that our books and records are accurate. If your job calls it for it, you should make sure that you're fully familiar with Google's policies, such as our revenue recognition policy for the recording of sales and our purchasing policy for purchases, and that you report to the Finance Department any transactions of which you think they may not be aware.

REPORTING IRREGULARITIES

Needless to say, you should never, ever in any way interfere with or seek to improperly influence, directly or indirectly, the auditing of Google's financial records; and you should never falsify any book, record or account, including time reports, expense accounts, and other personal Google records.

If in the course of your work you come to suspect accounting irregularities, no matter how small, you should immediately report them in accordance with our Reporting of Financial and Accounting Concerns Policy.

PROTECTING GOOGLE'S ASSETS

Google has (and intends to maintain) a well-earned reputation for generosity when it comes to employee benefits. But our long-term success will also depend on our ability to be smart about conserving company resources. Here are a few guidelines to follow in aiming to avoiding needless waste.

COMPANY EQUIPMENT

Googlers should always take care to conserve company assets and equipment. All Google employees are provided with every possible tool we need to do our jobs effectively and comfortably, which makes it even more incumbent on all of us to avoid needless waste. Nobody's going to complain if you snag an extra bagel on Friday morning, but as a general rule, company funds, equipment, and other assets should not be requisitioned for purely personal use. If you aren't sure whether or not a given usage of company assets is okay, please ask your manager or Human Resources.

COMPUTER AND OTHER COMMUNICATIONS RESOURCES

Google's computer, telephony, and other communications resources are a crucial aspect of our company's property, both physical and intellectual. Please take all due care to maintain the security and privacy of these resources, and if you have any reason to believe that our network security has been violated—if, for instance, you have reason to believe that your network password may have been compromised—please promptly report the incident to the senior director of Information Services.

NEED TO ACCESS AND MONITOR COMMUNICATIONS ON GOOGLE FACILITIES AND PREMISES

From time to time, Google is required by law (for example, a subpoena or warrant) to monitor, access and disclose the contents of email, voicemail, computer files, other messages or files in transit or storage on our electronic facilities, and other materials on Google facilities or premises. In addition, Google has a strong interest in protecting its employees and users and maintaining the security of its resources and property. Consistent with that interest, Google reserves the right to monitor, access and disclose communications made on or information stored in any and all of its work areas, work product and equipment, including technological resources.

This means that Google cannot guarantee the confidentiality of personal materials stored on our systems or facilities, including personal communications made on Google's email or voicemail systems or personal materials stored physically or electronically on Google's premises or on computers on Google's premises. This also means that for legitimate business purposes (such as the need to access business records, to administer electronic facilities, to investigate suspected misconduct or to prevent misconduct from occurring), we monitor, access, and disclose information or communications, including personal information and communications, made or stored on Google facilities or premises. Finally, it goes without saying that misuse of company property or resources or any other misconduct discovered through monitoring, access or disclosure, regardless of the reason for the monitoring, access or disclosure, is a violation of this Code and is subject to appropriate disciplinary action, up to and including termination of employment.

DATA PRIVACY

Google collects, stores, uses, and shares personal employee information from around the world. Use this data only in accordance with local data protection laws and Google's privacy policy.

THIRD-PARTY SUPPLIERS

As our company grows, we strike more and more deals with third-party suppliers of equipment and services—and we always strive to strike the best possible deal. If you're involved in selecting suppliers of goods or services, we strongly urge you to solicit competing bids to make sure that you're getting the best price. Still, price isn't the only factor worth considering; also take into account quality, service, and the terms and conditions of the proposed deal.

COMPANY CONTRACTS

Signing a contract on behalf of the company is a big deal. Please be sure never to enter into any contract unless you are authorized to do so (and if you are unsure if you are authorized, ask the Finance Department) and until it has been reviewed or approved as a form by the Legal Department. And even with these rules in mind, be careful never to sign a contract without first taking the time to study it yourself until you fully understand its terms.

OBEYING THE LAW

Google takes its responsibilities to comply with applicable laws and regulations very seriously. Although we recognize that it is probably impossible for you to understand all aspects of every applicable law, please take the time to familiarize yourself with the major laws and regulations that apply to your work and take advantage of our Legal Department to assist you and answer questions. We must all remember that our reputation is the foundation of our present and future success—and that earning, and maintaining, that reputation requires attention and effort to stay in compliance with the law.

IMPROPER PAYMENTS

Payments made to corruptly influence the recipient or to otherwise gain an improper advantage in any situation are never acceptable at Google. Such improper payments not only expose Google to possible criminal prosecution but may also result in the prosecution of any employees who may have been involved in the making of any such payments. In fact, even offering to make such an improper payment may be a crime. Google expressly prohibits improper payments in all business dealings, in every country around the world, with both governments and the private sector. Improper payments should not be confused with reasonable and limited expenditures for gifts, business entertainment, and customer travel and living expenses directly related to the promotion of products or services or the execution of a contract. These payments are acceptable, subject to specific Google guidelines.

EXPORT CONTROLS

The United States is among a number of countries that maintain controls on the destinations to which products or software may be exported. The United States regulations are complex and apply both to exports from the United States and to exports of products from other countries, when those products contain components or technology of American origin. Software created in the United States is subject to these regulations even if it's duplicated and packaged abroad. In some circumstances, an oral presentation containing technical data made to foreign nationals in the United States may even constitute a controlled export.

The bottom line here is, if you're in any way involved in the exporting of Google products, services, software, or any form of technology to a foreign country or countries, or if you're considering beginning such a transaction, you should work with your manager to be absolutely certain that the transaction or transactions in question stay well within the bounds of U.S. law. If you and your manager aren't sure, please contact the Legal Department.

ANTITRUST LAWS

Most countries have laws designed to encourage and protect free and fair competition. These laws often regulate a company's relationships with its distributors, resellers, dealers, partners, customers, and competitors. Generally speaking, these laws prohibit arrangements with competitors that restrain trade in some way, abuse intellectual property rights, or employ monopoly power, price discrimination, and other forms of unfair competition. Although the spirit of these laws, known as "antitrust," "competition," "consumer protection," or "unfair competition" laws, is straightforward, their application to particular situations can be quite complex. To ensure that Google complies fully with these laws, each of us should have a basic knowledge of them as they apply to our work, and should contact our Legal Department before questionable situations arise.

INSIDER TRADING

In the course of your employment, you may learn of material information about Google or other companies before it is made public. You may simply overhear a hallway conversation or come across a memo left at a copy machine. Using this information for financial or other personal benefit or conveying this information to others constitutes a violation of this Code and may even violate the law. This includes buying or selling the securities of Google or any other company about which you have material non-public information or giving this "inside information" to anyone else who might use it to buy or sell securities.

USING OUR CODE

It's impossible to spell out every possible ethical scenario we Googlers might face, so we rely on one another's discretion and judgment to uphold this policy. We expect all Googlers to accept and be guided by both the letter and the spirit of this Code. Often this will mean making judgment calls about situations. When it comes to ethical conduct, we believe in erring on the side of caution, but not all violations are equally serious. That isn't an easy call, so if you aren't sure, by all means don't be afraid to ask questions of your manager or our Legal Department.

We should all consider it part of our job at Google not just to follow this Code but to help enforce it as well. If you know of a situation or incident that you feel may violate this Code, please report it to your manager or to Human Resources. Your report will be reviewed, and any Googler found to have violated any of the terms of this Code will be subject to disciplinary action, up to and including termination of employment. We'll also take any appropriate steps to prevent any further violations.

Finally, Google enforces a strict "no retaliation" policy. Retaliation for reporting a possible violation of this Code, otherwise making a complaint regarding a possible violation of this Code or participating in any investigation of a possible violation of this Code, is strictly prohibited. If a complaint of retaliation is substantiated, appropriate disciplinary action will be taken, up to and including termination.

Chapter 13

The Audit Committee and Information Technology

Perhaps no governance subject has elicited as much commentary as that of the depth and extent of oversight participation in an organization's information technology (IT) systems appropriate for the full board. Because risk management is a well-recognized subject assigned by the board to the audit committee, this committee is likely to be deeply involved with oversight of IT activities. Heightening concerns over IT is the increased use of the Internet as a marketing tool, worries about IT security, and the fact that recent events have demonstrated the dependency of virtually every organization on its IT resources. For example, although the computer systems at several mainline U.S. air carriers were out of service for only a few hours, the operational aftermath of these misfortunes in terms of flight delays and cancellations lasted for days. The reputational damage suffered may be even longer-lasting. Additionally, numerous examples of data security breaches in both private industry and government have surfaced and have resulted in reputational damage, the long-term effects of which may turn out to be very significant.

INTRODUCTION

Since IT is viewed, perhaps sometimes wrongly, as totally concerned with technical matters, the argument has been raised that directors should be involved with matters relating to IT only on a limited and extremely high-level basis. The conclusion that the board should give limited attention to IT matters, however, is unwarranted. The risks associated with an organization's use of IT methods can be significant to the welfare of the entity. Regulatory burdens associated with data security are increasing. Additionally, the costs of IT represent a substantial portion of the total costs being incurred by firms, especially those in the financial services and other service organizations.

In view of these factors, it would seem evident that the board, and especially the audit committee, should provide active and informed oversight of IT issues. These include matters relating to the efficiencies that are involved with operating the IT function, including the costs of developing new applications as well as maintaining continuing services. Issues of data security and IT disaster recovery should be important aspects of the entity's risk management processes, the oversight of which is a critically important audit committee responsibility.

Opinions by governance thought leaders concerning board and thereby audit committee involvement with IT run a gamut of views. Some think of IT as merely a mechanism for achieving the strategic objectives agreed to by the board; they believe that having much meaningful involvement with IT issues is interfering with management responsibilities and should be virtually off the board's agenda as it is viewed.

On the other end of the spectrum, leaders in the field of governance believe that IT is tightly intertwined with and thus an integral and key element of the business strategies of many organizations today. They believe that most companies could not survive an IT disaster and will not be successful in the long term without effective and efficient IT applications. Therefore, these experts believe that the board should be well informed about the organization's IT strategies, plans, processes, and new investments.

The prudent course for audit committees and directors depends on many matters specific to their organizations. These factors include the sophistication of the entity's IT infrastructure; whether IT is utilized to provide a basic service to customers, as in online banking or brokerage; and how integrated IT is into the operating environment of the organization. Examples of the latter case include a retail organization that utilizes point-of-sale data to automatically reorder, track, and ship merchandise to its stores. A just-in-time manufacturing process would be another example of high IT integration.

Further factors to be considered in the committee's assessment of the level of IT risks include the strength of existing controls and the competence of the organization's IT professionals. What is clear, however, is that the oversight of IT issues cannot be totally delegated to IT professionals, but must receive the same board/ committee level scrutiny as other systems, strategies, and initiatives.

IT GOVERNANCE CONCEPTS

According to the IT Governance Institute (ITGI), organized by ISACA, formerly the Information Systems Audit and Control Association, a membership organization of IT professionals,

> IT governance is the responsibility of the board of directors and executive management. It is an integral part of enterprise governance and consists of the leadership and organizational structures and processes that ensure that the organization's IT sustains and extends the organization's strategies and objectives.[1]

The ITGI notes the importance of information necessary for decision making as well as the transaction management aspects of IT. The institute believes that this

[1] IT Governance Institute, *Board Briefing on IT Governance, Second Edition,* (2003), p. 10. See ISACA Web site http://www.isaca.org/Template_ITGI.cfm?Section=Business,_Management_and_Governance1&Template=/ContentManagement/ContentDisplay.cfm&ContentFileID=4667.

importance has resulted in IT becoming an integral part of businesses and is a fundamental asset necessary for support, sustenance, and growth. It thinks that successful enterprises understand and manage the risks and constraints of IT. Consequently, boards of directors and audit committees understand the strategic importance of IT and have made the governance of IT an important aspect of their total oversight responsibilities.

The definition of IT governance, according to the IT Compliance Institute (ITCi), is also expansive. IT governance needs to cover the structures, core definitions, and processes that shape all IT systems and efforts. The auditable areas also available for oversight that are on ITCi's list include:

1. Definition of what the IT organization is and does, including values and goals.
2. IT risk definition and management.
3. Definition of roles and responsibilities, including leadership structures.
4. Strategic planning, monitoring, and continual improvement.
5. Oversight of standards, policies, and procedures.
6. Oversight of technical foundations, such as IT infrastructure, architectures, a semantic baseline or glossary, and data management.
7. Asset management, including staff, systems, media, networks, and content.
8. Resource planning.
9. Investment management.[2]

OBJECTIVES OF IT GOVERNANCE

The *Board Briefing on IT Governance*, 2nd edition, by ITGI provides specific recommendations to make IT governance effective. Boards and management need to assess their capacity to:

- Take advantage of IT's enabling capacity for new business models and changing business practices.
- Balance IT's increasing costs and information's increasing value to obtain an appropriate return from IT investments.
- Manage the risks of doing business in an interconnected digital world and the dependence on entities beyond the direct control of the enterprise.
- Manage IT's impact on business continuity due to increasing reliance on information and IT in all aspects of the enterprise.
- Maintain IT's ability to build and maintain knowledge essential to sustain and grow the business.
- Avoid the failures of IT, increasingly impacting the enterprise's value and reputation[3].

[2] IT Compliance Institute, *IT Audit Checklist: IT Governance and Strategy* (2007), p. 4.
[3] ITGI, *Board Briefing on IT Governance,* p. 7.

The primary goal of IT governance is to make sure that the entity's expectations for IT are fulfilled while risks are mitigated.

According to ITGI, the IT issues of greatest importance that require governance attention from audit committees are:

1. *Strategic alignment* of the IT structure, with focus on aligning it with the business's strategies, objectives and solutions.
2. *Value delivery*, concentrating on optimizing expenditures and proving the value of IT to provide competitive advantage.
3. *Risk management*, addressing the safeguarding of IT assets including legal and regulatory compliance, disaster recovery and continuity of operations.
4. *Resource management*, optimizing knowledge and IT infrastructure.[4]

The general objectives for IT governance stated by ITCi are to ensure that technology assets and the information they contain are known, available, credible, and protected. Since regulatory legislation seeks the same objectives, good IT governance must be aligned with regulatory compliance. Beyond these general statements, ITCi sees the benefits of sound IT governance as:

1. Better alignment between business and IT strategy.
2. More informed, practical decisions about technology investments.
3. Greater agility in meeting shifting business demands, and a stronger foundation for innovation.
4. Better measurement and control of costs related to information systems and their protection.
5. Lower risk of noncompliance with regulatory requirements.
6. Lower risk of serious business disruption from events.
7. More healthy organizational relationships and reputation with directors, business staff, customers, and partner organizations.[5]

ITCi outlines the IT governance responsibilities of the board of directors as:

- Provide oversight: ask the right questions, encourage the right results.
- Set IT strategy and direction with executive input.
- Define IT governance culture[6].

---

[4] Id., pp. 22–29.

[5] IT Compliance Institute, *IT Audit Checklist*; IT Governance Institute, *Board Briefing*, p. 6.

[6] IT Governance Institute, *Board Briefing on IT Governance,* p. 9.

AUDIT COMMITTEE INVOLVEMENT WITH IT MATTERS

A survey of audit committee members performed by KPMG's Audit Committee Institute (ACI) and the National Association of Corporate Directors (NACD)[7] indicates that oversight of IT risks is ranked as one of the top three priorities for audit committees in 2007. Only Sarbanes-Oxley Section 404 compliance and oversight of accounting judgments and estimates ranked higher. But in terms of accomplishment, only 15% of the respondents were "very satisfied" with their oversight of IT, and about one in five said their IT risk oversight needed improvement. Some 90 percent of respondents said the audit committee should devote more agenda time to IT risk oversight.

"With IT supporting vital information about a company's finances, operations and competitive position—and with IT investments consuming a substantial portion of corporate budgets—more audit committees are recognizing that information and the technology driving it could pose significant risks to the company's financial reporting and compliance efforts," said Ed Smith, ACI's executive director.[8]

The results of a survey of more than 400 directors of U.S. companies conducted by Deloitte Consulting also shows the divergence of opinions over the optimal degree of board/audit committee involvement in oversight of IT matters.[9] According to the survey, implementing the right IT strategy is "very important" in successful compliance to 69% of respondents, in learning about and retaining customers to 66%, in managing risk to 57%, and in competitive positioning to 50%.

Yet the Deloitte survey notes a dichotomy between a belief that IT has high importance and the low level of directors' interaction with issues in the area. Only 14% of directors are "completely and actively involved" in IT strategy. Also, 66% say IT matters should be discussed at the board level, but only 11% have that discussion at every meeting. Only 10% say it is something they [consciously] leave to a committee. As to breakdowns in IT strategy that caused or contributed to a significant failure to achieve a particular goal, 28% blame the IT strategy itself, 44% a lack of alignment between IT strategy and business, and 43% due to missed deadlines in putting the strategy into effect.

The ITGI briefing paper notes the same disconnect between desirable and actual oversight. It states that in many enterprises, expectations of IT and reality often do not match, and boards are faced with:

---

[7] KPMG Press Release, "Audit Committees Stay Focused on Financial Reporting Oversight, but Awareness of Other Risks Grows, ACI/NACD Survey Shows," June 20, 2007. See KPMG Audit Committee Institute Web site, http://www.kpmg.com/aci/docs/News_Release--Annual_Audit_Committee_Member_Survey.pdf.

[8] Id.

[9] Deloitte Consulting, LLP/Corporate Board Member, "You're Talking, Not Walking." See https://www.corpgov.deloitte.com/binary/com.epicentric.contentmanagement.servlet.ContentDeliveryServlet/USEng/Documents/Board%20Governance/Information%20Quality%20and%20Technology/Big%20Conundrum%20DC%20032007.pdf.

- Business losses, reputational damage and a weakened competitive position
- Inability to obtain or measure a return from IT investments
- Failure of IT initiatives to bring the innovation and benefits they promised
- Technology that is inadequate or even obsolete
- Inability to leverage available new technologies
- Deadlines that are not met and budgets that are overrun[10]

Audit committee members that have a particular interest in the detailed and more technical aspects of the oversight of IT matters may find interesting the *IT Governance Implementation Guide: Using COBIT® and Val IT*, 2nd edition.[11] This guidance is published by ISACA—previously known as the Information Systems Audit and Control Association—and provides a generic road map for implementing IT governance using CobiT and Val IT frameworks.

20 QUESTIONS TO ASK ABOUT IT

The Canadian Institute of Chartered Accountants has published IT oversight guidance to directors in the form of questions directors should ask.[12] The questions are divided into three issue categories: Strategic, Internal Control, and Risk. Strategic issues include:

1. *Strategy and planning.* IT should not be omitted from the overall strategic planning process and should include the elements of the organizational-wide process, such as top management involvement and support, key employee involvement, and resulting action plans with appropriate time schedules.
   - Does management have a strategic information systems plan in place that is monitored and updated as required? Does this plan form the basis for the annual plans, annual and long-term budgets and prioritization of information technology projects?
2. *Technology trends.* Because IT is a rapidly changing field, organizations need to keep their systems current in view of the need to integrate with business partners, customers, and suppliers.
   - Have appropriate procedures been established to ensure that the organization is aware of technology trends, periodically assessing them and taking them into consideration when determining how it can better position itself?

[10] IT Governance Institute, *Board Briefing on IT Governance*, p. 8.

[11] Information Systems Audit and Control Association, *IT Governance Implementation Guide: Using COBIT® and Val IT, Second Edition.* See IASACA Web site www.isaca.org. http://www.isaca.org/Template.cfm?Section=Home&Template=/ContentManagement/ContentDisplay.cfm&ContentID=32290.

[12] Canadian Institute of Chartered Accountants, *20 Questions Directors Should Ask about IT* (Toronto: CICA, 2004).

3. *Performance*. Proper performance metrics point to areas that can be improved or that require change in order to be cost-effective and efficient.
   - Have key performance indicators and drivers of the IT department been determined? Are they monitored from time to time and are they benchmarked against industry standards?
   - Have relevant indicators been defined and monitored to manage the performance of the organization's third-party service providers?
4. *Personnel*. Productive IT personnel are difficult to obtain and retain. Effective governance assures that the organization has strong programs in place to control turnover, guide training, and promote professional development of IT personnel.
   - How has management identified the required technology expertise and how is top talent attracted?
   - Does management have appropriate procedures to address information technology employee turnover, training, and project assignment?
5. *Governance*. IT should be linked to the highest executive levels of the organization. Some organizations have appointed Chief Information Officers, reporting to the CEO or even directly to the audit committee or board.
   - Has the board considered the creation of an IT subcommittee or assigned a board member specific responsibility for the organization's investment in, and use of, information technology?
   - Has the responsibility for IT governance been assigned to a person in a sufficiently senior management position? How does management communicate IT policies to personnel?
   - What procedures are in place to ensure that the company's systems and management are in compliance with Sarbanes-Oxley [or similar rules] as appropriate?

The internal control category includes:

1. *Risk and controls*. Organizations should analyze threats to their information systems to determine the degree of risk that exists. Controls designed to reduce these risks to acceptable levels should be installed and operated. The governance structure should assure that an effective monitoring structure exists that regularly revisits the risk analysis, control implementation, and monitor of the IT system.
   - Does management have a plan to periodically conduct risk assessments covering the organization's use of information technology, including internal systems and processes, outsourced services and the use of third-party communications and other services? If it does, are the results of the assessments acted on where appropriate or required?
   - How does management ensure data integrity, including relevance, completeness, accuracy and timeliness, and its appropriate use within the organization?

- What arrangements does the organization have for the regular review and audit of its systems to ensure risks are sufficiently mitigated and controls are in place to support the major processes of the business?

2. *Personal Information Privacy*. Legal and regulatory requirements to safeguard the privacy of the information about individuals gathered throughout the organization mandate consideration of this issue as primary.
   - Has the organization assigned someone the responsibility for privacy policy, privacy legislation, compliance therewith?
   - Has the organization identified the various legislative and regulatory requirements for protecting personal information and developed a policy and procedures for monitoring compliance with them?

The risk category includes:

1. *E-business*. Utilization of e-business as a business strategy increases existing risks and adds new risks to the organization.
   - If the organization uses e-business to buy or sell products or services, has there been a specific review of the risks and controls over the e-business activities?
   - Are the organization's e-business activities appropriately protected from external and internal attack by unauthorized persons or others that, if successful, would result in loss of customer satisfaction or public embarrassment?
2. *Availability (continuity of service)*. It is paramount that plans and implementation mechanisms are in place to provide backup service in the event of a service outage. Formal recovery plans must be tested and in place to ensure that systems can be brought back into service as rapidly as possible.
   - Has the organization developed formal availability [continuity of service] policies? Has it implemented effective controls to provide reasonable assurance that systems and data are available in conformity with approved policies?
   - Does the organization understand the impact of an interruption in service and are there plans in place to deal with potential interruptions? Has a business continuity plan been adopted? If it has been adopted, is it tested regularly and are the test results used to improve the plan?
3. *Legal Issues*. Illegal copying and noncompliance with software licenses has resulted in fines and embarrassment. It is also essential that organization systems be used for acceptable purposes.
   - Has management considered and addressed legal implications that pertain to the use of software, hardware, service agreements and copyright laws?
   - Have policies covering licenses, agreements, copyright, and acceptable use been formulated and disseminated to all personnel?

ITCi CONTROLS FOR IT GOVERNANCE

The ITCi checklist of IT governance controls is organized into management controls, operational controls, and technical controls and is presented as Appendix13A.

KEY POINTS IN CHAPTER 13

1. The board, likely through its audit committee, is responsible for ensuring that the IT function, just like every other major function, is operating effectively and efficiently. Since so many operational processes now depend on IT, its security and continuity of service are among the most vital issues with which audit committees must contend.
2. IT governance should involve issues in three aspects of the business: strategy, internal control, and risk. Controls to ensure the effective performance of IT governance are necessary in three areas: management controls, operational controls, and technical controls.
3. Benefits from appropriate oversight of IT include:
   - Better alignment of the IT structure with business strategies and objectives.
   - Increased value from optimizing expenditures and improving competitive advantage.
   - Improved risk management, including regulatory compliance and disaster recovery.
   - Optimal IT resources and knowledge.
4. Proper IT governance should aim to avoid problems involving a wide gamut of issues:
   - Business losses, reputational damage, and a weakened competitive position.
   - Inability to obtain or measure a return from IT investments.
   - Failure of IT initiatives to bring the innovation and benefits they promised.
   - Technology that is inadequate or even obsolete.
   - Inability to leverage available new technologies.
   - Deadlines that are not met and budgets that are overrun.
5. A KPMG/NACD survey of audit committees reveals that oversight of IT risks ranked as one of the top three priorities for audit committees in 2007.

Appendix 13A

IT Governance Controls Checklist

MANAGEMENT CONTROLS

IT responsibilities and objectives

- A business model exists for the IT organization
- Management sets an appropriate "tone at the top" for IT activities, policies, and processes
- IT's organizational commitments and expectations are documented and communicated
- The IT organization adheres to corporate values
- The IT organization enforces a code of conduct

Roles and responsibilities

- Roles, responsibilities, and relationships of C-level officers (CEO, COO, CIO), executives, and management are defined, documented, communicated, and understood
- Roles and responsibilities are aligned with the execution and continuous improvement of short- and long-term plans
- An IT organization chart exists and includes management and reporting structures
- Accountability for policies and procedures is documented and acknowledged by management and staff

External influences

- IT leaders understand and monitor regulatory definitions and requirements
- IT leaders track industry processes and norms

Planning

- The IT organization maintains short- and long-term plans. Short-term plans execute the long-term plans
- Plans state objectives and performance metrics

- Plans indicate appropriate budget, timelines, and staff allocations
- Plans are evaluated by stakeholders for appropriateness and execution
- Strategic plans and changes to long-range plans are communicated to stakeholders
- Executive management is involved in critical decisions regarding information security, records management, operational management, business continuity, and other IT regimes

IT investment management

- IT management identifies business needs for new projects
- IT management evaluates new project proposals against IT and business objectives
- IT management tracks assets associated with new projects
- IT managers monitor project performance
- IT evaluates proposed new projects with deference to the entire project portfolio
- IT performs investment reviews and analysis to assess project performance versus expectations
- IT documents project selection criteria
- IT documents authority and alignment of managers responsible for project selection and oversight
- IT performs post-implementation reviews and evaluates stakeholder feedback
- IT management annually reviews project portfolios and identifies opportunities for improvement
- IT plans and documents system and technology succession
- IT benchmarks the investment process
- IT uses investment benchmarking to reduce risk associated with strategic business change

Resource management

- An IT budget is maintained. IT leadership is accountable to corporate management for budget adherence
- IT sets appropriate budgets for projects
- Appropriate staff, systems, and processes are dedicated to the IT governance effort

Monitoring and reporting

- Management monitors and measures organizational performance
- Management reviews short- and long-term plans compared to performance
- Reporting policies and mechanisms are well defined and understood
- Management receives and reviews project standards

- IT executives review key IT controls for financial reporting, transaction processing, electronic messaging, data and database management, information protection, and e-content management
- Contingency and failure reporting policies exist, escalation processes are documented, and policies and processes are communicated and understood
- Performance metrics are established and regularly measured against objectives
- Staff performance appraisals are completed regularly

Continuous improvement

- Plans and timetable exist to remediate identified IT governance control weaknesses
- Plans exist to standardize systems, policies, and processes across operations
- Management directs plan improvement based on monitoring results
- Management attempts to streamline redundant, incompatible, and overly complex processes
- Management ensures existence and adequacy of training programs

OPERATIONAL CONTROLS

Controls exist to meet compliance requirements

- Management sets levels and assurance metrics for information security
- Management is rapidly notified of security breaches
- Management tracks contractual definitions and requirements
- IT maintains an inventory of technology assets, including functions and relation to business processes. Assets include hardware, software, storage media, networks, and electronic content
- The IT organization has a standardized semantic baseline (glossary) for the development of policies and procedures
- The IT infrastructure is mapped and inventoried, infrastructure management documents are regularly updated and reviewed
- Data management and data stewardship policies and procedures are documented and enforced
- Management sets project scope and requirements prior to project start

TECHNICAL CONTROLS

- An enterprise architecture model exists and is enforced
- Management ensures that appropriate technical controls exist and are effective for major compliance practice areas, including data protection, content

management and e-discovery, and electronic messaging (e-mail, instant messaging, blogs, etc.)

- Management sets and enforces strategic data-management best practices, including policies for data dictionaries, master data management, and data integrity and quality controls
- IT automates controls in order to reduce resource requirements and ensure consistency and quality of results

---

Source: IT Compliance Institute: IT Audit Checklist Series, IT Governance and Strategy by Cass Brewer and Dan Swanson. Used with permission. http://download.101com.com/pub/itci/Files/ITCi_ITACL-Governance_0702c.pdf

Chapter 14

Audit Committee Issues in Not-for-Profit Entities

Not-for profit corporations are generally organized under a different state statute than those organized as for-profit. There is less commonality among state laws than is the case in for-profit corporations. Nevertheless, members of audit committees, directors and trustees of non-for-profit organizations should possess the same characteristics of good board and committee membership as the for-profit sector. Thus, this chapter covers only aspects of governance unique to not-for-profits.

The principal public outcry for governance reform occurred in the private sector and resulted in the enactment of the Sarbanes-Oxley Act of 2002, yet the not-for-profit sector has had its share of scandals as well. They include the bankruptcy of the Allegheny Health, Education, and Research Foundation as well as unfortunate incidents at The Nature Conservancy and United Way of the National Capital Area. Likewise, governmental agencies and entities doing business with federal, state, or local governments and agencies are subject to specific requirements that are designed to result in effective governance.

INTRODUCTION

Although most of the audit committee duties that are mandated by statute or regulation apply only to publicly held corporations, many of them are considered to be best business practices for all organizations. Few if any duties pertain to not-for-profit entities alone. One area that deserves more emphasis at not-for-profit enterprises is the need to establish and maintain an ethical culture within the organization. Accomplishing the mission of the organization requires the public perception that activities supporting that mission take precedence over every other motivation and that no personal enrichment or other benefit accrues to management, the board of directors, or staff.

It is well understood in all organizations that the key to good corporate governance is an ethical organizational culture. Culture depends on a strong tone at the top that permeates the entire organization. Also necessary is the motivation incentive for employees to report suspicious and possibly illegal or unethical behavior as well as the ability to do so without fear of retaliation. Recognition that reporting of unethical behavior supports the entity and should not be penalized or looked down on is important. Anonymous reporting is also an important part of the mitigating circumstances contained in the U.S. Sentencing Guidelines, which apply to all organizations. Fraud research shows that detection is most often accomplished through insider tips.

STATE STATUTES EMBRACE SARBANES-OXLEY REQUIREMENTS

California has enacted requirements that parallel some aspects of Sarbanes-Oxley. California SB 1262 is known as the Non-Profit Integrity Act. It requires nonprofits with gross revenues over $2 million, not counting amounts for which a governmental entity requires an accounting, to comply with these requirements:

1. Audit by an independent auditor
2. Audited financial statements disclosed to public
3. Independent audit committee
4. Review CEO [chief executive officer] and CFO [chief executive officer] compensation
5. Fundraising contracts must contain stipulated provisions[1]

Other states have joined the movement to impose stricter financial oversight and independence obligations on nonprofit boards as well. New Hampshire passed a law requiring nonprofit organizations with revenues in excess of $500,000 to submit audited financial statements with their Form 990s. Connecticut, Kansas, and Maine have passed similar laws. In other states, nonprofit accountability bills are in various stages of consideration.

FEDERAL VOLUNTEER PROTECTION ACT OF 1997 AND SIMILAR STATE STATUTES

The Federal Volunteer Protection Act was enacted on June 18, 1997.[2] It provides that a volunteer working for a 501(c)3 organization has a complete defense against tort claims. The General Rule is that "Punitive damages may not be awarded against a volunteer in an action brought for harm based on the action of a volunteer acting within the scope of the volunteer's responsibilities to a nonprofit organization or governmental entity unless the claimant establishes by clear and convincing evidence that the harm was proximately caused by an action of such volunteer which constitutes willful or criminal misconduct, or a conscious, flagrant indifference to the rights or safety of the individual harmed."[3]

[1] California SB 1262, Chapter 919, Statutes of 2004.
[2] P.L. 105–19.
[3] 42 USCS § 14503 (e).

A volunteer, for purposes of this act is anyone who:

1. performs services (including officers, directors, trustees, and direct service volunteers);
2. for a nonprofit organization or governmental entity; and
3. either: (a) receives no compensation (although reasonable reimbursement for expenses incurred is allowed), or (b) does not receive anything of value in lieu of compensation, in excess of $500 per year.[4]

In general, under the Volunteer Protection Act, a volunteer is protected from liability if all of these conditions are met:

- The volunteer was "acting within the scope of the volunteer's responsibilities" in the organization at the time of the act or omission.
- The volunteer is properly licensed, certified, or authorized by the appropriate authorities of the State for the activities taken, if such is "appropriate or required."
- The volunteer is not guilty of willful or criminal misconduct, gross negligence, reckless misconduct, or "a conscious, flagrant indifference" to the rights or safety of the individual harmed.
- The harm was not caused by the operation of a vehicle, vessel, or aircraft where the State requires an operator's license or insurance.[5]

In addition, the act provides that state laws may impose conditions that would preclude a volunteer from being covered by the act. The state may:

- Require an organization to "adhere to risk management procedures," including mandatory training of volunteers.
- Make an organization liable for the acts or omissions of its volunteers to the same extent as an employer is liable for the acts or omissions of its employees.
- Provide that there is no limitation of liability in actions brought by the state or a local government.
- Require the limitation of liability to be contingent upon an organization providing a financially secure source of recovery, such as an insurance policy, to pay losses up to a specified amount.[6]

Specific exemptions from coverage under the act may occur if there is misconduct by the volunteer:

1. That constitutes a crime of violence or terrorism for which the defendant has been convicted

---

[4] 42 USCS § 14505 (6).
[5] 42 USCS § 14503 (a).
[6] 42 USCS § 14503 (d).

2. That constitutes a hate crime
3. That involves a sexual offense for which the defendant has been convicted
4. Where the defendant has been found to have violated a federal or state civil rights law
5. Where the defendant was under the influence of drugs or alcohol at the time of the misconduct[7]

Many states have enacted similar laws that protect unpaid volunteers in not-for-profit and charitable organizations from being sued for damages due to their ordinary negligence. Directors and trustees of not-for-profit organizations are advised to obtain legal counsel as to the provisions of the laws in which their organization is organized.

IRS REPORTING BY NOT-FOR-PROFIT ENTITIES

Most not-for-profit entities that are exempt from income taxation are annually required to file Form 990, "Return of Organization Exempt from Income Tax." This is a document reporting the operations of the organization in three categories: Program Service, Management and General, and Fund Raising. It is used by the IRS to determine whether the entity is still eligible for its tax-exempt status under the Internal Revenue Code. The report is also used by independent organizations that evaluate and report on not-for-profit entities, such as GuideStar, which provides information to grant makers from its analysis of nonprofit filings. Schedule A of Form 990 requests eight pages of additional information dealing with support, compensation, and activities. In 2007, the IRS adopted revisions to Form 990 that substantially increase the amount of information reported by not-for-profit organizations.

Form 990-T must be filed by any tax-exempt organization that has gross income of more than $1,000 from activities that are not related to its tax-exempt mission. This form also requires payment of income tax on the net income from such activities.

ENTITIES RECEIVING FEDERAL FUNDING

Not-for-profit organizations, such as hospitals and universities that have federal government funding sources, are subject to most of the same audit requirements as federal agencies themselves. These requirements are different from those of a public company, but are likely to be just as extensive. White House Office of Management and Budget (OMB) Circular A-123, "Management's Responsibility for Internal Control," essentially adopted the essence of Sarbanes-Oxley and applies it to nonprofit organizations that receive federal funding.

[7] 42 USCS § 14503 (f).

OMB Circular A-133, "Audits of States, Local Governments, and Non-Profit Organizations," provides guidance for the audits of institutions of higher education and other nonprofit organizations. This document requires recipients of more than $500,000 in federal grants to undergo a single audit conducted using generally accepted government auditing standards (GAGAS) published by the U.S. Government Accountability Office and known as the "Yellow Book." Unless there is a program-specific audit guide, the circular requires an independent external auditor to:

(i) Perform an audit of the financial statement(s) for the Federal program in accordance with GAGAS;

(ii) Obtain an understanding of internal control and perform tests of internal control over the Federal program consistent with the requirements for a major program;

(iii) Perform procedures to determine whether the auditee has complied with laws, regulations, and the provisions of contracts or grant agreements that could have a direct and material effect on the Federal program consistent with the requirements for a major program; and

(iv) Follow up on prior audit findings, perform procedures to assess the reasonableness of the summary schedule of prior audit findings prepared by the auditee, and report, as a current year audit finding, when the auditor concludes that the summary schedule of prior audit findings materially misrepresents the status of any prior audit finding.[8]

NOT-FOR-PROFIT BOARD EVALUATION

Just like the boards and directors in for-profit corporations, the directors of not-for-profit entities should engage in self-evaluation and continuous improvement. Appendix 14A presents a Board Self-Evaluation Scorecard developed by the Society of Corporate Secretaries and Governance Professionals and the National Center for Nonprofit Boards. This organization notes that it is usually easy to spot an ineffective or dysfunctional board, as they are characterized by:

- The board does not have, or does not abide by, a regular meeting schedule.
- At board meetings nothing much happens, and many board members don't attend or are disaffected.
- Directors don't understand the mission or business of the organization and aren't passionate about either.
- Directors don't understand the financial underpinnings of the organization.
- Directors attempt to micromanage the staff.
- There's a lack of trust and confidence between the board and management.

[8] OMB Circular A-133 § 235(b) at OMB Web site www.whitehouse.gov/OMB/circulars/a133/a133.html.

- Directors or management speak disrespectfully of others on the board and/or of management.
- Directors or management speak publicly, without permission, about confidential board matters.
- A few directors dominate meetings.
- Directors don't understand basic governance principles.
- The organization is floundering.[9]

This same organization has developed a checklist of pertinent questions for individual directors to ask in evaluating the director's role and is presented in Appendix 14-B.

KEY POINTS IN CHAPTER 14

1. Almost all of the principles of good governance that apply to for-profit entities also apply to those organized as not-for-profit, including the U.S. Sentencing Guidelines.
2. Especially relevant is the need for a public perception of a fully ethical organization dedicated to the pursuit of its stated mission.
3. Some state statutes have embraced Sarbanes-Oxley requirements for not-for-profit entities in their state.
4. State statutes and the Federal Volunteer Protection Act of 1997 provide some protection against liability being assessed against directors in some circumstances.
5. Entities receiving funding from federal sources are generally subject to most of Sarbanes-Oxley requirements and are required to undertake audits under generally accepted governmental auditing standards.
6. As do the boards and directors of public corporations, those of not-for-profit entities should engage in activities of self-evaluation and continuous improvement.

[9] Society of Corporate Secretaries and Governance Professionals, *Governance for Non-Profits: From Little Leagues to Big Universities*, (New York: SCSGP, 2007) p. 14. www.governanceprofessionals.org/nfp/governance-for-nonprofits-2007.pdf.

Appendix 14A

Board Self-Evaluation Scorecard

Yes	No	
☐	☐	Does the board get enough information of the right kinds, at the right time, from the right members of management?
☐	☐	Do you have an effective director orientation program?
☐	☐	Does your board have active committees composed of a small, effective number of members to tackle audit, development/fund-raising, executive, finance, governance, nominations, personnel, program and other key matters?
☐	☐	Do you rotate committee members and chairs at appropriate intervals?
☐	☐	Are meetings conducted effectively, in appropriate frequency, on time and according to well-thought-out agendas circulated in advance?
☐	☐	Are meetings characterized by open communication and diligent questions on point discussed in a collegial manner?
☐	☐	Does your board meet regularly in private, apart from your executive director and other managers?
☐	☐	Are the board's actions motivated by and designed in furtherance of the mission statement?
☐	☐	Does your board periodically review your mission statement and implementation strategy?
☐	☐	Does your board act as if it is accountable to contributors and beneficiaries?
☐	☐	Does the board communicate effectively on a regular basis with its stakeholders, contributors and beneficiaries?
☐	☐	Does the board establish goals for management and review their effectiveness and performance on at least an annual basis?
☐	☐	Do you have effective processes and structures to evaluate, communicate with and counsel managers and staff?
☐	☐	Do you have guidelines for your managers, clearly specifying their authority?
☐	☐	Does your board micromanage your operations or, at the other extreme, does it ignore them and let management handle everything with little board oversight?
☐	☐	Has the board reviewed your operation's significant legal exposures and assessed your organization's legal compliance processes and record?
☐	☐	Do you have effective audit and financial oversight processes?

☐ ☐ Does your board review and adopt your capital and operating budgets?

☐ ☐ Do you have clear and effective procedures on handling funds, contributions and assets?

☐ ☐ Do you have effective standards and procedures to minimize and disclose potential conflicts of interest?

☐ ☐ Does your board governance and nominating committee regularly assess board practices and structures for effectiveness, evaluate current directors and counsel those whose performance is less than ideal, and continually look for talented potential new directors?

☐ ☐ Does your board have an appropriate level of turnover in its membership--new members and ideas balanced with experience and continuity?

Source: Society of Corporate Secretaries and Governance Professionals and National Center for Nonprofit Boards, www.governanceprofessionals.org/nfp/governance-for-nonprofits-2007.pdf.

Appendix 14B

Checklist for Directors of Nonprofits

1. Do you know why you were asked, or are being recruited, to serve on the board and what the board's expectations of you are, including any financial support or time commitment obligations?
2. Are you committed to being a good director and helping advance not only the mission of the organization, but the governance of the organization?
3. Do you have a copy of the organization's charter, bylaws and mission statement, and have you read them? Does the board periodically review these documents to make sure they are current with changes in law or practice, or strategy?
4. Is there a code of conduct for directors and do you have a copy? Do you understand your responsibility under the code and know who is responsible for enforcement of the code?
5. Is there a conflicts of interest policy (either in a code of conduct or a separate document)? Do you understand your responsibilities under the policy and know who is responsible for enforcement of the policy?
6. Does the organization provide Directors and Officers' Insurance?
7. Do you and other directors have copies of other critical board policies and are you aware of other policies that may be legally required for your organization (such as a document retention policy, or whistleblower policy)?
8. Who in the organization is responsible for filing tax forms related to the organization's nonprofit status and who reviews those forms?
9. Are financial performance and budget documents understandable and regularly monitored by the board or a committee of the board?
10. Are financial statements audited?
11. Are there policies in place to monitor donor designations on donations to the organization and who monitors compliance with them?
12. Do you know who else is on the board and how to contact other members?
13. Are you and other directors engaged in the work of the board and the organization?
14. How well do you and other directors understand the mission of the organization?
15. Do you and other directors preserve the confidentiality of material and information given or presented to the board?
16. Is the board functioning effectively, with regular well-attended and well-run meetings addressing important issues?

17. Does the board periodically review its own effectiveness?
18. Is the board up-to-date in its governance practices and, specifically, has the board considered the applicability to the organization of principles contained in Sarbanes Oxley and other governance legislation?
19. Do you and other directors understand your legal obligations as directors, including the duty of care and duty of loyalty, and the fact that board must act as a body, not through individual directors?
20. Do committees function well and serve the current needs of the organization?
21. Is there a well-understood process for recruiting new directors, with established criteria for seeking particular directors?
22. Is there a well-understood process for development and succession of officers of the board?
23. Is there a board orientation program or manual?
24. Is there a well-understood process for management development and succession planning?
25. Are key staff members formally evaluated by the chief executive and those evaluations shared with the board?
26. Are key staff salaries and expenditures approved by the chief executive and reviewed by the board or a committee of the board?

Source: Society of Corporate Secretaries and Governance Professionals and National Center for Nonprofit Boards, www.governanceprofessionals.org/nfp/governance-for-nonprofits-2007.pdf.

Chapter 15

Audit Committee Resources

Audit committee members may tap into a considerable number of sources if they wish to obtain more information about most aspects of their responsibilities as audit committee members. Each of the Big Four audit firms as well as other firms specializing in internal auditing have committed resources to help audit committee members. The contributions of firms and not-for-profit organizations are listed in alphabetical order. Some of these resources are limited to members of the organization, however.

AMERICAN INSTITUTE OF CERTIFIED PUBLIC ACCOUNTANTS

The AICPA, a membership organization of certified public accountants, has established the Audit Committee Effectiveness Center, which has three different methods for assisting audit committees. The center's Web site (www.aicpa.org/audcommctr/homepage.htm) contains a number of toolkits for download and use or customization. The toolkit for internal control evaluation is included as Appendix11A. Three other toolkits are available for corporations, not-for-profit, or government entities. They are a broad sampling of checklists, questions, reports, and guidelines that have been developed to help audit committees achieve best practices. The AICPA also provides guidance on matters of accounting, auditing, and financial reporting. Its monthly magazine is *Journal of Accountancy*.

ASSOCIATION OF AUDIT COMMITTEE MEMBERS

This membership organization promotes the professional interests of individuals who serve as members of public company audit committees by providing educational materials for and facilitating the exchange of information between members. The organization sponsors teleconferences and in-person meetings. Its Web site is www.aacmi.org

BOARDSOURCE

This membership organization specializing in governance of not-for-profit organizations. Its Knowledge Center at www.boardsource.org/Knowledge.asp contains references to papers, books, research, and other resources. The organization has a monthly e-newsletter.

CONFERENCE BOARD

This business membership and research organization provides a wide variety of publications on topics of interest to audit committees, including ethics, finance, governance, leadership, and risk management. Its Web site is www.conferenceboard.org.

CORPORATE BOARD MEMBER

Corporate Board Member magazine at www.boardmember.com frequently contains articles dealing with many aspects of the responsibilities of audit committee members.

COSO

COSO is the acronym for Committee of Sponsoring Organizations of the Treadway Commission. This group is a voluntary private-sector organization dedicated to the improvement of financial reporting through business ethics, effective internal controls, and corporate governance. It has conducted research and published guidance on these subjects. Its Web site is COSO.org.

DELOITTE CENTRE FOR CORPORATE GOVERNANCE

Deloitte has established a Centre for Corporate Governance, which has a section concerning audit committees. Deloitte publishes an online quarterly *Audit Committee Brief* and periodic white papers on various topics of interest to audit committees. The *Centre for Corporate Governance Update* is an email alert. The firm also publishes materials dealing with current accounting, auditing, and financial reporting issues. The center's Web site is www.corpgov.deloitte.com/site/us.

ERNST & YOUNG

Ernst & Young (E&Y) publishes guidance on current accounting and auditing matters as well as governance issues. E&Y publishes "Audit Committee Perspectives," "The Board Report," and other white papers on topics of interest to audit committees. The firm also publishes materials dealing with current accounting, auditing, and financial reporting issues. E&Y's Web site is www.ey.com.

FINANCIAL EXECUTIVES INTERNATIONAL

This membership organization of chief financial officers provides information on current developments in accounting and auditing. It also conducts research through its research foundation and publishes results on topics of interest to audit committees, including financial reporting. The organization's monthly magazine is *Financial Executive*. Its Web site is www.financialexecutives.org.

GRANT THORNTON

This firm publishes information on current accounting and auditing matters. The business advisory group in the firm publishes various publications concerning governance. Its Web site is www.gt.com.

HURON CONSULTING GROUP

This firm performs and publishes research concerning a broad range of topics, including governance and issues of financial reporting. Its Web site at www.huronconsulting group.com contains papers on a number of topics relevant to audit committees.

INSTITUTE OF INTERNAL AUDITORS, INC.

The Institute of Internal Auditors, Inc. (IIA), a global membership organization of internal auditors, conducts research through its research foundation and publishes results on topics of interest to audit committees, such as compliance, ethics, fraud, governance, internal controls, and risk management as well as internal auditing relationships with the audit committee. The organization's bimonthly magazine is *Internal Auditor*. The organization also distributes a complimentary governance newsletter, "Tone at the Top." Its Web site is www.theiia.org.

ISACA

ISACA, formerly the Information Systems Audit and Control Association, is a global membership organization serving professionals involved with the audit, control, and security of information systems (also known as information technology (IT)). ISACA performs research and publishes guidance on matters of interest to audit committee members. The organization's bimonthly publication is the *Information Systems Control Journal*. ISACA also sponsors the IT Governance Institute (ITGI), which is responsible for providing guidance on current and future issues pertaining to IT governance, security and assurance. The ITGI's guidance publication, *Control Objectives for Information and related Technology* (COBIT®), is said to be the world's leading IT governance and control framework. ISACA and ITGI are both accessible at www.isaca.org.

KPMG AUDIT COMMITTEE INSTITUTE

KPMG has organized an Audit Committee Institute (ACI), which, among other things, performs research on various audit committee issues and publishes results as well as other white papers on topics of interest to audit committees. The ACI cosponsors update sessions on audit committee issues twice yearly in many locations throughout the United States. The ACI's newsletter is called "Audit Committee Insights." ACI also publishes *KPMG Insights* at www.kpmginsights.com, a biweekly e-mail alert designed to help audit committee members keep up to date on important developments affecting audit committees, including accounting, auditing, and financial reporting issues. The ACI Web site is www.kpmg.com/services/audit/other/aci.htm.

NATIONAL ASSOCIATION OF CORPORATE DIRECTORS

The National Association of Corporate Directors (NACD), is a membership organization of corporate directors, whose mission is to improve corporate performance through better board practices. It sponsors research-oriented Blue Ribbon Committee Reports on governance issues including topics of interest to audit committees. The organization also sponsors conferences and educational programs on governance issues and has sponsored the Corporate Directors Institute which presents the Director Professionalism course that results in the Certificate of Director Education. The NACD publishes a daily membership news summary, *Directors Daily* and a monthly newsletter, *Directors Monthly*. The organization's Web site is www.nacdonline.org.

OCEG

The Open Compliance and Ethics Group is a nonprofit organization that uniquely seeks to help organizations drive performance by enhancing corporate culture and integrating governance, risk management, and compliance processes. It has published guidelines and standards, evaluation criteria and benchmarks, and an internal audit guide relating to these issues. Its Web site is www.oceg.org.

PRICEWATERHOUSECOOPERS

PricewaterhouseCoopers (PwC) publishes a number of materials dealing with corporate governance that can be accessed through the PwC U.S. Web site, www.pwc.com. The firm also provides guidance on emerging accounting and auditing issues.

Also, as part of its *ViewPoint* opinion series, PwC has published "Audit Committee Effectiveness," a white paper describing recommended actions that audit committees should take. This document is located at www.pwc.com/extweb/pwcpublications.nsf/docid/fc800243be0e3882852570500000c756/$File/vp04.pdf. In June 2007 PwC published a focus paper on full board effectiveness as a part of its Global Best Practices Series titled: "Building Blocks of Effective Corporate Boards." This document is located at http://cfodirect.pwc.com/CFODirectWeb/Controller.jpf?ContentCode=MSRA-76SLGR&ContentType=Content, which is part of the PwC Global Best Practices Web site—www.globalbestpractices.com/Home/Document.aspx?Link=About+us/Our+services.

PROTIVITI

This firm provides independent risk consulting and internal audit services. It also publishes research and commentary on issues of interest to audit committees including accounting and auditing, business law, financial reporting, information systems, internal auditing, risk management, and security. Its Web site is www.protiviti.com.

SOCIETY OF CORPORATE SECRETARIES AND GOVERNANCE PROFESSIONALS

This organization's corporate secretary members deal with issues such as public disclosure under the securities laws and matters affecting corporate governance, including the structure and meetings of the board of directors and its committees, the proxy process and the annual meeting of shareholders and shareholder relations, particularly with large institutional owners. It also conducts research, publishes monographs, and sponsors conferences on these subjects. Two evaluation tools for not-for-profit organizations are presented in Chapter 14. The organization's Web site is www.governanceprofessionals.org.

UNIVERSITIES

A number of universities provide educational programs for corporate directors and audit committee members. Others have centers of corporate governance that publish research and other commentary.

Glossary

All specialized professions and disciplines are filled with acronyms—initials that become words unto themselves—and specialized terms and references. Many of the special terms used in this book are defined when they appear in the text. Some other terms are defined in greater detail here.

ABA The American Bar Association. The professional member organization for attorneys in the United States. Its Committee on Corporate Laws, Section on Business Law publishes the *Corporate Director's Guidebook* which authoritatively sets forth guidance for boards of directors, including audit committees.

AICPA The American Institute of Certified Public Accountants is the professional membership organization for certified public accountants in the United States. Responsible for the CPA examination and, up until the Sarbanes-Oxley Act, for establishing and enforcing public accounting auditing standards through its ASB and CPA peer review programs.

ALI The American Law Institute, a group of judges, attorneys, and legal academics, published the *Principles of Corporate Governance: Analysis and Recommendations* in 1994.

Annual Meeting of Shareowners State incorporation laws require the shareowners to meet, allowing proxy representation, to elect directors, ratify the appointment of the external audit firm, and act on any other business that requires shareowner approval.

ASB The Auditing Standards Board is a committee of the AICPA and sets auditing standards for certified public accountant audits of entities other than those that are publicly held. Standards for audits of public company financial statements and internal control are set by the PCAOB.

Audit Committee A standing committee of the board of directors organized under the by-laws of the corporation. Duties of the committee are prescribed by statute, regulation, and best business practice. They involve oversight of financial reporting, auditing, ethics and compliance, and risk management processes.

Audit Committee Charter A formal document adopted by the full board of directors outlining the role and describing the detailed responsibilities of the audit committee. Audit committees should review their charters annually. SEC rules require that audit committee charters be included in a public company's proxy statement for the annual meeting of shareholders at least every three years, and oftener if revised.

BASEL II Accord An international banking capital regulation designed to encourage better and more systematic risk management practices, especially in the area of bank credit risk.

Blue Ribbon Committee A prominent study committee organized by the New York Stock Exchange and the National Association of Securities Dealers in 1998 to study and make recommendations for improving the effectiveness of corporate audit committees. Its recommendations were put into place through rules of the SEC and the AICPA.

Business Judgment Rule This rule states the legal concept that directors should be protected from liability if they have no financial interest in a transaction, and act on an informed basis, in good faith, and in the honest belief that the action taken was in the best interests of the corporation.

CAE A chief audit executive is the individual responsible for the internal audit function in an organization and reporting to the audit committee of the board. Previously, this person often was called the audit director.

Caremark Case Landmark Delaware court decision rendered in 1996 requiring directors to be sure that a system is in place to assure that all necessary information does reach the board for use in decision-making and oversight.

Certified Fraud Examiner An experience- and examination-based process that result in the professional designation CFE which is granted by the Association of Certified Fraud Examiners.

CoCo Criteria of Control The Canadian equivalent of the Committee of Sponsoring Organizations (COSO) internal controls framework or standards. Developed by the Canadian Institute of Chartered Accounts (CICA), an organization similar to the American Institute of Certified Public Accountants.

CobiT Control objectives for information technology is a comprehensive internal control framework developed by ISACA.

Conference Board A business membership and research organization that provides a wide variety of publications on topics of interest to audit committees.

COSO The Committee of Sponsoring Organizations of the Treadway Commission. The five organizations are: American Accounting Association, American Institute of CPAs, Financial Executives International, Institute of Internal Auditors, and Institute of Management Accountants. This group has published guidance on internal control and enterprise risk management.

COSO Internal Control COSO has defined internal control as a process, effected by an entity's board of directors, management and other personnel, designed to provide reasonable assurance regarding the achievement of objectives in:

- Effectiveness and efficiency of operations
- Reliability of financial reporting
- Compliance with applicable laws and regulations

COSO Risk Management COSO has defined enterprise risk management as a process, effected by an entity's board of directors, management and other personnel, applied in a strategic setting and across the enterprise, designed to identify potential events that may affect the entity, and manage risk to within its risk appetite, to provide reasonable assurance regarding the achievement of entity objectives.

Disclosure Controls Section 302 of Sarbanes-Oxley requires all publicly held corporations to certify the effectiveness of their controls designed to ensure full disclosure of all material facts are presented in quarterly and annual reports filed with the SEC and disseminated publicly.

Duty of Care Every director has the responsibility to become fully informed in making decisions affecting the corporation and in overseeing the performance of management.

Duty of Disclosure As fiduciaries, the courts have determined that directors have an obligation to ensure that decisions presented to shareholders for vote are accompanied by all relevant material information of which the directors are aware.

Duty of Loyalty Every director must act in good faith and in the best interests of the corporation and not in the interest of the director or someone else.

Enterprise Risk Management A term defining the processes an organization utilizes on a firm-wide basis to assess and then take actions to contain potential risks within the appetite set by the board of directors. Actions include avoidance, acceptance, mitigation, and transfer. Oversight of risk management is one of the audit committee's important responsibilities.

Ethics and Compliance Officer Association A membership organization of U.S. corporations having specific ethics and compliance related policies and procedures that address the requirements of the U.S. Sentencing Guidelines.

Fair Disclosure SEC rules require public corporations to disseminate all material and market-influencing information to everyone at the same time.

FASB The Financial Accounting Standards Board is the independent, nongovernmental agency that establishes U.S. accounting standards and rules. The board maintains U.S. generally accepted accounting principles.

FDIC The Federal Deposit Insurance Corporation is the U.S. regulator of banks and savings institutions that insures depositors against loss from failure of the institution, Individual depositors in U.S. bank and savings institutions are insured to a statutory limit.

FDICIA The FDIC Improvement Act of 1991 amended the 1934 Securities Exchange Act and began the movement to public reporting by management on internal control over financial reporting together with independent auditor attestation.

FEI Financial Executives International, a membership organization of CFOs and other senior financial executives of large corporations.

Fiduciary Duty A duty of persons holding positions of trust like directors who represent the interests of the shareowners.

GAAP Generally accepted accounting principles are the recognized U.S. standard for preparing financial statements. They are issued by the Financial Accounting Standards Board.

GAO The U.S. Government Accountability Office is headed by the Comptroller General of the United States and performs financial and operational audits of the executive branch of the federal government. It also sets auditing standards that must be used in audits of entities receiving government funding.

IIA The Institute of Internal Auditors, Inc. is the global professional organization of internal auditors. It develops the International Standards for the Professional Practice of Internal Auditing, the Code of Ethics for internal auditors and administers the CIA (Certified Internal Auditor) designation.

Insider Trading Directors are prohibited by the securities laws from purchasing or selling the securities of the corporation when they have material information not known by the public.

Internal Audit Charter A formal document, approved by the audit committee of the board of directors that describes the responsibilities and role of an organization's internal audit function.

ISACA Formerly called the Information Systems Audit and Control Association, IASACA is a global information systems membership organization. It is responsible for developing and maintaining the CobiT control objectives framework (see definition above), the CISA (Certified Information Systems Auditor) and CISM (Certified Information Systems Manager) designations.

ISO The International Standards Organization is a Geneva, Switzerland-based standard-setting body that issues worldwide standards in many areas.

M D & A Management's Discussion and Analysis of Financial Condition and Results of Operation is a required narrative filing with periodic reports to the SEC under Item 303 of Regulation S-K.

NACD The National Association of Corporate Directors is a membership organization of directors devoted to improving corporate governance in publicly held, private, and not-for-profit organizations through research and communication of best governance practices.

NASDAQ The National Association of Securities Dealers Automated Quotation system, is an electronic stock exchange, with many listed companies from the technology sector.

OCEG The Open Compliance and Ethics Group is a nonprofit organization that uniquely seeks to help organizations drive performance by enhancing corporate culture and integrating governance, risk management, and compliance processes. It has published guidelines and standards as well as measurement criteria and metrics relating to these issues.

PCAOB The Public Company Accounting Oversight Board is an independent governmental authority responsible to the Securities and Exchange Commission. It inspects the work and sets auditing, ethics, and quality standards for firms that audit public companies.

Pro Forma Financial Reports Financial reports that present an as-if picture of a firm's financial status by leaving out nonrecurring earnings expenses such as restructuring charges or merger-related costs.

Proxy Statement A document prepared in accordance with SEC rules containing disclosures considered necessary to inform shareholders so they can appoint proxy individuals to represent their interests at the annual meeting of shareowners.

Registered Public Accounting Firm An external auditing firm registered with the Public Company Accounting Oversight Board to audit the financial statements and internal control over financial reporting of a publicly held corporation.

Sarbanes-Oxley The Sarbanes-Oxley Act of 2002 regulates and oversees the performance of auditing firms with public clients, and establishes new disclosure rules and governance requirements for public companies. Another name for Sarbanes-Oxley is Public Company Accounting Reform and Investor Protection Act of 2002.

SAS Statements on Auditing Standards (SAS) are a series of statements that express auditing standards for audits of non-publicly held corporations and not-for-profit organizations. These are issued by the American Institute of Certified Public Accountants' Auditing Standards Board. CPAs who are members of the AICPA agree to follow these statements as part of their membership requirement.

SEC The Securities and Exchange Commission is the regulator of securities markets in the United States, including required standards of disclosure for publicly held companies. The SEC has oversight responsibility for the Sarbanes-Oxley Act and the Public Company Accounting Oversight Board (PCAOB), the regulator of auditing firms.

SEC Form 10-K The annual financial report mandated by the SEC to be filed by all publicly held companies.

SEC Form 10-Q The quarterly financial report mandated by the SEC to be filed by all publicly held companies.

Securities Act of 1933 Administered by the SEC, the Securities Act of 1933 is often referred to as the "truth in securities" law. It has two basic objectives:

- Require that investors receive financial and other significant information concerning [new] securities being offered for public sale; and
- Prohibit deceit, misrepresentations, and other fraud in the sale of [new] securities.

Securities and Exchange Act of 1934 With this Act, Congress created the Securities and Exchange Commission. The Securities and Exchange Act empowers the SEC with broad authority over all aspects of the securities industry. This includes the power to register, regulate, and oversee brokerage firms, transfer agents, and clearing agencies as well as the nation's securities self regulatory organizations (SROs), such as the stock exchanges.

SOX SOX is a frequently used abbreviation for the Sarbanes-Oxley Act of 2002. Some publications use this acronym, but this author believes that Sarbanes-Oxley is the better descriptor.

Treadway Commission An alternative name for the National Commission on Fraudulent Financial Reporting after its chair. One recommendation from its 1987 report led to the COSO study of internal control, named after the Treadway Commission's sponsoring organizations. Other recommendations concerning audit committees and governance have been adopted in subsequent legislation and regulation.

Volunteer Protection Act of 1997 The Volunteer Protection Act of 1997 shields volunteer directors from liability that could arise from a simple act of negligence.

Index